Late Ottoman Empire:
Freedom, Justice, and Slavery

Addie J. Hull

for Neş'e Karamürsel...

ABSTRACT

This dissertation concerns itself with the practice of slavery in the Ottoman Empire and the Turkish Republic in the second half of the nineteenth and early decades of the twentieth centuries. It places slavery at the intersection of the new liberal political order that began to form in the mid-1850s, the expulsion of the Caucasian peoples and their subsequent transplantation in the Ottoman Empire, and the international anti-slavery law that was taking shape simultaneously. It examines the social and legal (trans)formations at this particular juncture, traces the legal making and perpetuation of "Circassianness" as an "enslavable" ethnic category, and consequently argues that slavery bore a key significance in defining what citizenship came to mean in the Ottoman Empire and Turkish Republic.

Ottoman slavery comprised both male and female slaves, employed respectively for agricultural work in rural areas and for domestic and sexual services in the large urban centers of the empire. Their social destinies were markedly different from each other throughout the long course of the practice, but especially so in the "age of freedom," which was laden, above all, with the Ottoman state's promise of equality before the law. Male slaves demanded their "equality" in conspicuous ways by bringing lawsuits against their owners or through occasional armed resistance. Female slaves, on the other hand, whose flow towards the elite households of Istanbul did not cease at least until the second decade of the twentieth century, developed other forms of relationships both with their owners and slavery as a practice. Clinging on to the slave trade and at times wielding it as a weapon, they continued building extensive patronage networks across the empire, although their political participation became marginalized within an increasingly gendered political community, as the nineteenth century drew near its end.

Based on slave petitions, slaveholding elites' correspondences, police interrogations, legal records, and parliamentary minutes, this dissertation probes the entangled histories of slave emancipation and citizenship in the Ottoman Empire and Turkish Republic. Without dismissing its distinctive features, such as the multiple legal systems that governed it or the lack of its abolition, my aim is to place the Ottoman practice of slavery in its larger political context, not only within the Ottoman Empire but also the entire globe, and dismantle the categories of Islam and nationalism, which respectively essentializes Ottoman slavery and overcodes citizenship, along the way.

Table of Contents

Introduction.
The Children of the No-man's Land

This study began with broad range of inquiries on how such categories as gender, race, ethnicity, class, or age mattered and how their meanings and experience changed over time for the Ottoman state, slaveholders, as well as the slaves themselves. Navigating through slave petitions, slaveholding elites' correspondences, police interrogations, legal records, and parliamentary minutes from the late Ottoman Empire and early Turkish Republic, I tried to understand the ways in which the Ottoman slavery was different from other systems of slavery. Although not without overlaps with other systems, the Ottoman practice appeared highly distinct with 1) its loose racial and ethnic perceptions; 2) its traverse across different social classes which allowed manumitted slaves to own and trade in slaves as well as the permeability of class when slavery is taken into consideration; 3) its well-entrenched nature that even at the height of abolitionist sentiments the Ottoman palace could still consider buying new slaves; 4) its peculiar relationship with law that was made up of multiple legal systems; 5) difficulty or even impossibility of detecting it, in the presence of slavery-like practices; 6) its linguistic dimension; 7) its demand for mobility; 8) and last but not least, that it involved, mostly women.

The dissertation owes the present course it took, however, to a runaway slave named Fatma Leman and a document found at the Başbakanlık Ottoman Archives in Istanbul, which contains fragments of her life. The document, which opens chapter 4, recorded the voice of the young woman, who fled her mistress' house in the aftermath of the 1908 constitutional revolution to demand her freedom that she believed the newly promulgated constitution granted her. Firmly based on the liberal ideal of equality before the law, and with sound knowledge (or perhaps an instinctive conviction) that the Ministry of Justice was the primary responsible party in the affair, she stated that if the revolution brought freedom to each and every Ottoman individual as it claimed it did, then she too was free like the rest of her compatriots. Neither slave flights, nor claiming freedom was new or unusual in the early twentieth century. The Islamic *Şer'i* law technically allowed slaves to file complaints or demand to be manumitted at the *Şer'i* courts on the basis of ill treatment or fraudulent sale, so much so that students of Ottoman slavery had even argued that it had created a "culture of resistance" as early as the sixteenth century.[1] Yet these were almost all dispersed personal efforts, which mobilized personal strategies. Fatma Leman's claim, on the other hand, made specific use of the idiom of "freedom, justice, and equality," utilized by the constitutional regime to legitimize itself. The fact that her story, which she ingeniously placed at the complex

---

[1] Hayri Gökşin Özkoray, "Un 'culture de la résistance'?: Stratégies et moyens d'émancipation des esclaves dans l'Empire ottoman au XVIᵉ siècle," in *Mediterranean Slavery Revisited (500–1800)*, eds. Stefan Rank, Juliane Schlel (Zurich, Chronos Verlag, 2014).

intersection of the Ottoman practice of slavery, newly (trans)forming political order and its justice-administering institutions, ended with her alleged abduction, possible rape, and the eventual purchase by a high-ranking provincial officer is indicative of her subject position vis-à-vis the Ottoman state practice. In that respect, once Fatma Leman shifted the focus of this dissertation from slavery to freedom, the Ottoman practice of slavery appeared firmly embedded in the political developments not only within the Ottoman Empire, but in many respects, the entire globe.

Slavery had long been a practice in the Mediterranean, one that was deeply rooted in customs shaped by politics and the economics of war, territorial expansion as well as commercial circulations. The existence of the practice preceded the formation of the Ottoman state itself but in the later centuries the latter's own politics and the economics of war and expansion not only endorsed it but also built a bureaucratic system that relied heavily on slave recruits, creating, particularly from its frontier regions, "an almost ceaseless stream of prisoners of both sexes."[2] By the late eighteenth century, as the Ottoman state's expansionist advances were brought to a halt and the steady flow of slaves as products of war diminished, slave procurement relied more heavily on local tensions and larger conflicts in neighboring regions, such as the Caucasian War, 1817–1864 that caused a major upheaval in the Caucasus and rendered slave trade one of the

---

[2] Robert Brunschvig, "Abd," *Encyclopaedia of Islam, Second Edition* (Brill online, 2014), 11. The moments of war and economic boom notwithstanding, the enslaved population of the Ottoman Empire comprised mainly women in the nineteenth century. Gabriel Baer, "Slavery in Nineteenth Century Egypt," *The Journal of African History*, vol.8, No.3. (1967), 426; Kenneth Cuno, "African Slaves in 19th-Century Rural Egypt," *International Journal of Middle East Studies*, vol, 41, no.2, 186–87; Madeline Zilfi, *Women and Slavery in the Late Ottoman Empire: The Design of Difference* (Cambridge: Cambridge University Press, 2010), xi–xii.

region's most important sources of income in the first half of the nineteenth century.[3]

Throughout the war and the Circassian expulsion that followed,[4] during which "even

people of moderate means were able to pay for a slave with a few pieces of gold," the

imperial harem as well as many elite households consisted almost exclusively of young

Circassian women.[5] Coinciding with the Circassian expulsion were Britain's efforts in

---

[3] Liubov Kurtynova-D'Herlugnan, *The Tsar's Abolitionists: The Slave Trade in the Caucasus and Its Suppression* (Leiden: Brill, 2010); İbrahim Köremezli, "The Place of the Ottoman Empire in the Russo-Circassian War (1830–1864)," (Master's thesis, Bilkent University, 2004).

[4] In the first half of the 1860s, roughly a million Circassian refugees settled in various parts of the Ottoman Empire. For a detailed account, see David Cameron Cuthell, "The Muhacirin Komisyonu: An agent in the transformation of Ottoman Anatolia, 1860–1866" (Ph.D. dissertation, Columbia University, 2005). The word Circassian was and still is used as an umbrella term that denoted a variety of ethno-linguistic groups such as Adyghe, Chechen, Abkhaz, Kabarday, Ubykh, Ossetian, all originating from the Caucasus. In its proper designation and particularly in relation to the slaves brought from the region, it signifies those who lived in the area between the Black Sea and Sunja River to the west and east, the Caucasus mountains and the steppes north of Kuban and Pyatigorsk plains to the south and north. Köremezli, "The Place of the Ottoman Empire in the Russo-Circassian War," 5–6. For a detailed list of tribes and their geographic distribution at the beginning of the nineteenth century see Julius Von Klaproth, *Travels in the Caucasus and Georgia Performed in the Years 1807 and 1808* (London: Henry Colburn, 1814), 249–264; Fedor Fedorovich Tornao, *Bir Rus Subayının Kafkasya Anıları*, trans. Keriman Vurdem (Ankara: Kafkas Derneği Yayınları, 1999), 93–95. By the end of the nineteenth century, and especially following the 1908 revolution, the term Circassian was adopted by the Circassian intellectuals to signify what they deemed to be a "nation" based on a common Caucasian origin.

[5] Leyla Saz, *The Imperial Harem of the Sultans: Memoirs of Leyla (Saz) Hanımefendi* (Istanbul: Peva Publications, 1998), 58–59. Leyla Açba, *Bir Çerkes Prensesinin Harem Hatıraları*, Haz. Harun Açba (Istanbul: L&M Yayınları, 2004), 89. Harem, to briefly describe it, was a physically secluded section within the palace buildings or the elite households in Istanbul or provincial towns, where not only the women of the household, functioning as wives, concubines, handmaidens, servants or wet nurses resided but also where the sovereign himself lived. In the Ottoman Empire, by the end of sixteenth century, the imperial harem became an established institution, the powerful inmates of which took significant roles in politics. For an elaborate discussion on the topic, see Leslie Peirce, *The Imperial Harem: Women and Sovereignty in the Ottoman Empire* (New York: Oxford University Press, 1993). Largely removed from the political sphere by the second half of the nineteenth century, the imperial harem continued to function as an educational institution for enslaved women. In the late nineteenth century, it contained several hundreds of inmates, headed by *valide sultan* (the mother of the reigning sultan), *kadınefendi*s (official wives), *ikbal*s (concubines), followed by the staff of different ranks. While the imperial and elite harems differed from each other in size, organization and significance, they were connected through an extensive network of slave trade.

4

what Eve Troutt Powell has called "invasive abolitionism" that resulted in the abolition

of trade in African slaves in 1857.[6] However, neither the 1857 British-Ottoman

agreement nor later anti-slavery measures were automatically and fully extended to

include Circassian slaves, partly in response to the British insistence on a rigid definition

of abolitionism, in which the aristocratic or court slavery was lumped together with

menial or agricultural slavery.[7] In the ensuing decades, this discord helped to depict

African and Circassian slaves as two distinctly separate groups, the abolition of the

former being a humanitarian issue with an international dimension and regulated by

numerous conventions and acts, whereas the latter remained largely a domestic matter.

Different from earlier works on the Ottoman practice of slavery and in accordance

with the above-mentioned concerns and questions, this dissertation moves away from the

discursive field of the Ottoman state policy and conception of slavery and emancipation

(and how that shaped the practice of slavery and slaves' lives) and focuses on what sense

slaves, and occasionally slave holders themselves, made of slavery, emancipation, as well

as the social and political developments at the time. The aim here is not simply to give

agency to the slaves, or as Ehud Toledano suggests, to put the "'cameras […] in the

hands of the enslaved, rather than in those of the slavers, where they have rested in most

---

[6] Eve M. Troutt Powell, *A Different Shade of Colonialism: Egypt, Great Britain, and the Mastery of the Sudan* (Berkeley: University of California Press, 2003), 136.

[7] Ehud R. Toledano, *Slavery and Abolition in the Ottoman Middle East* (Seattle: University of Washington Press, 1998), 113. This situation, according to Toledano, perpetuated the suffering of domestic and agricultural slaves in the country, as it made the abolition of one type of slavery impossible without the abolition of the other.

5

standard documentary accounts,"[8] but to have a better grasp of the ways in which their subject positions as victims or perpetrators came into contact with the social and political change that took place in the second half of the nineteenth and early twentieth centuries and the Ottoman state as its main instigator. This is not to write off the concept of agency by any means, but rather to point at, as Walter Johnson well elaborates, its negative capacity to "overcode" intricate and interconnected layers of "human subjectivity and political organization" and dangers in obscuring related questions "about the contexts and consequences of human activity..."[9] Thus, the question, which Johnson characterizes as "persistently mis-posed," of whether the slaves "were agents of their own destiny or not" is not a concern of this dissertation. Rather, it aims to explore slaves' participation in the making of the social and political order in the Ottoman Empire, during the period in question. The slaves wrote petitions, used both local and higher courts extensively, informed themselves about international legal developments and strategically demanded, in compliance with what the increasingly liberal Ottoman governance promised, their freedom, equality, justice, and citizenship. That their attempts largely failed determined not only their own destiny but also the destiny of the Ottoman society as a whole, as well as the very limits of the "liberal governmentality" that the Ottoman Empire was in the process of forging.[10]

---

[8] Ehud R. Toledano, *As If Silent and Absent: Bonds of Enslavement in the Islamic Middle East* (New Haven: Yale University Press, 2007), 8.

[9] Walter Johnson, "On Agency," *Journal of Social History*; Fall 2003; 37, 1, 114. A

[10] Patrick Joyce, *The Rule of Freedom: Liberalism and the Modern City* (London: Verso, 2003), 2.

By studying the slaves' attempts and failures, this dissertation aims to unearth and highlight the major fault lines in the social and political forces that governed the Ottoman Empire and early Turkish Republic. One such fault line that runs through the dissertation, and that is particularly central to the second and fourth chapters, is the coexistence of multiple legal systems during the period in question. Some Ottoman historians take this pluralistic legal order as the manifestation of "flexibility, pragmatic decision making, and a measure of freedom that can encourage adaptation and peaceful coexistence."[11] Viewed from the slaves' and slavery's perspective, however, it becomes clear that this composite structure was not made of legal practices that existed in and of themselves but always in relation to power.[12] Other fault lines include "Ottoman conservatism" in relation to the Ottoman government's strict adherence to Islamic law, as well as their corporate notions of citizenship, which crystalized in slaves' claims to emancipation, and in an indirect yet intensifying way, to citizenship.

Bent, fractured, and at times invented anew along those fault lines were the categories of race, ethnicity, and gender. I follow the process that delineated (or, at least perpetuated) "Circassianness" as an enslaveable ethnic category and the ways in which it interacted with the newly emerging international anti-slavery law, which had the primary aim, at least in the Ottoman Empire, of abolishing the trade in African slaves. The questions, which this dissertation deals with, spring from the complex intersection of the

---

[11] Karen Barkey, "Aspects of Legal Pluralism in the Ottoman Empire," in *Legal Pluralism and Empires, 1500–1850*, eds. Lauren Benton and Richard J. Ross (New York: New York University Press, 2013), 84.

[12] For an elaborate criticism of the concept of legal pluralism, see Kamari Maxine Clarke, *Fictions of Justice: The International Criminal Court and the Challenge of Legal Pluralism in Sub-Saharan Africa* (Cambridge: Cambridge University Press, 2009).

Ottoman Reform Edict in 1856 and the subsequent legal reforms; the trade ban of African slaves in 1857 and its transforming effects on Islamic law; and the Circassian expulsion in the 1860s and the "transplanted" *adat* (customary law) in the Circassian settlements across the Ottoman Empire. I argue that these different, and at times conflicting, legal systems interplayed with or worked against each other in delineating the categories of race and ethnicity explicitly, setting the limits of slavery and emancipation, and cultivating a form of political power that would last for decades to come in the Ottoman Empire and its successor states. In this, I offer not only a brand new conceptualization of the Ottoman practice of slavery and an insight into the complexities of Ottoman citizenship law, but also an intervention to the scholarship on state and citizenship in the Ottoman Empire and Turkish Republic, which traditionally approaches the matter from the perspective of religion, the corporate structure considered to be the primary category that ordered these relationships. Circassian slaves were after all Muslims, whose enslavement took place in accordance with the Caucasian customary law, but not necessarily in compliance with the Şer'i law, which the Ottoman legal system was, or at least deemed to be, largely based on. The very fact that the Ottoman government could approve their slave status despite apparent sanctions against enslaving Muslims and despite numerous tenacious campaigns run by Circassian slaves starting immediately after the Circassian expulsion of the early 1860s, rendered their case no less than a "state of exception," defined at times as "a point of imbalance between public law and political fact," "a no-man's-land [...] between the juridical order and life" that emerges within an "ambiguous, uncertain, borderline fringe, at the intersection of the legal and the political."[13] Here, in place of the suspension of one unitary law and the state as the sole authority that exercises it (as the state of exception is usually defined), we encounter competing sovereignties and legalities, the careful selection and elimination of which determined who could and could not be enslaved in the Ottoman Empire. This way of limit setting, in Veena Das's rendition, determined "what or who is recognized as human within a social form and provide[d] the conditions of the use of criteria as applied to others," pointing at "the dangers [... of] withhold[ing] recognition from the other, not simply on the grounds that she is not part of one's own community but that she is not part of life itself."[14]

Slavery in the Ottoman Middle East lingered well after the empire's collapse in 1918. It existed officially until the early 1930s, when the newly founded republic of Turkey became a member of the League of Nations and by that virtue a signatory to the 1926 Slavery Convention that made it liable "to bring about, progressively and as soon as possible, the complete abolition of slavery in all its forms."[15] While the practice involved, especially in the urban areas such as Istanbul or Cairo, mostly women whether as victims, like Kazal and in others as perpetrators, like Um Mazed, they were not always the main actors within it. Nevertheless, they emerged as key agents through which the newly

---

[13] Giorgio Agamben, *State of Exception* (Chicago: The University of Chicago Press, 2005), 1. Agamben draws respectively from François Saint-Bonnet and Alessandro Fontana for these definitions: François Saint-Bonnet, *L'état d'exception* (Paris: Presses Universitaires de France, 2001), Alessandro Fontana, "Du droit de résistance au devoir d'insurrection" in *Le droit derésistance*, ed. Jean-Claude Zancarini (Paris: ENS, 1999).

[14] Veena Das, *Life and Words: Violence and the Descent into the Ordinary* (Berkeley: University of California Press, 2007), 15–16.

[15] Slavery Convention, signed at Geneva on 25 September 1926, article 2b. Accessed through http://www.ohchr.org/EN/ProfessionalInterest/Pages/SlaveryConvention.aspx

(trans)forming Ottoman "rule of freedom" reached its limits. Scholars of gender and

sexuality have long been engaged in exploring these limits in other geographic areas.

Linda Kerber, for instance, examined the extent of what she called the "mythic space" of

"We the People," that drew "much of its power by its egalitarian spirit," in so far as it

excluded the poor, black men, and women, "whatever their race or class. "[16] Pamela

Haag, on the other hand, explored the meanings of consent and coercion to demonstrate

how liberal thought and tradition was not only complex but also internally

contradictory.[17] Most recently, in her work on the traffic in women in late imperial

Russia, Philippa Hetherington treads along similar lines of thought when gauging the

limits of "governmental freedom" at a time when the "state and social understandings of

the subject's freedom, to move across borders or to consent to sex, were being

reconceptualized."[18] Hetherington emphasizes the importance of "highlighting

continuities in the development of 'liberal' and 'illiberal' approaches to a particular

political question" in non-European and non-Western settings, such as Russia where

"strict binaries (between liberal and illiberal, *sonderweg* and shared heritage) obscure

more than they reveal, embedded as they are in ideological assumptions about the

'backwardness' of Russia and the progressiveness of the West."[19] For Hetherington,

---

[16] Linda Kerber, *No Constitutional Right to be Ladies: Women and the Obligations of Citizenship* (New York: Hill and Wang, 2000), 8; Kerber, "The Paradox of Women's Citizenship in the EarlyRepublic: The Case of Martin vs. Massachusetts, 1805," *The American Historical Review,* vol. 97, no. 2 (Apr., 1992), 350.

[17] Pamela Haag, *Consent: Sexual Rights and the Transformation of American Liberalism* (Ithaca: Cornell University Press, 1999), xviii.

[18] Philippa Hetherington, "Victims of the Social Temperament: Prostitution, Migration and the Traffic in Women from Imperial Russia and the Soviet Union, 1885–1935," Ph.D. diss., Department of History,: Harvard University, 2014, iii.

[19] Hetherington, "Victims of the Social Temperament," 16.

accentuating the similarities and differences between Russian and non-Russian contexts is useful "not so much to say that Russia was liberal like the West, but that liberalism was itself an incomplete project in continental Europe and North America, an observation that makes binary oppositions and claims of special paths of limited utility."[20] My objective and concerns are similar to those expressed by Hetherington, in that at the core of this study lies a desire to look at the ways in which liberalism did or did not take root in the Ottoman Empire, but not without acknowledging that it was a form of governmentality with intrinsic flaws and contradictions, that habitually treated "the poor, black men, and women," as "not part of life itself."

In the past five decades of Ottoman slavery studies, the issue of Ottoman or Middle Eastern slavery (at times referred to as Islamic slavery) has been largely treated, with few exceptions, as an anomalous, even exotic, phenomenon removed from contemporary social and political developments. The earlier studies of introductory character were followed by those that took the form of general surveys that covered "the traffic from Africa and the Caucasus," as Ehud Toledano put it, "described the main routes, determined the types of slaves, their prices, the customs duties levied on them, the jobs they performed, the social roles they played, [...] and the problems of suppression and abolition."[21] Yet, only few treated slavery not in its own terms but in connection with

---

[20] Ibid., 16–17.

[21] Ehud Toledano, *As If Silent and Absent*, 39–40. Earlier works on Ottoman and Middle Eastern slavery comprise Baer, "Slavery in Nineteenth Century Egypt," (1967); Bernard Lewis, *Race and Colour in Islam* (New York: Harper Torchbooks, 1971); Alan Fisher, "Chattel Slavery in the Ottoman Empire," *Slavery & Abolition: A Journal of Slave and Post-Slave Studies* 1, no. 1 (1980). Ehud Toledano's "Slave Dealers, Women, Pregnancy, and Abortion: The Story of a Circassian Slave-girl in Mid-nineteenth Century Cairo," *Slavery & Abolition*, Volume 2, Issue 1, 1981 was the first to introduce gender and slave agency in Ottoman slavery studies, although

larger structures of power.[22] All these works examined the Ottoman policy of slavery and abolition, but touched upon the politics of slavery only tangentially. They all made an emphasis on the legal aspect of it but they rarely delved into the messiness of the legal practice. They heeded Islamic law to be the primary legislative body that regulated all phases of slavery, from slave raiding to manumission, and disregarded power dynamics, which allowed ample amount of extra-legality particularly within the trade. Last but not least, while the importance of gender within the Ottoman practice of slavery has been acknowledged from the very start, only a few studies put emphasis on it, and when they did, it was to portray women mostly as victims,[23] even though a significant portion of the Ottoman slave trade was overseen and controlled by powerful women in the nineteenth century. Queen mothers and consorts in the imperial harem, wives of bureaucrats across the empire, and not the least ordinary matchmakers here and there all extensively

---

Ronald C. Jennings' 1975 article "Women in Early 17th Century Ottoman Judicial Records: The Sharia Court of Anatolian Kayseri," in the *Journal of the Economic and Social History of the Orient* (Vol. 18, No. 1) featured numerous legal cases that involved enslaved women's use of the Şer'i courts. Survey studies include Ehud Toledano, *The Ottoman Slave Trade and Its Suppression, 1840–1890* (Princeton: Princeton University Press, 1982) and *Slavery and Abolition in the Ottoman Middle East*, 1998; Ronald C. Jennings, "Black Slaves and Free Blacks in Ottoman Cyprus, 1590–1640," *Journal of the Economic and Social History of the Orient* 30, no. 3 (1987); Ralph A. Austen, "The Mediterranean Islamic slave trade out of Africa: A tentative census," *Slavery & Abolition: A Journal of Slave and Post-Slave Studies* 13, no. 1 (1992); Y. Hakan Erdem, *Slavery in the Ottoman Empire and its demise, 1800–1909* (New York: Palgrave Macmillan, 1996). There is also a fairly large body of apologetic literature on Ottoman/Islamic slavery in Turkish that is left outside the scope of this dissertation. For a good example of this literature, see Ahmet Akgündüz's recent book where he reiterates the major apologetic argument that Islam did not introduce slavery, but gave its practice a "humane" character. Ahmet Akgündüz, *Ottoman Harem: The Male and Female Slavery in Islamic Law* (Rotterdam: IUR Press, 2015).

[22] Powell, *A Different Shade of Colonialism*; For a more recent study that similarly examines imperial hierarchies in the eastern Mediterranean through Ottoman slavery and abolition, see Alison Frank, "The Children of the Desert and the Laws of the Sea: Austria, Great Britain, the Ottoman Empire, and the Mediterranean Slave Trade in the Nineteenth Century," *The American Historical Review* (2012) 117 (2).

[23] Zilfi, *Women and Slavery in the Late Ottoman Empire*.

exploited the system they knew so well. Their story was not only about despair but also power, in which the dividing lines between the victim and the culprit, were at best thin, if they existed at all. The chapters that follow bring these issues to the fore.

Largely an overview of the Caucasian customary law and the practices of blood revenge, princely plunder, and bride kidnapping associated with it, the first chapter examines the Caucasus region during the Caucasian wars, particularly at the end of its intensified phase between 1817–1864. It places these slave-producing practices in the larger social and political context of wartime Caucasus and looks at how they interfered with the Islamic Şer'i law, at a time when the meaning of Islam itself was going through significant changes in the region. The chapter also establishes that procurement of and trade in slaves were two separate processes, not necessarily organized by the same legal systems or orders. Ultimately, it offers a "prehistory" for later chapters that traces the making or perpetuation of Circassianness as an enslaveable ethnic category.

The second chapter follows the process of displacement and transplantation of Circassian tribes within the Ottoman domains. Building on the previous one, the chapter focuses on the complex intersection of 1) the Ottoman Reform Edict in 1856 and the subsequent legal reforms, 2) the trade ban in African slaves in 1857 and its transforming effects on Islamic law, and 3) the Circassian expulsion in the 1860s and the "transplanted" *adat* (customary law) in the Circassian settlements across the Ottoman Empire. In doing that, it aims to trace how legal practices were carried over with Caucasian refugee-immigrants to the Ottoman domains and how these different legal systems interplayed with or worked against each other in determining the limits of slavery and freedom. Secondly, navigating within a set of what was literally called "freedom suits" (*hürriyet davaları*), it explores how slaves built their claims in relation to different legal terrains, problems, and concepts. Finally, it touches upon the ways in which these processes continued to bend the categories of ethnicity, race, and gender in the decades that followed the expulsion.

While women were often central to the claims in these slave petitions, which constitute the main source base for the second chapter, they are hardly visible in the official documentation that described these legal processes. In fact, the reports on instances of conspicuous resistance always listed men as leaders within the Ottoman practice of slavery, whether they took up arms or pursued their claims through legal channels at the local or higher courts. Women and young girls on the other hand, whose flow, especially towards big cities like Istanbul or Cairo, had not ceased until the early twentieth century, developed other forms of relationships both with their owners and slavery as a practice. The third chapter looks at a diverse group of women, with different racial, ethnic, and class associations to offer a glimpse of how slavery was understood, slave trade practiced and at times wielded as a weapon by them.

Focusing on the immediate aftermath of the 1908 constitutional revolution, the fourth chapter explores in what sense slaves, particularly women slaves, made of freedom and how they positioned themselves vis-à-vis the new regime's emancipatory efforts and failures that determined the limits of citizenship in the Ottoman Empire. Examining the idiom of freedom used by the Ottoman state, slave owners and slaves in distinct and often conflicting ways on the one hand and the bifurcated nature of the Ottoman legal system

14

on the other, it offers a glimpse of the social and political conditions that determined who was entitled to claim freedom and who was not at the time.

The fifth and final chapter explores the "republicanization" of slavery and freedom after the inauguration of the Turkish Republic in 1923 and how the latter dealt with what the contemporary press called the "burdensome inheritance" of slaves and slavery in general. Focusing on the portrayals of the "twin relics," that is slavery and polygamy, of an unwanted past embodied in the institution of harem, the chapter traces how the republican "project of regulated amnesia"[24] dealt with the physical disposal of items found in the imperial harems. It also probed the republicanization of the law, in the sense that the republic eliminated at least the institutional bifurcation in the legal realm and became the sole authority in administering what was now understood as universal justice.

---

[24] Murat Ergin, "'Is the Turk a White Man?' Towards a Theoretical Framework for Race in the Making of Turkishness," Middle Eastern Studies, 44:6 (2008), 837.

Chapter One.
Barbarians by Design

"Their subsistence routines, their social organization, their physical dispersal, and many elements of their culture, far from being the archaic traits of a people left behind, are purposefully crafted both to thwart incorporation into nearby states and to minimize the likelihood that statelike concentrations of power will arise among them. State evasion and state prevention permeate their practices and, often, their ideology as well. They are, in other words, a "state effect." They are "barbarians by design." They continue to conduct a brisk and mutually advantageous trade with lowland centers while steering clear of being politically captured."

James C. Scott, *The Art of Not Being Governed*[1]

In late 1887, a group of newly immigrated Georgian families petitioned the palace secretariat in Istanbul to complain about an ongoing situation, "known to everyone native or foreign," perpetrated by one of the aides-de-camp to Sultan Abdülhamid II, Çürüksulu Ali Pasha. Ali Pasha, himself of Georgian origin from Çürüksu (Kobulety, in today's Georgia), allegedly threatened and frightened many families, particularly those who were poor and vulnerable like the ones who filed the petition, and forced them to hand their daughters to him. Coercing a number of these girls into slavery each month, the petition reported, Ali Pasha ran a slaving business with the help of his family members (most notably his brother-in-law, Arslan) between the settlements of Georgian immigrants in the eastern Black Sea coast and Istanbul, where the enslaved girls were subsequently

---

[1] James C. Scott, *The Art of Not Being Governed: An Anarchist History of Upland Southeast Asia* (New Haven: Yale University Press, 2009), 8.

brought to, either to be sold in exchange of money or to be presented as gifts to various grandee households.[2]

The two reports that accompanied the petition, addressed to the palace secretariat and the governor of Trabzon, both cautioned the authorities to give utmost care not to "favor anyone when looking into the matter," pointing at Ali Pasha's high rank and close connections to the palace but also hinting at his ill repute, which he inherited from his family, known to be "at the center of a lucrative slave trade business" during most of the second half of the nineteenth century.[3] Shortly after the authorities began investigating the case however, favor was no longer necessary for Ali Pasha's part. During their interrogation, the families denied altogether that they filed such a petition and with what seems to be a series of false (or at best inconsistent and suspicious) statements, they tried to assure the police that they came to Istanbul of their own account. They were left with no means to make a living in their (newly adopted) hometown; so, far from being forced to leave, they said, they voluntarily traveled to Istanbul in search of jobs as servants or wet-nurses. As for their children, that is the three young girls mentioned in the petition, they were to be given away as *evlatık*, which meant fostering or adoption with the implicit purpose of servitude, a practice that often constituted a safe haven to all those who traded in slaves clandestinely.[4]

---

[2] Başbakanlık Osmanlı Arşivleri (The Ottoman Archives of the Prime Minister's Office, hereafter BOA), Y.MTV 29/112, 1305.R.26 (11 January 1888).

[3] Oktay Özel, "Migration and Power Politics: The Settlement of Georgian Immigrants in Turkey (1878–1908)," *Middle Eastern Studies*, vol.46, no.4 (July, 2010), 487.

[4] BOA, Y.MTV 29/112, 1305.R.26 (11 January 1888). Nazan Maksudyan talks about an order issued by the Council of State in 1887, and an investigation carried out in 1899, against the widespread practice of deceiving "destitude girls or some poor and weak parents," though which young female children were "continuously *sold* from one master to the next, such that they were

At the time of this incident, Çürüksulu Ali Pasha held a substantial amount of political power (as those who wrote the above mentioned reports were well aware), not only because of his high ranking position as the aide-de-camp and the brigadier general (his honorific title), but also because of his close connections to the palace and the sultan. His power was also due to his former position as the district governor of Ordu province in the eastern Black Sea coast, which blended with his services as the military commander in the Batum-Çürüksu/Kobulety area during the 1877–78 Russo-Turkish War,[5] as well as his duties as the chief immigration officer for settling Georgian immigrants in the region in its aftermath. In the years that followed the war and the subsequent Treaty of Constantinople signed in 1879, Ali Pasha assumed the responsibility of settling approximately 150,000 Georgian immigrants in the region.[6]

That an Ottoman statesman of Georgian origin was appointed to oversee his "fellow" Georgian immigrant subject-citizens was not unprecedented as far as the Ottoman state's Caucasus policies went. In fact, the Ottoman state was accustomed to use its subjects of Caucasian origin or ancestry as the mediators in their dealings with the Caucasus region and its people. Paul B. Henze pointed out that, as early as the Treaty of

---

engulfed by misery and prostitution." See Nazan Maksudyan, "Foster-Daughter or Servant, Charity or Abuse: *Beslemes* in the Late Ottoman Empire," *Journal of Historical Sociology*, vol. 21 no., 4 December 2008, 500–501.

[5] The 1877–78 Russo-Turkish War was a watershed moment in late Ottoman history both in terms of international developments like the territorial loss and internal political shifts such as the prorogation of the 1876 parliament it instigated. It has further significance in relation to the scope of this study, as it brought on a second wave of Circassian migration from the Balkan provinces towards the Anatolian and Arabian Peninsula in its aftermath, a point revisited in the second and third chapters below.

[6] Özel, "Migration and Power Politics," 478–79. The Treaty of Constantinople finalized the provisions of the San Stefano Treaty signed in 1878 and revised by the Congress of Berlin later that year, according to which Batumi, among several other south Caucasian localities, was ceded to Russia.

18

Küçük Kaynarca in 1774, when Ottomans decided to establish a formal representation in the Caucasus, they appointed a former Georgian slave, Ferah Ali Pasha as the first governor in the region.[7] Later, in the 1860s, when the Ottoman government founded the Emigrant Commission to oversee the large inflow of Circassian refugees, it recruited its chief officials almost exclusively from among those who had Caucasian ancestry.[8] Çürüksulu Ali Pasha fit in this long-standing pattern. Yet unlike Ferah Ali Pasha, who governed parts of the North-Western Caucasus or Hafız Mehmet Ali Pasha who headed the Emigrant Commission, "Ali Bey Kobuletskiy"[9] was nobility on his own account and in the late 1870s, the chief of his family, namely the Tavdgiridze family of Georgian nobility. Throughout the process of settling Georgian refugees as well as his earlier dealings with the people in his district, Ali Pasha acted not solely within the "classic frames of state power," as Bruce Grant called it, but rather within the framework of a mixture of his powers as a statesman and his "princely" privileges and entitlements that referred back to the more complex, "varied and often competing Caucasus modes of power and authority."[10] Thus, "us[ing] and direct[ing] his fellow Georgian immigrants in their new homeland" as Oktay Özel argued, Ali Pasha established a power base for

---

[7] Paul B. Henze, "Circassian Resistance to Russia" in *The North Caucasus Barrier: The Russian advance towards the Muslim world*, ed. Marie Bennigsen Broxup, (New York, St. Martin's Press, 1992), 74.

[8] David Cameron Cuthell Jr., "The Muhacirin Komisyonu: An Agent in the Transformation of Ottoman Anatolia, 1860–1866" (Ph.D. Dissertation, Columbia University, 2005), 103–104.

[9] Candan Badem, "The Ottomans and the Crimean War (1853–1856)" (Ph.D. Dissertation, Sabancı University, 2007), 139.

[10] Bruce Grant, *The Captive and the Gift: Cultural Histories of Sovereignty in Russia and the Caucasus* (Ithaca: Cornell University Press, 2009), xv–xvi.

himself."[11] The extensive slave trade network that he inherited from his family (most notably his mother) and operated vigorously does not correspond solely to the image of a corrupt statesman, but also to what he thought was his noble privileges and entitlements, within a larger spectrum of competing sovereignties in the region.

The incident that opens this chapter was not the first, nor only, recorded instance in which Ali Pasha's name was mentioned in relation to the slave trade. Almost two decades prior, in the summer of 1859, Ali Pasha's mother and the matriarch of the Tavdgiridze family, Dendine Hanım filed a petition to the office of the Grand Vizier with the purpose of denying all allegations against her son, who was being accused of murdering a man named Ibrahim, also a recent immigrant from Georgia to the Ottoman empire, and reportedly a recent convert to Islam. According to the brothers of the victim, Ali Pasha not only murdered Ibrahim, but also kidnapped two of his children whom he subsequently sold into slavery in Istanbul.[12] In his defense, Dendine Hanım, "one of the most inveterate dealers in slaves" as Frederic Millingen called her,[13] refuted on behalf of her son, not only the allegations of murder but the very existence of the victim himself. The plaintiffs, on other hand, claimed otherwise and by providing ample detail, reported that one of Ibrahim's children, a 7-year-old girl named Ayşe, was sold to a certain Hacı

---

[11] Özel, "Migration and Power Politics," 482. Özel rightly sees the pervasiveness of Georgian banditry in the region in the 1880s, which coincided with the process of settlement under Ali Pasha's supervision as the indicator of this power.

[12] BOA, MVL 589/64, 1276 S 30 [sic] (possibly 27 September 1859).

[13] Frederic Millingen, "The Circassian Slaves and the Sultan's Harem," *Journal of the Anthropological Society of London*, 8 (1870–1871): cix–cxx, cx. Dendine Hanım's name has several different spellings in archival sources, such as Dendene and Dendane. Millingen calls her Dindine.

Ismail Ağa in Istanbul by no other than Dendine Hanım herself.[14]

Both Dendine Hanım, who "was most highly connected, and intimate with the Seraglio, as well as with many of the grandees,"[15] and her equally "highly connected" son were aware of the illegal nature of their slave capturing and trading activities. In another case from October 1863, Dendine Hanım (who already had a bad reputation by that time for wrongfully seizing and enslaving Georgian girls from "both sides" of the border) reportedly perpetrated the smuggling of four Georgian girls, who were Russian subjects, and thus were being requested by the Russian consulate to be returned at once.[16] When the girls were seized in the Trabzon port by the customs authorities, Dendine Hanım, well aware of their unlawful enslavement, did not claim them nor pursued their recovery; in fact, she did not even bother to leave the boat that brought her to Trabzon, but continued her way to Istanbul.[17] Likewise, Ali Pasha was aware that what he was doing was not necessarily compliant with Ottoman state policies against the slave trade, which prohibited or at least brought limitations to trade both in Caucasian and African slaves, beginning with the imperial edicts of 1854 and 1857 respectively.[18] Those two edicts and subsequent vizirial correspondences were followed by a series of draft laws, conventions and acts signed internationally.[19] Yet none of these hindered Ali Pasha and his family in

---

[14] BOA, MVL 589/64, 1276.S.30 [sic] (27 September 1859).

[15] Millingen, "The Circassian Slaves and the Sultan's Harem," cx.

[16] BOA, MVL 658/80, 1280.Ca.1 (14 October 1863).

[17] Ibid.

[18] For a detailed overview of both documents, see Hakan Erdem, *Slavery in the Ottoman Empire and its Demise, 1800–1909* (New York: St. Martin's Press, 1996), 102–113. FO 195/946, Consular Dispatch #35, 28 September 1869; Memoranda Re: White Slaves and Firman of 1854, 1970; Consular Dispatch #36, 30 August 1870.

[19] Erdem, *Slavery in the Ottoman Empire and its Demise*, 125–151.

their pursuit of their "princely" entitlements and privileges.

It was not that the Ottoman government or the palace was strictly enforcing the prohibition of the trade in slaves. In an earlier example, for instance, when the British consul effected the capture of fifty Circassian slaves at Trabzon port in 1858 and used his "endeavours to persuade the Governor General" to stop their shipment to Istanbul and "send them back to Circassia" in the following two weeks, the government allowed their passage on a Turkish steamer, simply stating that they were families emigrating to Istanbul.[20] In a more striking example, when the British consular officials asked khedive Isma'il Pasha to enforce the prohibition on white slave traffic from Istanbul to Egypt, he stated that such traffic was carried mainly in Istanbul, "by the high dignitaries of the Turkish Empire," that at least eighty percent of the pashas had made money by purchasing and reselling white slaves and that he himself had bought slaves from the present Grand Vizier Aali Pasha.[21] Nevertheless, Ali Pasha and his family, and their acts of plunder, extortion, and other coercive means in slave procurement (enslaving freeborn Georgian girls "as if they were slaves or *cariyes*," the families exclaimed in the above mentioned petition), stood apart from those manipulations or violations.[22] They were

---

[20] FO 84/1060, Consular Dispatch #34, 15 April 1858, 130.

[21] FO 195/946, Slave Trade #5, from Colonel Stanton to the Earl of Clarendon, 14 October 1869. Similarly, a consular report from Jerusalem mentions a Turkish functionary sending for "a white slave from Constantinople itself, where his communication was duly respected." FO 195/946, Moore to Foreign Office, 28 October 1869.

[22] It is important to note that the Tavdgiridze family in general and Ali Pasha in particular were not alone in slave procurement business. A consular report issued in Trabzon in 1869 noted that the local chiefs were the principal agents in the traffic ("a profitable one, it is said," as it stated) in Georgian slaves, "kidnapped and sold from the Turco–Russian frontier provinces." FO 195/946 from Palgrave to Clarendon, 21 September 1869. Just as the slave trade constituted the primary tie between the Caucasian princes and nobles and the Ottoman empire, İbrahim Köremezli pointed out that in the first half of the nineteenth century, the 370 families that immigrated to and

rather embodiments of, to invoke Bruce Grant once again, "competing sovereignties" in what can be called an extensive borderland and the vacuum that formed in between the conflicting realms of state, religious and customary law that stemmed from them. This chapter aims to trace enslaved bodies as "products" of these competing modes of sovereign power; modes that were not always pitted against each other, but sometimes cooperated in their coercive practices which Bruce Grant has listed as "raiding, the exchange of human proxies during warfare, and bride kidnapping, alongside related experiences of voluntary self-abnegation and exile."[23] As Grant further has argued, "to understand sovereignty in the Caucasus [of which, the eastern Black Sea coast as well as other refugee settlements of the Ottoman empire often functioned as extensions], one has to think historically not only about the practices of Russian governance [or Ottoman advances to form military or trade alliances] over time but with the equally historicized archive of the Caucasus' many social worlds."[24] Briefly stated, the purpose of this chapter is to unpack some of these social worlds and draw connections from such practices as blood vengeance, raiding, bride kidnapping, and slavery to larger contexts of power and exploitation, with the aim of presenting a prehistory of coercive power that shaped not only the slaves' experiences and their delayed emancipation in the Ottoman lands but also, as this dissertation aims to demonstrate, informed such categories of gender, age, beauty, as well as ethnic and racial classifications in the decades that followed.

---

settled along the Black Sea coast of the empire drew their main source of income and wealth from slave trading with the Caucasus. İbrahim Köremezli, "The Place of the Ottoman Empire in the Russo-Circassian War (1830–1864)," (Master's thesis, Bilkent University, 2004), 42, note 103.

[23] Grant, *The Captive and the Gift*, xvii.

[24] Ibid.

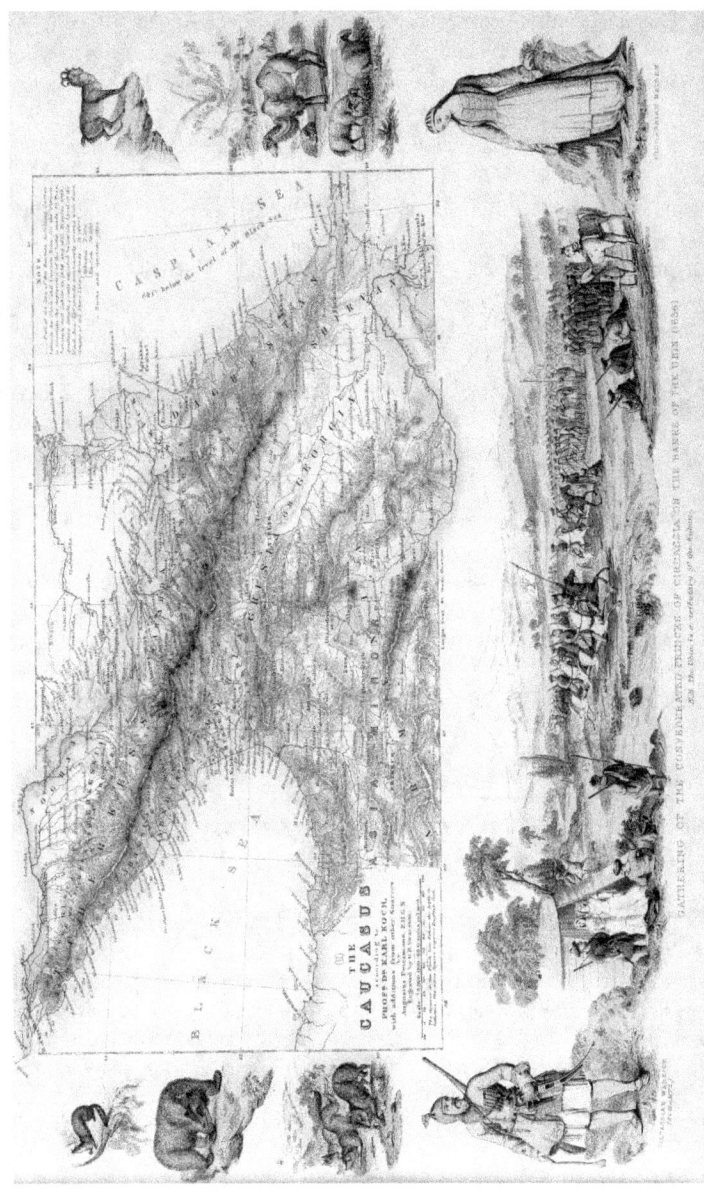

Image 1.1 The Caucasus, divided diagonally by the Caucasus mountain range. The well -known and widely referenced figures of the 'Circassian maiden,' the 'Circassian warrior,' as well as the 'confederated princes' all made their way to accompany the map. *The Royal Illustrated Atlas, Of Modern Geography*, with an Introductory Notice by Dr. N. Shaw, Secretary to the Royal Geographical Society &c. A. Fullarton And Co. London And Edinburgh. 1872.

Tracing the Origins of Slave Trade in the Ottoman Borderlands

In his short story "Two Months in the Village," the nineteenth century Adyghe[25] author Kalambii depicted a scene in which a group of young Adyghe girls go strawberry picking in the mountains, accompanied by the young men of their village.[26] In this customary performance of implicit wooing, the narrator of the story (himself a young man who had just returned from his military education in St. Petersburg) pairs up with Zaliha, the beautiful, orphaned daughter of a noble family. When the group rushes altogether up around the hill, where strawberries were said to be plentiful, the narrator offers Zaliha a ride on his horse. When Zaliha accepts the offer and attempts to mount the horse, however, the horse becomes restless and rears up to throw her off of its back. The young man apologizes to Zaliha for his horse's behavior, but for her it is not his or his horse's fault. "The horse is not accustomed to 'women's skirt,'" she says, "apparently no girl was abducted by it." Abduction, or bride kidnapping as it is often called, first appears in passing in the story, as a flirtatious comment,[27] but then returns to haunt the lovers, when Zaliha is abducted by the prince of the village, to be kept hidden and away from the

---

[25] Köremezli, "The Place of the Ottoman Empire in the Russo-Circassian War," 5–6; Julius Von Klaproth, *Travels in the Caucasus and Georgia Performed in the Years 1807 and 1808* (London: Henry Colburn, 1814), 249–264; Fedor Fedorovich Tornau, *Bir Rus Subayının Kafkasya Anıları*, trans. Keriman Vurdem (Ankara: Kafkas Derneği Yayınları, 1999), 93–95.

[26] Kalembiy (Kalambii, Adil-Girei Keshev, 1837–1872), "Köyde İki Ay" in *Kalembiy'den Adıge Halk Öyküleri*, trans. Abaze Ibrahim (Ankara: Kafdav Yayınları, 2010), 26. The story first appeared in 1860 in Russian (with the title "Dva mesiatsa v aule") in the influential literary magazine *Biblioteka Dlya Chteniya* (The Reader's Library), published in St. Petersburg from 1834 to 1865. Writing largely for an urban middle-class Russian audience, and at a time when Great Reforms were in progress both in central Russia and the Caucasus, Kalambii's writings were not untouched by the ideological currents of his time. He was presumably in dialog with the Russian romantic literature on the Caucasus, in one part transcribing Adyghe cultural practices and in another reinscribing Russian views of the Caucasus. Here, I read his stories against the grain and in most cases only for the details he mentions in passing.

[27] Zaliha's comment also playfully mocks the narrator's lack of knowledge or care of the local customs and practices.

narrator, a commoner and a Russian educated soldier, deemed unsuitable for the noble Zaliha.

Bride kidnapping, a custom widely practiced in the entire region, appears in almost all of Kalambii's stories also. In his most famous one "Abrecler" (Abreks), the kidnapping of a girl serves as the decisive event that shapes the story. When a young man kidnaps a girl against her will[28] and hides her in his friend's house, the villagers, particularly the elders and the girl's family, demand the host to give the girl back, to which the host finally, and grudgingly, consents. In what follows however, he sets out to avenge all those who forced him to act contrary to the customary law (*adat* or *xabze*, as called by the Adyghe), which orders a host to protect his guests under any circumstances.[29] In another story, "Kukla/Pipxe" (Puppet), the issue of bride kidnapping appears more directly related to a sovereign's power and authority.[30] When an elderly and powerful prince uses his power and influence to marry the young and beautiful noble girl

---

[28] As opposed to an arranged abduction, which happened occasionally to circumvent the parents' or elders' opposition to the marriage or a high bride price set for the girl.

[29] Kalembiy, "Abrecler," 106–109. "Abreks" was first published with the title "Abreki" in 1860, in *Russkii vestnik* for a similarly urban middle-class audience. See Rebecca Gould, "Transgressive Sanctity The Abrek in Chechen Culture," for a brief note on the author in *Kritika: Explorations in Russian and Eurasian History* 8, 2 (Spring 2007), 272. A similar case is recounted by John Baddeley, *The Rugged Flanks of the Caucasus* (Arno Press, New York, 1973), 2: 136–7, quoted in Kristin Collins-Breyfogle, " Negotiating Imperial Spaces: Gender, Sexuality & Violence in the Nineteenth–century Caucasus," (Ph.D. Dissertation, The Ohio State University, 2011), 15. For the significance of the notion of host (or *konag*) see J.A. Longworth, *A Year Among the Circassians*, vol. 1 (London: Henry Colburn Publisher, 1840), 224, quoted in Paul Manning, "Just Like England: On the Liberal Institutions of the Circassians," *Comparative Studies in Society and History*, vol.51, no.3 (2009), 600. For its connection to slavery, see Liubov Kurtynova-D'Herlugnan, *The Tsar's Abolitionists: The Slave Trade in the Caucasus and Its Suppression* (Leiden: Brill, 2010), 30.

[30] The original medium that this story first appeared remains unclear, but it is very likely that like the other two stories that are mentioned above, this one was also published in Russian and for similar audience.

Naziha, he realizes that what he himself has extorted could easily be snatched away by another.[31] Not that he particularly cared about Naziha, the author noted. The prince was concerned about his own power and authority, which was eventually violated by his son with horrific consequences.[32]

What also appears as a recurring theme in Kalambii's stories is stealing, or rather the obligation to steal, particularly for the Adyghean aristocracy. Again in "Kukla (Pipxe)," when boasting about his righteous life, Prince Tépserıque admits to have "driven off nine or ten heads of cattle in his youth." However, he did not do it to improve his property, he explicates, but to keep his name and honor as a prince, unblemished. Contrary to what Kalambiï exemplifies with Prince Tépserıque, however, stealing was more than a heroic act in the Caucasus. In addition to establishing their reputations, the princes and the nobility in the Caucasus did in fact make their fortunes or ensured privileged status for their offspring through plunder.[33] "The ideal image of a Circassian noble," Liubov Kurtynova-D'Herlugnan noted "was that of a lucky predator, who spent his time robbing and plundering his neighbors but who was never caught."[34] While being caught brought "infinite shame," Kurtynova-D'Herlugnan added, successful expeditions were considered to be the proof of "gallantry and virility." Writing in the late 1830s, James Stanislaus Bell stated:

> [the princes and the nobility] still indulged in one of the ancient privileges
> of "their order"; that of assembling for exploits of plunder, either in

---

[31] Kalembiy, "Kukla/Pipxe," 87.

[32] Ibid., 96.

[33] Kurtynova-D'Herlugnan, *The Tsar's Abolitionists*, 19.

[34] Ibid.

neighbouring provinces or in Russia (notwithstanding their *quasi* peace with her), having their faces masked for fear of discovery, and speaking together a language not understood by others, or perhaps a mere "slang" of the craft, to prevent the intrusion of the uninitiated.[35]

Moreover, since the main source of their wealth was slaves, the primary export commodity of the region, they stole, more often than not, people and they were, as Kurtynova-D'Herlugnan called them, slave traders.[36] There were some tribes or clans that were ruled by councils of elders, or as Kurtynova-D'Herlugnan noted, popular assemblies and elected magistrates. Those too, however, valued "military prowess and gallantry" as civic virtue and thrived upon slave raiding and pillaging. The main difference, as Kurtynova-D'Herlugnan pointed out, was that raiding, warfare, and as their product, slave trading, were not the privilege of the princes and the nobility, but open to all free commoners, as well.[37]

Abduction, raiding, and pillaging were not particular to the Caucasus but endemic to all societies that were "caught up in a process of extreme social stratification," who customarily reduced their less powerful neighbors to slavery, as Pierre Clastres asserted, to benefit from a steady inflow of captives, as well as a substantial supply of labor power.[38] For James C. Scott, economies of raiding and pillaging pertained not only to the societies that aimed to circumvent chronic labor shortages, but also those who aimed to

---

[35] James Stanislaus Bell, *Journal of a Residence in Circassia during the Years 1837, 1838, and 1839*, vol.1 (London: Edward Moxon, 1840), 357.

[36] Kurtynova-D'Herlugnan, *The Tsar's Abolitionists*, 19.

[37] Ibid., 20.

[38] Pierre Clastres, *Society Against the State* (New York: Zone Books, 1989), 34; Scott, *The Art of Not Being Governed*, 67.

keep larger states (as the Russian or Ottoman empires for the case at hand) always "at arm's length." "Barbarians by design," as Scott described them, they maintained "a brisk and mutually advantageous trade with lowland centers while steering clear of being politically captured."[39] Like their North African counterparts, the Berbers, who considered raiding as their "agriculture,"[40] an economy based on plunder was more than incidental in the Caucasus:

> "Most, if not all, the characteristics that appear to stigmatize hill peoples—their location at the margins, their physical mobility, their swidden agriculture, their flexible social structure, their religious heterodoxy, their egalitarianism, and even the nonliterate, oral cultures— far from being the mark of primitives left behind by civilization, are better seen on a long view as adaptations designed to evade both state capture and state formation. They are, in other words, political adaptations of nonstate peoples to a world of states that are, at once, attractive and threatening."[41]

The Caucasian societies did not always neatly fit into the description of the nonstate peoples where "sovereignty and taxes ended" and "ethnicity and tribes began,"[42] as the coercive power of the sovereign seems to be a principle aspect of the social relations. Bell asserted:

> "[their] princes and the higher class of nobles still possessed considerable power over their own serfs *even that of life and death*, and of *transference*

---

[39] Scott, *The Art of Not Being Governed*, 8.

[40] Berber saying "raiding is our agriculture," is quoted in ibid., 150.

[41] Ibid., 9.

[42] Ibid., 30.

by sale to others, when they have committed crimes. They also preside at public trials and decide upon the fines to be imposed upon persons who commit offences; but these fines, and also the proceeds of the sale of culprits as slaves, by way of punishment, are appropriated as here. They raise no revenue from the people...[43]

Yet they did not clearly fit into the picture depicted by Paul E. Lovejoy in relation to emerging or expanding Muslim states in Africa either, which used raiding, plunder, and the slave trade as a means to coercive state-making and integration into the regional economy and politics.[44] Slaves procured in the Sahel in Africa and sold both to the Ottoman market and Atlantic system were products of these raiding economies that constituted the integral part of their state-building processes. In the Caucasus, on the other hand, there was no equivalent to Usman dan Fodio and the Fulani Jihad, but the local princes and nobles there too used raiding, plunder, warfare, and the slave trade to maintain the existing hierarchies and their own power and authority.

---

[43] Bell, *Journal of a Residence in Circassia*, 357. Emphasis added.

[44] Paul E. Lovejoy (ed.), *Slavery on the Frontiers of Islam* (Princeton: Markus Wiener Publishers, 2004), introduction.

Image 1.2 "Cotes de la Mer Noire. Parti tcherkesse allant faire du butin," in *Le Caucase pittoresque dessine d'apres nature par le prince Gregoire Gagarine* (Plon, 1847). IMAGE ID: 1241838, NYPL Digital Archives.

The act of abduction itself, particularly of women had been, as Leslie Peirce argued for the case of the early modern Ottoman world, the core of sovereign power, so much so that "to validate [any] dynasty's claim to "distinguished origin," [a chronicle] listed six points, the second of which was that "the hand of a conqueror never touched their spouses."[45] The implication was, Peirce argued, "the unstated presumption of using

---

[45] Leslie Peirce, "Abduction with (Dis)honor: Sovereigns, Brigands, and Heroes in the Ottoman World," *Journal of Early Modern History*, vol.15 no. 4 (2011), 314. Drawing from Thomas Blom

them for sex," but the humiliation could also be related to sovereigns' dependents, particularly his wife, being reduced to slavery, as was the case with the wife of Bayezid I, who was reportedly forced to perform menial services.[46] In fact, the very first military victory of Osman ("the eponymous first ruler of the nascent state" as Peirce described him) had an abduction story at its center; abduction of a village woman, "the first and precipitating event in Osman's path to power."[47] "By abduction and adultery," Georges Duby argued, "male sexuality undermined the rules governing the society. Abductors of women destroyed marriage contracts, committing a public crime that caused hatred between families, gave rise to reprisals, and defiled and divided the community."[48] In a similar vein, in the Caucasus, abduction of women was tightly knit with the political

---

Hansen and Finn Stepputat, Bruce Grant has argued that individual bodies have always been "at the center of sovereign logics [...] especially at times when questions of power and authority are most in flux." Grant, *The Captive and the Gift*, 2. Grant also refers here to Giorgio Agamben's discussion on the intersections between juridico-institutional and biopolitical models of power in which he argued that "the inclusion of bare life in the political realm constitutes the original –if concealed– nucleus of sovereign power." For Agamben, "*the production of a biopolitical body is the original activity of sovereign power*" (emphasis in the original). Agamben, *Homo Sacer: Sovereign Power and Bare Life* (Stanford: Stanford University Press, 1995), 6; Grant, *The Captive and the Gift*, 8.

[46] Peirce, "Abduction with (Dis)honor," 313–315.

[47] Ibid., 315–316.

[48] Georges Duby, *The Knight, the Lady and the Priest: The Making of Modern Marriage in Medieval France* (Chicago: The University of Chicago Press, 1983), 68. On a separate note, Claude Meillassoux argued in relation to the Sahel that the domestic societies preferred to abduct and incorporate women, for the obvious advantages and simplicity. Especially in cases when abduction did not result in marriage, Meillassoux further argued, "the abducted woman, withdrawn from her native milieu, deprived of arbitration through the intervention of her family, without rights over her progeny, and, furthermore, assigned to hard agricultural labor and household tasks, might seem to be the forerunner of the slave." Claude Meillassoux, *The Anthropology of Slavery: The Womb of Iron and Gold* (London: The Athlone Press, 1991), 31. Kristin Collins-Breyfogle argued that the nineteenth century Caucasian writers made similar observations in relation to the women of the region. Even when the marriage took place, the Caucasian women entered their new family "not as a member, but as a worker." They were seen as their husbands' slaves, and even a small error on the woman's side could result in divorce, stripping women of any rights they may have. See Dzhannat'-Bagi quoted in Breyfogle, "Negotiating Imperial Spaces, 28.

32

realm, also serving as one of the main causes that triggered and exacerbated blood feuds and blood revenge,[49] which, according to Paul Manning, constituted the main pretext for pillage and the economy that was largely based on it.[50] Both Paul Manning and Georges Charachidze identified blood revenge, pillage, and in an indirect way abduction, as the core of what they called the "princely commerce" or "princely economies" of the Caucasus:

> Commerce was controlled and organized by the nobility, run by the
> intermediation of commercial buyers who were strangers (Turks or Tatars)
> installed on the coast of the Black Sea. The nobles imported manufactured
> goods, weapons, prestige objects, which they redistributed to their
> 'vassals.' . . . But the 'commercial balance' of the Circassian princes
> would have remained in the deficit . . . If they had not had another source
> of revenues, namely pillage. The aristocracy devoted themselves to this
> nearly half of the year, from spring to the end of summer, procuring thus
> regularly weapons, horses, slaves. This surplus allowed them to engage in
> exportation, especially of horses and slaves, also to entertain their vassals,
> an indispensable mechanism for maintaining the social structure. This
> complex and diversified cycle of exchanges combining agricultural

---

[49] Grant, *The Captive and the Gift*, 17, 81. Amjad Jaimoukha argued that in the case of the Vainakh society (comprised mainly of the Chechens and the Ingush), failure in delivering a "promised" fiancée, especially after the presentation of gifts, gave the injured party the pretense to "wreak vengeance on [the male relatives of the bride] as if it were a blood feud." Amjad Jaimoukha, *Chechens: A Handbook* (London: Routledge, 2005), 84. Klaproth argued that among the Karachay, as well as other Tatars, the bride price was termed as the "price of blood." Klaproth, *Travels in the Caucasus and Georgia*, 286. Although an important triggering event, abduction of women was not the only cause of blood feuds in the Caucasus. Anna Zelkina listed the shortage of arable land and pastures as factors that perpetuated enmities and caused constant clashes between rural communities, which "lead to the emergence of the deeply-rooted enmity and centuries-long confrontation between the various North Caucasian tribes and political formations." Anna Zelkina, *In Quest for God and Freedom: Sufi Responses to the Russian Advance in the North Caucasus* (New York: NYU Press, 2000), 25.

[50] Manning, "Just Like England," 600.

production, commerce and pillage has exercised considerable influence on the Circassian vendetta, provoking distortions, 'anomalies,' . . . distortions accentuated by the very nature of political and juridical power, left to the discretion of the aristocracy.[51]

One of these distortions had to do with the corporate nature of the blood feuds. Charachidze argued that when a prince, or a member of the aristocracy, was involved in such a feud, either as the victim or the perpetrator, all of his dependents (sometimes an entire clan or a tribe) took part in taking vengeance.[52] "The revenge of the princes and nobles," as Charachidze stated, "was not limited solely to their personal enemies but extended to all of their dependents," as well as their property, and as a result "entire villages were decimated, crops destroyed, and people were left without houses or food."[53] Avenging parties customarily invaded villages of what they deemed the enemy territory, burnt everything, killing and capturing prisoners, "seizing the cattle and taking anything that could be taken."[54] Blood revenge did not have an expiration date, either. In 1853, a prince attacked a village (vassal of another prince with whom the former had a long existing feud) and took about forty women and children as slaves. Forty years later, a descendant of the wronged prince attacked the village of the opposing party,

---

[51] Georges Charachidze, "Types de Vendetta au Causase," in *La Vengeance. Etudes d'ethnologie, d'histoire et de philosophie.* ed. Raymond Verdier (Paris: Editions Cujas, 1980), 89. Quoted in Manning, "Just Like England," 601. Translation is Manning's.

[52] Charachidze, "Types de Vendetta au Causase," 86. This is also mentioned in Zelkina, *In Quest for God and Freedom,* 16.

[53] Ibid.

[54] Ibid.

"exterminated all the men and boys, cut the breasts of women and took a great number of slaves, most of whom were sold to Turks afterwards."[55]

Unceasing or prolonged blood feuds were not reserved for princes and nobility. In one case from 1830, an Ossetian peasant was reportedly gagged, "tied to a pole [...] taken to Dagestan, and sold into slavery."[56] The victim's son, who deemed vengeance not only his right but also his obligation, avenged his father's abduction and sale into slavery by killing the abductor's son thirty-five years later.[57] However, both the corporate character and the potential long durations of the feuds (particularly when thought in combination with the "substitutionability" of slavery for death, which Orlando Patterson talked about,[58] and vice versa, as illustrated in the previous example) had important consequences, due to sharply varying blood prices between princes, nobles, commoners or slaves, and helped, as Manning argued, building a "princely monopoly on foreign trade, particularly the trafficking of harem slaves to the Ottoman empire."[59] The trade in these "prestige slaves," for Manning "accounted for a major impetus for the transition to "market-based" feuding system amongst coastal Circassian princes."[60] Thus, the economy of slavery, closely knit to abduction, pillaging and blood feuds, "enabled the

---

[55] Ibid., 87.

[56] Breyfogle, "Negotiating Imperial Spaces," 43.

[57] Ibid.

[58] Orlando Patterson, *Slavery and Social Death* (Cambridge: Harvard University Press, 1982), 5.

[59] Manning, "Just Like England," 601. Although Manning's article is not about the Caucasian society but about possible British (mis)interpretations of it, the sections about pillaging, slave trading, and feuding systems bring in ethnographic or historical works of such scholars as Georges Charachidze or Ehud Toledano to provide an analysis about the Caucasian (or, specifically Circassian) society.

[60] Ibid.

proliferation of princely retainers, considerably augmenting the prince's ability to continue pillaging," and rendering the princes and the aristocracy in general, not as the "agents of order but disorder,"[61] in which blood money and slaves appeared as a "universal measure of exchange."[62] A passage on the Abkhaz customary law, which appeared in the Russian state-sponsored newspaper *Kavkas* in 1866 and quoted by Kurtynova-D'Herlugnan, is illustrative of this particular point:

> The decisions of the courts of law usually involved a customary penalty (according to *adats*), which was paid by the guilty party to the plaintiff. For example, the penalty for the murder of a prince was 38 young boys, a horse with a saddle and full set of mountaineer's armaments. Someone, who had killed a nobleman had to pay 16 young boys, a horse with a saddle and armaments; for the murder of a free commoner the penalty was 2 young boys, a gun and a saber. The height of the above mentioned boys had to satisfy the requirements of the *adats*: they were measured by a certain number of palm lengths of the plaintiff. Sometimes the boys could be substituted for cattle.[63]

George Charachidze similarly demonstrated the differences in blood pricing for the Adyghe and other Circassian societies, whose social structure and stratification was similar to that of the Abkhaz. In the formers, however, the distinction between the two ends of the hierarchical order, that is, between the prince in one end and the serf or the slave on the other, was more accentuated. Thus the blood price varied more sharply,

---

[61] Ibid.

[62] Kurtynova-D'Herlugnan, *The Tsar's Abolitionists*, 31.

[63] Ibid.

sometimes rendering the blood price of a prince practically incalculable.[64] As

Charachidze exemplified, in around 1860, when a Kabardian prince of Atazhukin clan (in

the eastern part of Circassia) was killed by the Karachay (Tatar people of the North

Caucasus), the Atazhukin clan set the blood so high that the entire Karachay clan

combined would not be able to pay it.[65] As a contemporary put it in 1826 "the horrible

custom of blood revenge gives rise to an unstoppable series of murder and plunder which

in the end would reduce the people to the level of African tigers and lay low the

population of this region like the plague if the related customs of hospitality and the

peculiar spirit of the bonds of friendship that is famous in the Caucasus under the name of

kunachestvo did not place several limits to this torrent of destruction."[66]

Entangled Legalities

Witnessing a blood feud-related murder in Abkhazia in the 1830s, Fedor

Fedorovich Tornau stated that in the event that both parties agreed, the matter could be

brought to a court; that of customary or Islamic law, to be decided and agreed upon by

---

[64] Charachidze, "Types de Vendetta au Causase," 89–91. Klaproth argued that as former subjects of the Circassian princes, who, at the beginning of the nineteenth century, "still arrogate[d] themselves and apparent superiority, the Abkhazian princes were considered equal only to the Circassian/Kabardian nobles and could not marry women who had a higher rank than a noble's daughter, which added further complexities to inter-communal relations in the region. Moreover, if a Kabardian prince or any oneunder his protection was robbed by an Abkhazian, the latter paid three slaves (of either sex) as a punishment; if anyone under Kabardian princes' protection got murdered, the punishment was the payment of nine slaves. Klaproth, *Travels in the Caucasus and Georgia*, 249.

[65] Charachidze, "Types de Vendetta au Causase," 91.

[66] S.D. Nechaev, *Moskovskii telegraf* quoted in Thomas M. Barrett, *At the Edge of Empire: The Terek Cossacks and the North Caucasus Frontier, 1700–1860* (Boulder, CO: Westview Press, 1999), 147.

each party. According to Şer'i law, Tornau noted, all Muslims were deemed equal and thus, the blood of a prince had the same value as the blood of a serf. According to *adat*s on the other hand, as argued above, a prince's life was more expensive than a peasant's or serf's. Thus, he concluded, the princes and nobles always opted for customary law, and the peasants and serfs, for the religious Şer'i courts, and since an agreement was rarely reached on this, very few of the blood feud cases (especially if they were not likely to turn into a prolonged, total tribal warfare) were actually brought to a court.[67] This was the case even in more distinctively Muslim (hence deemed more egalitarian)[68] parts of the Caucasus like Dagestan (in North-East Caucasus) and Chechnya, which, had a long history and tradition of *muridism* (more so than any other part of the Caucasus), which implied, at least in theory, that Islamic religious legal code had the upper hand, rather than customary law. There too, however, the relationship between the customary and Islamic legal codes remained in flux and was far from following a linear progress. They too commonly raided neighboring communities and abducted people, "as rather a pleasant plunder, [took] them away, and [sold] them as slaves," to Turkish or Crimean slave-merchants and made considerable profits.[69] Like in the rest of the Caucasus, they converted their "*kanly*s and needy debtors into slaves."[70]

---

[67] Tornau, *Bir Rus Subayının Kafkasya Anıları*, 49–50.

[68] Köremezli, "The Place of the Ottoman Empire in the Russo-Circassian War," 15.

[69] Elena Inozemtseva, "On the History of Slave-Trade in Dagestan," in *Iran & the Caucasus*, vol.10, no.2 (2006), 185.

[70] Ibid., 186. *Kanly* (literally meaning bloody or blood stained in Turkish) is a term used to describe those who killed a person and thus owed either his life or a corresponding blood money; Kurtynova-D'Herlugnan, *The Tsar's Abolitionists*, 14.

Paul B. Henze argued that Islam, like Christianity that reached the region before it, was merely a "veneer over traditional beliefs and customs."[71] One reason for this was that Islamization of the Caucasus people was relatively a recent phenomenon. As late as 1760s, Circassians, As Klaproth stated, "proved themselves Mohammedans by little else than by their abstinence from swine flesh and wine."[72] Even in Dagestan and Chechnya, Islam became an official religion only in the second half of the eighteenth century. Ingush people, described as an "incredible picture of complete religious chaos," converted to Islam only in 1862.[73] Drawing from the nineteenth century Russian scholar Andria Shegren, Anna Zelkina described the degree of religious syncretism among the Ingush as follows: "The mullahs feel free to call upon Muslims when the bells ring, the Kist [Ingush] idol Gel-erda stands in peace in an old church built by Queen Tamara, which now lies abandoned."[74] Religious syncretism was not particular to the Ingush alone. Tornau wrote that there were many families among the Abkhazians that had both Muslim and Christian members and that this situation was never deemed unusual or harmed family relations.[75] Abkhazians, according to Tornau, had not forgotten their Christian mores after they were proselytized by the Turks in the sixteenth century.[76] Muslim Abkhazians drank wine and ate pork, while the newly (re)converted Christians sought out ways to take a second wife. They celebrated Christmas together, and both

---

[71] Henze, "Circassian Resistance to Russia," 67–68.

[72] Klaproth, *Travels in the Caucasus and Georgia*, 316.

[73] Zelkina, *In Quest for God and Freedom*, 34–35.

[74] Ibid., 39.

[75] Tornau, *Bir Rus Subayının Kafkasya Anıları*, 39.

[76] Ibid. It is important to note that Tornau observes and writes as a Russian colonial officer, respresenting the Russian colonial project, which contained, among other things, an objective to convert Caucasus people into Christianity.

respected the "holy forests," and feared the "spirit of the mountains."[77] Klaproth made a similar argument in relation to the Abazeh, that they had "strictly speaking, no religion, and [ate] pork," although nobles reportedly began professing Islamism in recent years.[78] Klaproth stated that likewise the Tatars had no religion either, and that the common people worshipped "whom they call Tägri and not Allah, as the giver of all good, and the prophet Elijah (*Nebi Ilia*), who, according to them, frequently appears on the summits of the highest mountains, and to whom they offer sacrifices of lambs, milk, butter, cheese, and beer (ssra), accompanied with singing and dancing."[79] Klaproth further argued that under the influence of the Circassians, the Tatar chiefs embraced the Mohammedan faith, although except for the Karachay they neither had mosques, nor priests; the latter having been converted to Islamism in 1780s, by a Kabardian priest named Isaak Effendi, who was "in the pay of the Porte."[80] "Ever since the peace of Kütschük Kanardshi in 1774," Klaproth wrote, "the Porte has endeavored to spread the religion of Mohammed, by means of ecclesiastical emissaries, in the Caucasus, and especially among the Circassians..."[81]

Anna Zelkina argued that the degree of Islamization in Dagestan and Chechnya (with implications for other parts of the Caucasus) could be observed through its

---

[77] Ibid. Klaproth mentions that the Karachay, Barlkarians and the *Tschegem* exhibited traces of Christianity. Klaproth, *Travels in the Caucasus and Georgia*, 10. Nogays were, according to Klaproth, "Mohammedans, of the sect of the Sunni, and have priests of mullahs of their own nation, who partly pursue their studies among the Turks, and in five or six years return to the Ckuban," 162, 254.

[78] Klaproth, *Travels in the Caucasus and Georgia*, 257.

[79] Ibid., 282.

[80] Ibid., 285. Even they, however, had "recourse to divination" and believed in mountain spirits, 290–91.

[81] Ibid., 316–317.

reflection in these communities' legal systems and "the balance between *shari'a* and *'adat* legislature within it." The common claim of the contemporaries who assumed the civil matters and criminal offences were neatly settled in accordance with Şer'i law and *adat* respectively, did not always hold, nor did it do justice to the complexities of the ways in which Islam had penetrated to the region.[82] Zelkina notes that the more accessible lowland settlements, such as the Chechen villages, Şer'i law had a more discernable influence on the codes of *adat*, whereas in the highland areas, it existed only superficially and the legal system remained largely based on customary law.[83] While family matters, such as marriage, divorce, or burial were under the jurisdiction of Islamic law, for instance, this did not mean that old practices were completely abandoned. "Thus," Zelkina exemplified "throughout the North Caucasus the tradition of *umykanie* (kidnapping) of a bride by a groom, persisted, although even in these cases, the marriage was considered to be valid only after approval by a religious official."[84] More importantly, however, these two legal orders were at odds with each other:

> There are a number of fundamental differences between the Islamic and pre-Islamic tribal legal systems. The most important are, firstly, differentiation between personal and collective responsibility for a crime (one of the main characteristics of tribal society being the principle of shared responsibility – 'one for all and all for one' – while Islam introduced the notion of personal responsibility); secondly, differentiation

---

[82] Zelkina, *In Quest for God and Freedom*, 40.

[83] Ibid., 41. See page 43–44, for appointment of additional *kanly*s, for instance, for a good example of a "middle ground" for religious and customary laws.

[84] Ibid., 45. In complete violation with Şer'i law, the customary law allowed marriage between milk brothers and sisters, 46. Amjad Jaimoukha also mentions the *adat-Şer'i* law opposition, which he deems still unresolved in the present day. Jaimoukha, *The Chechens*, 84.

between deliberate and accidental crimes and the establishment of different degrees of punishment for them, a concept which was wholly alien to the pre-Islamic tribal societies; thirdly, the concept of balance between the damage inflicted and the punishment; and fourthly, legal procedure and the means of carrying out justice (i.e. judges, executive officers, type of oath etc.).[85]

The differentiation between these two legal systems in terms of accidental-deliberate crimes and collective-personal responsibilities were particularly important for crimes involving blood-revenge. Although Şer'i law recognized the legitimacy of blood-revenge, Zelkina argued, it prohibited taking revenge on collective basis, and prefered settling the dispute in peaceful ways. For the Dagestanis, Chechens, and the Ingush, accepting blood money was a dishonor and humiliation. In other parts of the Caucasus, as discussed above, uneven blood pricing claimed more bodies and instigated even more violence. Thus, there existed a certain degree of irreconcilability between these two orders, which strictly kept such practices as blood revenge, bride kidnapping or abduction in general, and as their product, slave procurement, trade, and slavery itself, outside of the jurisdiction of Islamic law.[86] As Zelkina further notes: "with the collective responsibility and no distinction being made between murder and manslaughter, long-lasting blood-feuds involving whole clans and tribes could lead to the mutual extermination of their

---

[85] Zelkina, *In Quest for God and Freedom*, 40–41.

[86] See Klaproth, *Travels in the Caucasus and Georgia*, 287. For example, *ümm-i veled* principle of Islamic slavery did not hold among the Karachay, one of the more distinctively Islamized tribes in the Caucasus, and one that had close connections with the Ottomans as well. The sons born to slave mothers were declared bastards by the legitimate offspring, and put to death by them "as no person will avenge his blood, because he is related to nobody."

entire male population [and female population, needless to say, by abduction/ enslavement]."[87]

Students of Ottoman slavery have often been perplexed by the fact that Ottomans enslaved, in violation of the *Şer'i* code, their fellow Muslim peoples of the Caucasus. One explanation given was that the preexisting slave caste and the corresponding legal status made the trade in fellow Muslims permissible vis-à-vis Islamic law.[88] However, both the question and explanation not only fail to notice that the slave procurement and slave trade were separate mechanisms, but also presume a uniform Islamic identity through all stages of the trade, as well as adherence to Islamic legal order among the Caucasus communities, with ample attention given to the problem of "just enslavement," which did not exist.[89] What has also been argued was that it was common practice that the slave-holding classes sold their slaves and non-slave holding commoner/peasants

---

[87] Zelkina, *In Quest for God and Freedom*, 44.

[88] Hakan Erdem, *Slavery in the Ottoman Empire and its Demise, 1800–1909* (New York: St. Martin's Press, 1996), 50. Ehud R. Toledano, *The Ottoman Slave Trade and its Suppression: 1840–1890* (Princeton: Princeton University Press, 1983), 148. For Kurtynova-D'Herlugnan, the assumption that the number of born slaves in the Caucasus sustained such a large scale, long standing trade is questionable. Kurtynova-D'Herlugnan, *The Tsar's Abolitionists*, 27–28.

[89] It is important to note that this too readily presupposes that Islamic law was clear on the subject of slavery also. The classic divide of *Dar-ul-Islam* and *Dar-ul-Harb,* the slave-producing frontier between the world of Islam and the land of Unbelief (hence, war), respectively, has often been taken as a clear-cut line that divided the Muslim and non-Muslim, particularly idolatrous societies. Paul E. Lovejoy demonstrates that this divide was highly contextual and subject to constant debates, along with the problem of "just enslavement," among Muslim scholars since the very early stages of Muslim expansion in Africa. Islam and slavery were linked through *jihad* and *ghazawat* (slave producing war and raiding activities within a specific Islamic context), which were deployed at will by emerging and expanding Muslim states (such as the Sokoto Caliphate in the early nineteenth century) to enslave Muslims and idolaters alike. Paul E. Lovejoy (ed.), *Slavery on the Frontiers of Islam* (Princeton: Markus Wiener Publishers, 2004), introduction.

their children.[90] Quoting from a Russian survey from 1823, however, Liubov Kurtynova-D'Herlugnan demonstrated that was rarely the case:

> Although bonded people can be sold [...] it is generally regarded as a
> dishonor to the master and, since custom here is stronger than the law, it is
> rarely done. Such a humanitarian attitude may seem contradictory because
> slave trade is an ancient and a respected occupation in the Caucasus. It
> may be explained by saying that slaves for sale are taken as spoils of war
> and later they change hands and are eventually sold [to the traders]. Such
> are the customs not only of the mountaineers, but also of the Mingrel
> princes. When they make war with each other, their first goal is to take as
> many prisoners as possible. Later the prisoners are taken to Poti, to
> Anaklia, to Anapa or other ports for sale. Therefore, everybody sells not
> his own bonded people, but somebody else's.[91]

Kurtynova-D'Herlugnan concluded that except "in perceived dire need or in case of blatant disobedience," princes and nobles did not sell their slaves, nor did fathers sell

---

[90] Toledano, *The Ottoman Slave Trade and its Suppression*, 18. He writes: "the sale of children was widespread among the Circassians, mostly among those who belonged to the slave class. With the consent of the master and parent, girls were sold and taken to the harems of Istanbul to enjoy the great opportunities believed to be awaiting them there. In many cases, all parties involved—not least among them the slave girl herself—were eager to effect the deal. As put by an upper-class Istanbul lady sold by her widowed mother at a tender age: 'One day, however, my mother came to us with joy in her face and said to me: 'My children, your father must be having in his favor the ear of the Prophet. Here comes to us a miraculous help. A rich *Hanoum* wishes to buy six or seven little girl slaves. I am going to sell you three little girls, and with the money go back to the mountains to bring up your brothers as true Roumeliotes, not like mice in a city.' We were very happy..."; Also see Erdem, *Slavery in the Ottoman Empire and its Demise,* 104–105 and Madeline Zilfi, *Women and Slavery in the Late Ottoman Empire: The Design of Difference* (Cambridge: Cambridge University Press, 2010), 126–128, 211. Zilfi argues that many of the enslaved Circassian *cariyes* in Istanbul were Muslim born, and that the Islamization of the Circassians had been going on for many centuries, 210.

[91] Kurtynova-D'Herlugnan, *The Tsar's Abolitionists*, 28.

their children.[92] Klaproth argued that "the common notion, that the Turkish seraglios are chiefly supplied with [Circassian women], is totally unfounded; for the Circassians very rarely sell people of their country to the Turks, but only captive slaves."[93] In Kalembiy's story " Kukla (Pipxe)," Naziha's father refers to slave trade as a curse or at best a source of humiliation. Rather than marrying her beautiful and talented daughter to someone less than a prince, he exclaims, he would rather sell her to a Turkish slave trader![94] Tornau also mentioned that Circassians did not sell their daughters, but only those who they captured in raids and occasionally their own slaves. In one instance, he meets Han, one of the enslaved servants of a local Abezeh prince, a fifteen year old girl "with fair hair," who was kept apart from other servants, dressed and trained "to be sold to the Turks."[95]

"To Constantinople—to be sold!"

It is not possible to argue the wholesale inexistence of such cases of self-enslavement or enslavement by relatives, as there is documentary evidence, particularly in British archives, which underlines the pervasiveness of Caucasian parents selling their

---

[92] Ibid. Apart from dire need, following the Circassian expulsion and the resettlement after the Russo-Turkish war in 1877–78, the Abkhaz chiefs relocated in Ottoman Anatolia became interested in sending their daughters to imperial harems as enslaved servants. By the end of the nineteenth century, the *cariyes* employed in imperial harems, as well as the wives and consorts of the sultan were predominantly Abkhazian.

[93] Klaproth, *Travels in the Caucasus and Georgia*, 322. Klaproth adds that most of the women sent to Turkey were from Imerethi and Mingrelia.

[94] Kalembiy, "Kukla/Pipxe" in *Kalembiy'den Adıge Halk Öyküleri*, 76.

[95] Tornau, *Bir Rus Subayının Kafkasya Anıları*, 167. In James Stanislaus Bell's account, two young Circassian girls appear, themselves "eagerly desire to go to Stambul to push their fortune—what we call being sold for slaves, and, with [Sir William]Allan's romance of a picture before us, think of with sympathetic horror." Bell, *Journal of a Residence in Circassia during the Years 1837, 1838, and 1839*, vol.1 (London: Edward Moxon, 1840), 28–29, 44.

children into slavery. A consular report from Erzurum, for one, discussed (after stating that there was discernable trade in Georgian, Chechen and Circassian slaves in the province) the ways in which these slaves [most of whom were children aged between eight and fourteen] were obtained. According to the report, they were procured "from that part of the Russian territory touching the Turkish border between Batoom [Batumi] and Akhalsik [Akhaltsikhe]." It continued:

> The people engaged in the trade are dependents or servants of the local Beys of Ajerreh [Adjara]—a district of the Trebizond [Trabzon] *vilaiet* [province]—who, either by raid into the Russian territory kidnap them secretly, or buy them openly from their parents. [...] They are not generally disposed of in this *vilaiet* but are sent away for sale to the contiguous *vilaiets* of Diarbekr, Aleppo, and Baghdad. I may add that Turkish subjects as well, native of Ajerreh as also the Tchetchen and Circassian immigrants from Russia, sell their children into slavery—the females under the *Nikkah* [marriage contract] system and the males for servitude—and that, when official reclamations are made by Foreign Authorities for the restitution of kidnapped Georgians to their families, the local government authorities invariably assert and attempt to prove their assertion, that they belong to the latter classes—consequently Turkish subjects—and are not Georgians, while at the same time, the main question of slavery itself is invariably overlooked...[96]

Another report, this time written by the consular office in Istanbul, stated that white slavery "was not accompanied with cruelty" and that the parents were in the habit of breeding the "girls for sale, they themselves look to it for position and settlement in life—

---

[96] FO 195/946 Consular Dispatch from Consul Taylor to Earl Clarendon, 20 September 1869.

46

as do girls in other countries."[97] Similarly, a draft of a pamphlet, submitted to Yıldız

Palace in 1883, repeated the same claim, particularly in regards to Georgians, stating that

their habit of selling their children to various countries has been in effect for a long

time.[98] Klaproth made the same argument earlier in the nineteenth century, only in

relation to the Mingrelia, Imereti, and Guria parts of Georgia, that the inhabitants of these

places subsisted through agriculture and the sale of their children.[99] Liubov Kurtynova-

D'Herlugnan observed that such romantic ideas were common in the nineteenth century,

among the European travelers to the region, who "visited the Caucasus were, apparently,

also left under the impression that slavery was the most desirable fate for any Circassian

girl."[100] August von Haxthausen's account of the recovery and manumission of six

Circassian enslaved women, which he claimed to have witnessed, is a good example of

this particular reasoning:

> In announcing to the girls their liberation, the [Russian] General ordered
> them to be informed, that the choice was open to them, to be sent back to
> their homes with the Prince of their own race, or to marry Russians and
> Cossacks of their free choice, to return with me to Germany, where all
> women are free, or lastly to accompany the Turkish Captain, who would
> sell them in the slave-market at Constantinople. The reader will hardly
> credit that, unanimously and without a moment's consideration, they
> exclaimed, "To Constantinople—to be sold!" There is scarcely any people

---

[97] FO 195/946 From P. Francis to Lord Clarendon, 28 September 1869.

[98] BOA, Y.PRK.AZJ 7/57, 1300.Z.29 (31 October 1883).

[99] Klaproth, *Travels in the Caucasus and Georgia*, 402. It is worth noting that most of the information Klaproth has on Imereti, Mingrelia and Guria, he seemingly obtains from a Russian officer while being quarantined in Ananuri on his way to Georgia.

[100] Kurtynova-D'Herlugnan, *The Tsar's Abolitionists*, 40.

more proud and jealous of their liberty, and yet this was the voluntary answer of these women."[101]

Von Haxthausen concluded that if one looked at the views, thoughts and habits of "this Eastern people," the answer given by the women would be in complete agreement with their notions:

> The purchase and sale of women is deeply rooted in the custom of the nation: every man buys his wife from the father or from the family. On the part of the women no feeling of shame is attached to the transaction, but rather a sense of honor; and indeed, before we can pronounce on the subject, we must be intimately acquainted with the circumstances, and must be able to place ourselves exactly in the position of the Circassians. In her own country, a Circassian girl lives in a state of slavish dependence on her father and brothers; her position is therefore raised when a man demands her in marriage, and stakes his fortune to obtain her, at the same time that he liberates her from the servile constraint of her family.[102]

Ivan Golovin, on the other hand, argued that the supporters of Count Vorontsov and the concessions he made to the Circassians were also responsible for these perceptions. According to them:

> "The slave-trade is indispensible to the existence of the mountaineers, and the daughters of the Caucasus are too happy to dwell in the harems of

---

[101] August von Haxthausen, *Transcaucasia: Sketches of the Nations and Races Between the Black Sea and the Caspian* (London: Chapman and Hall, 1854), 8. Also quoted in Charles King, *The Black Sea: A History* (Oxford: Oxford University Press, 2005), 118. Haxthausen's account of the Russian peasant commune has also been found highly inaccurate. See Dennison, T. K. and A. W. Carrus. "The Invention of the Russian Peasant Commune: Haxthausen and the Evidence." *Historical Journal* 46, no. 3 (Sept. 2003).

[102] Von Haxthausen, *Transcaucasia*, 8–9.

Constantinople, as in fact, the sisters and the mothers of the Sultans are Circassian women; being brought up in the religion of Mahomet, their fate would not be different if they remained in their own country; besides can they grieve for parents who sold them?" The supporters of the slave-trade are not, it must be admitted, scrupulous about principles. But what would they answer if we told them that life in harems is not so happy as they are pleased to say? [...] The slave trade was sanctioned by a treaty of 1847, between Russians and Circassians. During part of the year it is carried on openly on the Black Sea. Every year more than 1,000 young girls are carried from Circassia to Turkey; and the obstacles opposed to that trade have had no other result than to quadruple the price of slaves. Even Austrian steam boats are employed to for carrying Circassian girls; and whenever the Russians capture any of these slave boats, they either give the girls in marriage to the Cossacks, or they allow them to be violated by the soldiers of the regiments garrisoned in the neighboring forts.[103]

Whether this was merely an attempt to reason with what seemed to be a strange custom on Von Haxthausen's and other foreign travelers' side (they understood it as the sale of the nation's women by the nation)[104], or it was the proliferation, as Golovin suggested, of an official justification of Russians' acts, particularly failures, in the region is difficult to say. In either case, such presumptuous descriptions attributed a unity, as well as ethnic and religious uniformity to the Caucasus that it did not have, even during the Shamil War, and failed, according to Kurtynova-D'Herlugnan, to recognize the fact that the majority of the Caucasian slaves transported to the Ottoman Empire were captured in

---

[103] Ivan Golovin, *The Caucasus* (London: Trübner & Co., 1854), 22.

[104] Note that this particular perspective haunted the Circassian nationalists in early twentieth century, as will be discussed in the fourth chapter of this dissertation and constitutes one of the main reasons that slavery is virtually erased from the collective memory of diaspora Caucasians.

raids. Moreover, in a region, which was called by Thomas Barrett as the "land without labor," whose most definitive feature was chronic labor shortages, made worse by disease and constant fighting, raiding, and plunder,[105] voluntary release of family members, except in cases of necessity, does not seem plausible.[106] Klaproth reported that such tribes as the Abezeh strengthened themselves not solely by reproduction, but also by "carrying off captives from among the neighboring tribes, whom they employed in the operations of agriculture," pointing at the fact that the objective of raiding was not always (and only) obtaining captives for slave trade but also the compensation of labor shortages.[107] Moreover, that the Caucasian settlements were often founded in remote places (difficult to locate without the help of a guide) and the village houses were arranged to form a circle in the middle where the "defenseless people are held in case of attack," or that the villages reportedly kept watchmen, all hinted at the pervasiveness of predatory raids in the region and defense strategies developed against them.[108] The fact that slaves were almost always bartered in exchange of such scarce or controlled commodities as salt, arms, and ammunition makes it more likely that the impelling factor of slave procurement comprised larger mechanisms than the sporadic sale of children by their parents and

---

[105] Barrett, *At the Edge of Empire*, 89.

[106] It is important to note that such an action also meant expulsion of the sold person from the community, which was, as Kurtynova-D'Herlugnan argued, "never taken lightly." Kurtynova-D'Herlugnan, *The Tsar's Abolitionists*, 29. For a discussion on the "sovereign ban," see Grant, *The Captive and the Gift*, 9.

[107] Klaproth, *Travels in the Caucasus and Georgia*, 256–257.

[108] Shora Bekmurzin Nogmov, *Adighe-Hatikhe Çerkes Tarihi*, trans. Dr. Vasfi Güsar (Istanbul: Baha Matbaası, 1974); Klaproth, *Travels in the Caucasus and Georgia*, 323; Bell, *Journal of a Residence in Circassia*, 89–90. This goes against Zilfi's argument of the largely voluntary character of Caucasian slave trade. Zilfi, *Women and Slavery in the Late Ottoman Empire*, 211.

involved a highly organized system of trade, as well as raiding groups, whose numbers, depending on the target of the raid, could reach hundreds or even thousands.[109]

Thomas Barrett argued that a successful raiding expedition typically involved small numbers of attackers, either mounted or on foot, depending on the purpose of the attack.[110] If the raiders aimed at capturing only few people and a few head of cattle, the raid would be undertaken on foot.[111] Those parties focused mainly on traveling women and children, particularly girls, who worked the fields or ran such errands as carrying foodstuff or water, "outside the village or settlement walls, with little or no armed cover," which made them easy targets.[112] The mounted parties attacked larger groups or settlements guarded by men and/or "drove off large herds of cattle and horses and flocks of sheep..."[113] In Kalembiy's "Abreks," the narrator describes their raid into a village as follows:

> Children were playing tip-cat at the verge of the ditch. When they saw us
> they stopped playing and started staring at us. It seemed as if they were
> about to get suspicious. Yismel and I got closer, grabbed two of them, and
> clutching them tightly under our arms we got out. The others ran away
> screaming. Hearing their scream, two or three men came running near the
> ditch and emptied their bullets after us. They flew whistling, left and right.

---

[109] Grant, *The Captive and the Gift*, 28; Barrett, *At the Edge of Empire*, 157. Barrett mentions service records from Chervlennaia settlement that reported raids that involved 3,000, 4,000, and 8,000 attackers, between 1840 and 1845. Klaproth states that in their expeditions, the Circassians even used "secret languages, founded on a pre-concerted arrangement." Klaproth, *Travels in the Caucasus and Georgia*, 328.

[110] Barrett, *At the Edge of Empire*, 137–138.

[111] Ibid.

[112] Ibid.

[113] Ibid.

A group [of men] started chasing us on their horses but our horses had

been in the barn in the past two weeks, they were fast as an arrow. Still,

they got nearer; we could hear their cursing. Harıçet was behind us; he

turned around and shot at them. Smoke of the gunpowder concealed

[Harıçet] and the followers for a while. Then we heard gun shot again, two

or three times. We turned around to look and saw three horses with empty

saddles heading back to the village...

The raiders finally go into hiding in the forest and shortly after set out to rid themselves

off of their spoils (for the narrator maintains that such booty should not be kept near the

enemy), trading them with a local prince in exchange of two horses, garments, and a

Turkish revolver.[114] Klaproth wrote that the tribes that lived near Kuban River did not

"venture to retain their prisoners, lest they should seek refuge in the Russian territory, and

therefore sell them to the Abazeh, who again dispose of them to the yet more remote

Kubichan inhabiting the country beyond the snowy mountains contiguous to the sea."

"They are thence," Klaproth added, "transported to Anatolia and Egypt."[115]

Regardless of its size and purpose, raids were never "indiscriminate burning and

plunder,"[116] but always well planned and involved more people than those who did the

raiding. For campaigns of military character, Barrett argued, "the raiders learned the

troop strength, weakness along the line, and other opportunities from spies, Russian

deserters, native villagers who lived close to the Terek, native traders, and others familiar

---

[114] Kalembiy, "Abrecler," 118–121. In a few days the raiders go back to the same village and drive off thirty heads of cattle, which they sell to Armenian merchants, who eventually sell them to Russian soldiers, 121.

[115] Klaproth, *Travels in the Caucasus and Georgia*, 258.

[116] Michael Khodarkovsky, *Russia's Steppe Frontier: The Making of a Colonial Empire, 1500–1800* (Bloomington: Indiana University Press, 2002), 17.

with the Russian side."[117] The raiders planned both the entry and exit of their attack very carefully for weeks; attacked very swiftly and more often than not, at night.[118] Primary goal was to take as many captives as possible. Some raids had specific and decisively limited targets. In one instance, told by Tornau, an impoverished noble family called upon a meeting and decided to pursue a blood feud they previously had with an Abezeh family, to rid themselves off of their poverty. Consequently, a small group consisting of the clan's young men raided the family, stole a "young, beautiful" girl whom they sold to the Turks afterwards.[119] In rare occasions, the "Turks" themselves did the raiding. In one of these cases, three children, aged twelve to sixteen, were kidnapped by small bands of armed infantry, reportedly "in Ottoman outfit." Captured in different times, while traveling alone in the countryside surrounding the city of Ozurgeti (in Georgia's Guria district on the Ottoman border), the children were quickly disposed of: first brought to the house of a local man (possibly from nobility as his name, Bayraktar, indicates), predetermined as a safe keep, and then sold to Ottoman slave traders, destined for Erzincan district of Ottoman Anatolia.[120] Not only were the villagers, the peasants, or the free folk residing in the Caucasus targets of the local raiders, but anyone passing by or sojourning in the vicinity were equally vulnerable to such attacks. In one famous example, which occurred in 1854 and according to John Ussher, "created a great

---

[117] Barrett, *At the Edge of Empire*, 158.

[118] Grant, *The Captive and the Gift*, 28.

[119] Tornau, *Bir Rus Subayının Kafkasya Anıları*, 182–183.

[120] BOA, HR.MKT 266/49, 1275.R.18 (25 November 1858). Candan Badem talks about Ottoman irregular troops, *başıbozuk*s (commanded by Çürüksulu Ali Paşa who opens this chapter) and even regular men were involved in kidnapping children from the neighboring Georgian villages during (and possibly after) the Crimean war. Badem, "The Ottomans and the Crimean War," 139–140.

sensation at the time throughout Russia," princesses Orbeliani and Nina Baratoff were captured in a circumstantial raid by Lesghians, in a village called Tsenondahl, where the former was visiting the latter in her summer residence. The Caucasus pillaging economies connected to the Ottoman state via slave trade and to the Russian state through ransom business. Thus, anyone who could be captured was a desired commodity.[121]

Ultimately, slaves were obtained, through "a variety of domestic raiding systems" which evidently converged to the trade network that tied the Caucasus to the Ottoman Empire, but nevertheless was different from it. To add to what Liubov Kurtynova-D'Herlugnan argued in relation to the fundamental difference between slavery and slave trade, "the *trade* in slaves, and the raiding that produced them" were also two different mechanisms.[122] Raiding systems, as an "expedient to control a lucrative trade route or to safeguard privileged access to valuable markets,"[123] were governed by the local princes and nobility's desire to maintain their privileges and existing hierarchies and were regulated largely by customary law, modified at will. In trade, on the other hand, "mutually accepted" and "immutable" laws of commerce prevailed.[124] The Turkish merchants were always present, but never as close to question the "just enslavement" of the slaves they bought and sold.

---

[121] John Ussher (F.R.G.S.), *A Journey from London to Persepolis: Including Wanderings in Daghestan, Georgia, Armenia, Kurdistan, Mesopotamia, and Persia* (London: Hurst and Blackett, 1865), 29–32.

[122] Grant, *The Captive and the Gift*, 23.

[123] Scott, *The Art of not Being Governed*, 22.

[124] Alison Frank, "The Children of the Desert and the Laws of the Sea: Austria, Great Britain, the Ottoman Empire, and the Mediterranean Slave Trade in the Nineteenth Century," *The American Historial Review*, vol.117, no.2 (April 2012), 444.

In most cases, "the Turk" was not on the ground but rather concealed in such items as a "Turkish revolver" and ammunition, tokens of Ottomans' virtual colonization in the Caucasus,[125] that were bartered, as a prerequisite, only with young girls and children.[126] Or, they waited in shops, lined up in port cities, such as Soukhum-kale or Anapa, along the Black Sea coast in the Caucasus, where the sale of women was a daily occasion.[127] There they sat comfortably and calmly, as Tornau depicted them, and smoked their long tobacco pipes, pretending that they were indifferent towards everything around them.[128] Some took up residence in villages and hamlets. İbrahim Köremezli noted that until the Russian annexation of Anapa, there were sixty villages where only merchants resided,[129] some of them exceedingly rich and powerful. For one, James Bell mentioned a certain Hassan Bey, a wealthy man whose family was originally from Turkey, who "collected" young women for Constantinople, with the help of other "Mussulmans."[130] He was not a native chief, yet had a fortune (which included three vessels that he used to trade with Istanbul) comparable "with that of most of them."[131] The Turkish traders' immunity and the ease with which they traveled, or had access to their merchandize are exemplified in an incident related by Tornau. When a local prince

---

[125] Zilfi, *Women and Slavery in the Late Ottoman Empire*, 127; Klaproth, *Travels in the Caucasus and Georgia*, 292, 323.

[126] Tornau, *Bir Rus Subayının Kafkasya Anıları*, 182; George Leighton Ditson, *Circassia; or A Tour to the Caucasus* (London: T.C. Newby, 1850), 188; Von Haxthausen, *Transcaucasia*, 3, 7.

[127] Tornau, *Bir Rus Subayının Kafkasya Anıları*, 111.

[128] Ibid., 25; Klaproth, *Travels in the Caucasus and Georgia*, 265–266.

[129] Bell, *Journal of a Residence in Circassia*, 94; Köremezli, "The Place of the Ottoman Empire in the Russo-Circassian War," 41–42.

[130] Bell, *Journal of a Residence in Circassia*, 52.

[131] Ibid., 53, 66.

needed to travel to a port city, to accompany and guarantee a safe passage for the author, he devised to take an Abazin slave woman to travel with them. Thus, he assured that their travel did not seem "unnatural" to the onlookers, for, as Tornau stated, the mountaineers had to account for their movement in the region and descended to the shore either for the purpose of pilgrimage or emigrating/ traveling to the Ottoman lands only.[132] Slave traders, on the other hand, could roam about freely. The Turkish/Ottoman presence in the Caucasus was so extensive and slave-producing mechanisms so deep-rooted that despite the intensifying blockade efforts by the Russians, particularly after the Treaty of Adrianople in 1829 and the completion of the Black Sea Coastal Military Line (which had the specific aim to cut off ties between the Caucasus and the Ottoman Empire), the trade continued.[133] Reportedly, the number of Turkish vessels that ran between the Caucasus and the Ottoman ports diminished by the end of the 1830s, but even then, as Bell stated, one hundred and fifty ships found constant employment in the trade between the Caucasus and Ottoman lands.[134]

Financing the Holy War

With the onset of the Caucasian Wars during the first decades of the nineteenth century, Caucasian communities began systematically raiding Russian military settlements, as well as neighboring tribes that formed alliances with them. These raids

---

[132] Tornau, *Bir Rus Subayının Kafkasya Anıları*, 105.

[133] Barrett, *At the Edge of Empire*, 3; Köremezli, "The Place of the Ottoman Empire in the Russo-Circassian War," 41.

[134] Bell, *Journal of a Residence in Circassia*, 72. Also see Köremezli, "The Place of the Ottoman Empire in the Russo-Circassian War," 42, particularly note 99 and 100.

were not only larger in scale, better planned, and organized but also rendered already widespread raiding, ransoming, and slave capture (parts of a "formal system of local conflict resolution," as Barrett called it and as already, if partially, discussed above) an everyday event, elevating these communities to the level of total mobilization.[135] Muriel Atkin argued that as the war progressed, not only there were more tribes "rallied around a single objective than before but also more people at all levels within the tribes were involved."[136] "Unlike many of the Caucasian wars," Atkin argued, "this was not simply a rivalry among elites" but a defense of a "whole way of life."[137] Starting with the tenure of General Ermolov as the commander in the region in 1817, the Russo-Circassian War intensified and gradually turned into a war of attrition. Ermolov's infamously harsh policies and brutal measures, designed to "fight fire with fire" as Bruce Grant described it, included retaliation of the mountaineers' raids with even more aggressive ones, sometimes "completely razing entire villages he judged to be complicit and cementing his reputation for merciless determination through a series of public executions."[138] Contrary to the Russian administrators' estimation or expectations, these aggressive policies produced only more blood feuds, an "implacable enmity" towards the Russians, increasing the number of both the raiding and the slaves obtained from them. These blood feuds also determined who formed allies with whom during the war, adding to the

---

[135] Barrett, *At the Edge of Empire*, 160.

[136] Muriel Atkin, "Russian Expansion in the Caucasus" in *Russian Colonial Expansion to 1917*, ed. Michael Rywkin (London: Mansell Publishing, 1988), 161.

[137] Ibid., 161.

[138] Grant, *The Captive and the Gift*, 29.

already highly fractured nature of the region.[139] As early as 1807 and 1808, the messiness

of the situation was apparent in Julius Von Klaproth's following description:

> [The] Abasses [Abkhazes], who are at enmity with Russia, have
> nevertheless friends and kindred on the Russian side, who secretly cross
> the Ckuban to visit them [and raid every village and rob any traveler on
> the way, Tornau adds]. When a favorable opportunity offers, they likewise
> make excursion beyond the Cossack *statnitzas*, in order to plunder the
> adjacent villages, in company with the Nogays, and divide the booty with
> them and the Abasses who dwell within the Russian boundaries. Here the
> Kabardian banditti find an asylum; and such is the connection subsisting
> between them and these people, that they frequently bring their booty,
> consisting of captives and cattle, for sale, across the Ckuban. All these
> abuses might easily be prevented by the neighboring Nogays, who are
> subject to Russia, were they not also in alliance with the Abasses. [...] The
> leaders of the Beslen go out to plunder with the Kabardians and the
> Nogays residing in the Russian territory, and share the booty with them.
> The captive Russians they sell to the inhabitants of the more remote
> mountains, reserving children for themselves.[140]

Quoted in Grant, Bronevskii sketched a similar picture in 1823:

> Some tribes such as Kabards and Lezgins gained the glory of conquerors,
> pursuing almost constant battle with their neighbors: Cherkess with
> Abkhaz, Kabards with Ossetians and Chechens, Ossetians with Kists,
> Chechens with almost everyone around them, and Lezgins with Georgia

---

[139] İbrahim Köremezli argued that Russians took advantage of the existing rivalries also. Köremezli, "The Place of the Ottoman Empire in the Russo-Circassian War," 14.

[140] Klaproth, *Travels in the Caucasus and Georgia*, 250–251, 253.

and Shirvan. In a word, war is the normal state of affairs and a way of life for these peoples.[141]

Tornau also depicted a scene that points at the commonplaceness of raiding, in which two raiding groups casually crossed paths on their way to their respective raids; Nogays were heading towards the Urup River, to raid the Kabardians on account of revenge and the Ubykh, with a group of several hundred men, were on the way to raid the Besleney; on the spot, the Nogay prince managed to trade an enslaved woman from Bashilbay tribe, in exchange of two horses.[142] Another example from Soukhum-kale, from almost the end of the war points at the turmoil among those on the Russian side:

> Hasan Marghani, a powerful native chief and much protected by the reigning prince of Abkhasia, availing himself of his master's absence at Piatigorsk [Pyatigorsk], has recently attacked and set fire to a village near Attara [Atara], the property of Prince Gregory Shervashidze, killing eight of his serfs and carrying off into slavery some forty women and children, besides seizing a number or cattle and horses. Shortly afterwards and while Hasan was returning to Soukoum Kale he was attacked by two of Prince Gregory's brothers and their followers, but as Prince Alex. Shervashidze (brother of the reigning prince) happened to be with Hasan at the time, the attack had to cease, but it is expected that further uprisals will take place on some future day. Both Prince Gregory and Hasan hold Russian military rank but the local authorities do not appear to interfere in the matter so far, and leave to the Prince of Abkhazia to deal with the case as he may seem fit."[143]

---

[141] Grant, *The Captive and the Gift*, 29.

[142] Tornau, *Bir Rus Subayının Kafkasya Anıları*, 107.

[143] FO 195/762, Confidential dispatch No.5, from C.K. Dickson to Earl Russell, 9 August 1863. The note underlines the pervasiveness of brigandage in the region, which renders "communication by land with Migrelia and Georgia dangerous."

This, in essence, was what the Caucasus War was. It did not comprise "military operations for the purpose of destroying the enemy and conquering territory." It meant the increased frequency and intensity of raiding, kidnappings and plunder, with "minimum confrontation and battle."[144] Despite considerable military and economic potential on the Russian side, fundamental discordances between each party's fighting techniques or strength, as well as the difficulty of the terrain, hindered the possibility of quick, decisive results. Instead, Russia was dragged (or perhaps inserted itself) into a local system of infamously unresolvable blood feuds and Caucasus people on the other hand, were pushed into a costly war sustained largely by slave trade.[145] The response to and engagement with the Russian presence in the region differed from one tribe to the other. In the North-West Caucasus, Anna Zelkina asserts, secular leaders led the resistance, in close cooperation with the Ottomans, whereas in the east, the movement had a more apparently Islamic character, which eventually managed to unite the resistance to a great extent under the leadership of Sheikh Shamil. Shamil's "State of God," Zelkina argues, brought on administrative, legal, and fiscal reform, such as the efforts to replace *adat* with *Şer'i* legislature, systematic or planned redistribution of military booty, or introducing taxation, with the aim of attaining a centralized government.[146] Perhaps more important than the military effect was that the Russian expansion in the Caucasus transformed the region, where, at least initially, Bruce Grant

---

[144] Barrett, *At the Edge of Empire*, 148.

[145] George L. Ditson, *Circassia; or A Tour to the Caucasus* (London: T.C.Newby, 1850), 193; Köremezli, "The Place of the Ottoman Empire in the Russo-Circassian War," 98.

[146] Zelkina, *In Quest for God and Freedom*, 204–206.

asserted, "raiding was done without special prejudice toward national character;"[147] it stimulated and hastened its Islamization, united many of the Caucasian tribes (which were customarily "not only disunited, but also were not stable in their choices," as Köremezli put it),[148] and turned the war into a holy war, *jihad*, and raiding into *ghazawat*, the original (and vis-à-vis Islamic jurisprudence, only) source of slave procurement, in a strictly Islamic context.

Conclusion

James C. Scott has described the Caucasus as a shatter zone, where "expansion of states, empires, slave-trading, and wars, as well as natural disasters, have driven large numbers of people to seek refuge in out-of-the-way places..." Shatter zones were, to invoke Scott's description once again, places where "ethnicity and tribes began" and "sovereignty and taxes ended." However, the Caucasus did not always fit into this clear-cut picture. Even though there never existed a "fully articulated," or even a discernable state formation, princes and nobles, to recall Bell's description, had "considerable power over their own serfs even that of life and death, and of transference by sale to others," and presided at public trials and "decide[d] upon the fines [and punishments] to be imposed upon persons who commit offences."[149] They set blood prices, judged peoples' alienability, substituted their death with slavery, and above all made laws and exceptions to those laws; hence embodied, by definition, the sovereign power. Even in so-called

---

[147] Grant, *The Captive and the Gift*, 31.

[148] Köremezli, "The Place of the Ottoman Empire in the Russo-Circassian War," 11–12.

[149] Bell, *Journal of a Residence in Circassia*, 357.

democratic societies, where such decisions were made by councils of elders or other similar assemblies, coercive means of maintaining power and authority were present.

What happened with the Russian military expansion or the Ottoman commercial encroachment was not necessarily the conquest of the "ethnic and tribal" by the sovereign who taxed. It was rather a clash of different models of coercive power. Like Tolstoy's Hadji Murat, who got caught between Nicholas I and Sheikh Shamil, enslaved bodies in the Caucasus were caught between local princes and nobles, self-made religious leaders, and Russian and Ottoman states. The civilizing mission brought to the region at gunpoint by the Russian army or Shamil's *murshids*, omnipresent merchants or paid religious dignitaries deployed by the Ottoman government, even the image of the beautiful Circassian maiden contributed. The Caucasus War ended in 1859, with the eventual defeat of the Caucasian army and the capture of Shamil, although occasional clashes and rebellions continued for two more decades, "culminating in the extensive rebellion of 1877 that coincided with the outbreak of another war between Turkey and Russia."[150] Starting in 1860, the Caucasus peoples had been expelled from the region mainly on account of their Muslim identity, paradoxically carved out, for most part, throughout the Caucasus War.

In 1861, a Nogay prince, expelled from the Caucasus and settled near Constanza, in today's Romania, wrote to the Ottoman officials to complain about the "rebellious

---

[150] Austin Lee Jersild, " From Savagery to Citizenship: Caucasian Mountaineers and Muslims in the Russian Empire," in *Russia's Orient: The Imperial Borderlands and Peoples, 1700–1917*, eds. Daniel Brower and Edward J. Lazzerini (Bloomington: Indiana University Press, 1997), 103.

behavior" of his five slaves, whom he brought with him.[151] Canpolat Bey was one of many Caucasian chieftains who were dislocated from their native Caucasus lands during the war and settled in the Ottoman domains. Like many other Caucasian slave holders at the time, he sought ways to suppress his slaves' pursuit of freedom, inspired particularly by the abolition of trade in African slaves effected a few years prior. When Canpolat Bey submitted his formal complaint however, to his dismay, he was asked to pay *pençik* tax on the slaves he owned.[152] Utterly perplexed, he objected, claiming that *pençik* tax was not known to them in their native lands in *Kuban*. Nor was his ownership of the slaves a *Şer'i* matter, he contended, which could be litigated or settled at the court, for in Canpolat Bey's "transplanted" perception of law, his ownership of his slaves was regulated primarily by *adat*. The following chapter will look at the ways in which the slave owners like Canpolat Bey and slaves themselves faced the Ottoman state, which not only had to take an active stance against slavery for the first time, but also delineate its categories of race and ethnicity more explicitly as well.

---

[151] BOA, A.MKT.UM 507/61, 1278.R.14 (19 October 1861).

[152] Hakan Erdem gave the description of *pençik* as "one fifth of booty due to the sovereign." Erdem, *Slavery in the Ottoman Empire and its Demise*, xiii. Erdem further described it as an *ad valorem* import tax on slaves, which Ehud Toledano argued was abolished with the 1857 trade ban. Erdem, *Slavery in the Ottoman Empire and its Demise*, 19; Toledano, *The Ottoman Slave Trade and its Suppression*, 70.

Chapter 2.
Transplanted Slavery, Contested Freedom

> He is tall, his hair is erect and eyes red. Like the beak of an eagle, his forbidding
> nose neatly descends down from among his eyebrows, halts in hesitation and
> bends to form a hook. In keeping with his frightening reputation, when his
> sparsely grown beard and moustache is added to all his ugliness, the indistinct
> figure of his pockmarked face becomes clear.
>
> -Krikor Zohrab, "Ceyran"[1]

As his train readied to leave Haydarpaşa station, thus young Krikor Zohrab pictured his

client Krandük. A recent refugee from Dagestan and a *zabtiye* officer,[2] Krandük was

being accused of first-degree murder in Izmit. On his train ride there, where the trial

---

[1] Krikor Zohrab, "Ceyran," in *Öyküler* (Istanbul: Aras Yayıncılık, 2001), 139–140. The story was
first published in *Hayrenik* in 1892.

[2] Referred to as "jandarma onbaşısı" here. Many male Circassian refugees became low ranking
gendarme officers after their settlement especially in Tuna province. See Vladimir Troyansky
"Tuna Vilayeti'nde Çerkesler," paper presented at "Çerkes Diasporası Konferansı" (9 May 2015,
Bahçeşehir Üniversitesi, Istanbul) for a detailed account of "integration" strategies of refugee
Circassians. Eugene Rogan mentions that in Jordan too the Circassian and Chechen settlers were
active in the police, a fact that he attributed to the formal military training many of the Circassian
settlers received in the Balkans, particularly during the 1877–78 Russo-Ottoman war. Eugene
Rogan, *Frontiers of the State in the Late Ottoman Empire: Transjordan, 1850–1921* (Cambridge:
Cambridge University Press, 2002), 67. Also see the brief note in Grattan Geary, *The Times*,
Letters to the Editor, July 25, 1878. Issue 29316, p.4, in regards to the Ottoman government
recruiting 500 Circassian to be employed as gendarme officers.

would be held,[3] the young lawyer reviewed the official documentation that contained the details of the case (as well as his own defense) over and over again. He knew the difficulties involved in defending the case and once again regretted taking it on in the first place. Krandük's testimony gave everything away, he wrote, and his "naivety beyond belief" left no room for the lawyer even to plead not guilty.[4]

Upon his arrival in Izmit, Zohrab's feelings were those of a burning desire to leave this messy case behind and return to Istanbul at once on the one hand and a deep fascination with the discordant (if not outright chaotic) air among the Circassians he found waiting for him ("the *abukat* from Istanbul") on the other. His fascination grew even bigger as he got acquainted with strange sounding names (Krandük and Nüş, the murderer and his victim respectively, to begin with), a rich variety of languages spoken in the courtroom, and the person of Krandük himself, who had nothing to do with what Zohrab imagined him to be. A frail looking man of pale complexion, the murderer had "slender hands, long graceful fingers, and eyes as blue as an English girl's."[5] Far from being a calculating murderer as Zohrab imagined him to be, he appeared more as

---

[3] Along with Sivas and Canik, Izmit was a province/district where Circassian refugees were settled in great numbers, especially following the 1877–78 Russo-Turkish war, when the Circassians tribes who settled in Tuna and other Balkan provinces once again had to be relocated within the Ottoman Anatolian and Arab provinces, such as Qunaitra in Syria or Amman in Jordan. It should be noted here that despite the two decades that separate those peak moments of displacement, I treat them as two stages of the same event. Needless to say, in these two decades, both the political and material conditions for settlement and resettlement changed. After the 1877–78 war, for instance, the loss of territory made it more difficult to accommodate the immigrants with agricultural land and presumably caused more friction between the incoming Caucasian groups and the native peasant populations. However, viewed from the perspective of the legal transplantation and assimilation processes, as this chapter aims to do, the second wave of migration that took place after the 1877–78 war appears as the continuation of the first in the aftermath of the Caucasus War.

[4] Zohrab, "Ceyran," 140.

[5] Ibid., 142.

someone who acted in accordance with the custom or circumstances, and was now confused with what it turned into. "Are they going to hang me?" he asked Zohrab, to which the latter answered in the negative. But he would possibly be sentenced to hard labor. Despite the impending danger however, what really mattered to Krandük was not the destiny waiting for himself but what would happen to Ceyran. "Who is Ceyran?" the lawyer asked. He was Nüş's wife. "What business do you have with someone else's wife?" Zohrab sternly rebuked.

Just as he was wrong in the way he imagined Krandük's appearance, Zohrab misinterpreted his "business" with Nüş's wife and miscalculated his naivety, too. Krandük's understanding of murder was essentially different than how the criminal law ("which could be anything but taken lightly" Zohrab noted) described it or the lawyer himself defined it. His act of killing was triggered by a personal incident of vengeance/retribution, that involved his childhood friend Nüş and his beloved Ceyran, implied to have been "appropriated" by the former in ways not described in the story. The animosity (even, feud) that started between Krandük and Nüş was consequently carried over to the Ottoman lands upon their expulsion from the Caucasus and subsequent settlement there, as was their "savage" ways. "A great many accepted the Ottoman state's protection as it were the divine order," Zohrab noted with a touch of exoticism, and others kept with their "nomadic and bellicose habits," and the news of their bloody adventures echoed in the Ottoman lands as well.[6] Nüş, as one ringleader among them, invoked fear all over Sapanca,[7] whose criminal acts evidently gave Krikor Zohrab the

---

[6] Ibid., 144.

[7] Ibid.

edge he needed for his defense. "After all, the killing of the bandit is no loss to the society," he maintained at the court, demanding Krandük's acquittal, which he consequently managed to obtain through his further claims that the murder was a case of self defense. Learning that he was acquitted, Krandük's disoriented despair turned into a confused contentment and he gave his "Circassian dagger" to Zohrab as a gift, bringing his multi-episode life that began on the "slopes of the Caucasus mountains," presumably continued along the Danube river for brief period of time, to an end in the Izmit criminal court.

Starting roughly around the mid-nineteenth century, such criminal offences as murder or theft (raiding, pillaging, or banditry in general) and the conflicting Circassian and Ottoman views on them, were addressed and dealt with in accordance with the (trans)forming criminal law and legal institutions that adjudicated criminal cases. Particularly, after the wholesale adoption of the French Criminal Code by the Ottomans in 1879 and the emergence of the office of public prosecutor ("as facilitator of the law," Avi Rubin described it), the legal procedures for these cases were left virtually with no room for any negotiation but called for a definitive decree of punishment.[8] There were other legal practices, categories, and procedures still, particularly pertaining enslavement, slavery, and manumission, the exact definition of which the Ottoman state and Circassian slave owners did not necessarily agree upon but those rarely came to contradict one another. In fact, on the contrary, as this chapter aims to demonstrate, they often worked in support of each other, delineating a system of slavery which could be defined neither as a

---

[8] Avi Rubin, *Ottoman Nizamiye Courts: Law and Modernity* (New York: Palgrave Macmillan, 2011), 136; Kent F. Schull, *Prisons in the Late Ottoman Empire: Microcosms of Modernity* (Edinburgh: Edinburgh University Press, 2014), 22–25.

Caucasian life-term type of slavery nor exactly an Islamic one, but a strange combination of those two, whose bind was virtually impossible to break out of for the slaves, as well as the reformers that aimed for general abolition.

What did not pose a contradiction for the Ottoman state and Circassian chieftains' perception of law, however, was complicated yet by another legal system that was in the making at about the same time. In that, the international anti-slavery law added yet another layer of complexity to the post-Circassian expulsion Ottoman Empire and how slavery, freedom, and in a less direct way citizenship were understood and handled there. These international developments and the emerging law provided the incoming slave-refugees the incentive not only to question their status as slaves and claim freedom (which they deemed to be their right) but also to challenge the supposed sacred (thus, immutable) character of the *Şer'i* law. Building upon the previous chapter, which looked at different legal practices (pertaining to customary law, known as *adat* or *xabze*) of the Caucasian communities that produced slaves, such as blood revenge, bride kidnapping, and raiding/pillaging, this chapter has three objectives. First and foremost, it aims to trace how these legal practices were carried over with Caucasian refugees to the Ottoman Balkans and Anatolia and negotiated there during the elongated crisis of the Circassian expulsion. Secondly, navigating within a set of what they literally called "freedom suits,"[9] (*hürriyet davası*), it aims to explore how slaves built their claims in relation to different legal terrains, problems, and concepts. All in all, it examines the ways in which

---

[9] "A retail rather than wholesale approach to ending slavery," as Catherine Adams describes them, freedom suits were legal claims to freedom that slaves made often on the basis of such legal technicalities as fraudulent sale/resale in colonial and antebellum America. Catharine Adams et al., *Love of Freedom: Black Women in Colonial and Revolutionary New England* (Oxford: Oxford University Press, 2009), 127–128.

these processes, which took place against the backdrop of a general prohibition in African slaves, bent the categories of ethnicity, race, and gender in the decades that followed the expulsion.

The Circassian Expulsion and Transplanted Legalities

Kirkor Zohrab was not the first to provide an account of the chaotic air among the immigrant-refugees from the Caucasus, although he may have been the only one to depict it in a courtroom. Not only the hardships, such as the diseases and destitution that the refugees encountered during their passage and settlement, but also a good amount of information from the profuseness of the languages they spoke to the strangeness of their customs appeared in journals and newspapers worldwide. "In our age, perhaps, nothing has occurred so melancholy, so appalling, as this vast and gradual extirpation of the Circassian race," the London Journal exclaimed in 1864, "finished by exile, fever, famine ague, and, far worse than all, cruelty."[10] Their interest shaped by strong anti-Russian sentiments, the British public read and wrote a great deal about "the brave and hardy" people of the Caucasus who "have at last fallen under the yoke of a people far inferior to them in every way."[11] A variety of others reported on the integration problems they encountered upon their settlement as well. Around the same time as Krikor Zohrab published his story on post-expulsion Izmit, the *English Illustrated Magazine* reported on the conditions of Syria, a province of the Ottoman Empire where Caucasian refugees

---

[10] "National Extinction of the Circassian People," *The London Journal*, July 23, 1864, 61.

[11] "The Circassian Exodus," *The Quiver*, June 1864, 214.

were "transplanted" in large numbers especially following the Berlin Treaty in 1878, that

brought limitations to the Ottoman state's deployment of then as a "demographic

weapon" in the Balkan provinces.[12] Described as a "country [...] infested with Bedouins

and Circassian thieves who went unpunished except when the exasperated villagers in

sheer desperation resisted,"[13] Syria was seen as an opportunity by the Ottoman state, and

a solution to the crisis in the Balkans, materialized in the program of settlement at its

periphery.[14] Both Tuna and Syrian provinces were in fact at the margins of the empire

and populating those with the incoming Caucasian refugees was advantageous not only

on the account of an outside threat (as was the case in Tuna province, in relation to

Russia, for instance) but also for managing the native populations of the empire.[15] The

highly fractured nature of the refugees (and the hostilities and feuds amongst them)

nullified any possibility of forming a unified Caucasian community.[16] As the British

---

[12] For a comprehensive discussion on this matter, see Mark Pinson, "Demographic warfare : an aspect of Ottoman and Russian policy, 1854–1866," (Ph.D. Dissertation, Harvard University, 1970) ; Also see Rogan, *Frontiers of the State in the Late Ottoman Empire*, 72.

[13] *The English Illustrated Magazine, 1891–1892* (London: MacMillan and Co.), 903.

[14] Rogan, *Frontiers of the State in the Late Ottoman Empire*, 73.

[15] Janet Klein, *The Margins of Empire: Kurdish Militias in the Ottoman Tribal Zone* (Stanford: Stanford University Press, 2011), 165–166; Klein here is drawing from Roderic H. Davison's argument in *Reform in the Ottoman Empire, 1856–1876* (Princeton: Princeton University Press, 1963), 151–152. Also see Ryan Gingeras, *Sorrowful Shores: Violence, Ethnicity, and the End of the Ottoman Empire, 1912–1923* (Oxford: Oxford University Press, 2009), 26.

[16] See BOA, A.MKT.MHM 168/33, 1276.Ra.23 (20 October 1859) for an official correspondence which points out to the governors of Silistra and Varna that a Bzhedug tribe consisting of 44 households and 365 individuals was not to be mixed with the Tatars when settled in Dobruca (Dobrich, in today's Bulgaria). David Cuthell specified the Russo-Circassian war under Shamyl's leadership as the last [and possibly the only] "meaningful organized resistance" among the Circassians. David Cuthell, "The Circassian Sürgün," *Ab Imperio*, no.3 (2003), 145. However, there was also a simultaneous vigilance about Caucasian immigrants becoming a unified group, which began much earlier than the Circassian expulsion. See for instance BOA, A.MKT 17/14 1260.N.25 (8 October 1844) for a note written by the Grand Vizier to the governor of Filibe (Plovdiv), cautioning him to keep a close eye on a Circassian chieftain named Safer, not to let

consul in Soukoum-Kalé, Dickson, reported to Earl Russel in February 1864, "the absence of all political cohesion between the northern tribes, or such remnants thereof, and those inhabiting other parts of the Caucasus, and, indeed, the almost utter impossibility of bringing about such a consummation" was one of the major misfortunes that fell on the people of the Caucasus. "Each and all cannot be made to forget their blood feuds," Dickson noted, "still less to unite in a common cause..."[17] However, formidable addition to the empire's "Mahomedan population," they proved useful in destabilizing existing structures of power and networks of influence.[18] This situation, producing ample amount of tension between the refugees and local populations particularly in relation to the distribution of land, caused frequent clashes across the empire.[19]

---

him travel outside of Edirne or communicate with other Circassians. After Safer Paşa's death, his son reportedly kept on appearing in public, dressed in traditional Circassian clothing and giving speeches of political content, in Circassian language. BOA, A.MKT.MHM 249/57 and 250/57, 1279.C.17, 1279.C.25 (10 December 1862, 18 December 1862). In a later but more famous example, Sultan Abdülhamid ordered Gedikpaşa Theater demolished on the account that a group of Ottoman pashas of Caucasian origin went to see Ahmed Midhat's play *Çerkes Özdenler* (The Circassian Nobles) in full Circassian traditional outfit. Musahipzade Celal, *Eski İstanbul Yaşayışı* (Istanbul: İletişim Yayınları, 1992), 90.

[17] Note no.2, Consul Dickson to Earl Russell in Papers Respecting the Settlement of the Circassian Emigrants in Turkey: Presented to the House of Commons by Command of Her Majesty, in pursuance of their Address dated June 6, 1864 (London: Harrison & Sons, 1864)."Papers Respecting the Settlement of Circassian Emigrants in Turkey," presented to the House of Commons on June 6, 1864. It is important to note that both the first and second wave immigrants comply with the chaotic image provided by a wide array of observers throughout the settlement process.

[18] David Cuthell argued that particularly the initial wave of the refugees were armed, as in many instances they did not have to surrender their weapons to the Russians when they were forced to leave the Caucasus. Cuthell, "The Circassian Sürgün," 150. Also see B. Philpot, *The Times*, *Letters to the Editor*, June 17, 1864, p.7. Also see a note sent to the governor of Vidin in 1861, cautioning him against the armed Crimean, Nogai and Circassian settlers. BOA, A.MKT.MHM 238/12, 1278.Ca.28 (1 December 1861).

[19] See the brief note no.7 written by Sir H. Bulwer to Earl Russell on this issue in "Papers Respecting the Settlement of Circassian Emigrants in Turkey." Also see "Report from Select Committee on East India Communication," July 20, 1866, page 620 for a brief note on an insurrection at a Circassian settlement that caused interference with British communications

In many instances these hostilities and clashes were circumstantial, forced upon the refugees by the difficult conditions of refugee life or on the native peasant populations trying to make ends meet.[20] However, in other cases, the correspondences, petitions, and other types of documents on these social explosions made references to the ancient laws (*kanun-i kadim*) of the Caucasian immigrant-refugees, to be understood as the customary law that governed (as discussed at greater length in the previous chapter) the entire Caucasus. As we have seen in the previous chapter, the customary law known as *adat* differed from one tribal organization to another, particularly in regards to the ways and degrees it was affected by the *Şer'i* law, producing a largely arbitrary legal regime that favored primarily princes, nobles, and in general, the powerful. Despite its arbitrariness, it constituted the primary legal system in settling both criminal offences and civil matters in the region, some of which had been carried to the Ottoman domains and made some Circassians famous "for their fierce independence and banditry," which generated, according to Reşat Kasaba, a strong reaction from the Ottoman center.[21] As one Armenian villager put it, new coming Caucasians had "hazy ideas as to the difference between *meum* and *tuum*." Similar to what the *English Illustrated Magazine* reported on Syria, such incidences of robbery were common near immigrant settlements in Anatolia

---

system. In addition, there were ongoing/chronic clashes with the existing tribes around the settlements. See numerous files on the hostilities between Circassian settlers near Sivas/Kayseri and the Afşar tribe, one of the most powerful tribes in the region. A more detailed account can been seen in Georgi Chochiev and Bekir Koç,"Migrants from the North Caucasus in Eastern Anatolia: Some Notes on Their Settlement and Adaptation (Second Half of the 19th Century-Beginning of the 20th Century) in *Journal of Asian History*, vol.40, no.1 (2006), 94–95, 97. Gingeras, *Sorrowful Shores*, 29.

[20] Reşat Kasaba, *A Moveable Empire: Ottoman nomads, migrants, and refugees* (Seattle: University of Washington Press, 2009), 117–118.

[21] Ibid., 118.

also. As the Armenian villager further reported to Fred Burnaby, several of their cows had recently disappeared and "it was strongly suspected that some Circassians were implicated in the robbery."[22]

Besides the hostilities and clashes that took place between the refugees and native populations, or among different Caucasian tribal groups with ongoing feuds, what posed a major concern for the Ottoman government in regards to the incoming refugees had to do with the disputes/conflicts within the tribes and clans themselves. As will be further explored below, that the refugees moved to the Ottoman Empire organized as tribes and clans did not mean that they saw themselves as homogenous units. As discussed in the previous chapter, the Circassian, or in general Caucasian, social order was peculiar in that, as Paul Manning describes it, they "contained 'feudal' distinctions of hereditary caste but situated within a generally egalitarian 'acephalous' segmentary political structure," which could be interpreted as highly hierarchical (thus ripe for indirect rule, with the co-optation of the princes and chieftains) or "a miniature Liberal revolution," depending on who looked at them.[23] The Adyghe, for instance, had four castes composed of the princes, nobles, freemen, and serfs/slaves. One slave petition from 1872 (of unidentified tribal affiliation) noted that even the slave class was stratified and consisted of two types of slaves. The *abd-ı memluk* was responsible for giving half of their crop to the chieftain every year and could also be sold. The *abd-ı hür*, on the other hand also had

---

[22] Fred Burnaby, *On horseback through Asia Minor* (London: Sampson Low, Marston, Searle, & Rivington, 1877), 277. Burnaby also visited the Sivas prison, to see that out of 102 prisoners kept there, the majority were Circassians and Kurds for horse and cattle stealing, 285. Fred Burnaby was a British army officer who was on an expedition to inspect the Russian border prior to the 1877–78 War, whose observations may have been strategically mediated.

[23] Paul Manning, "Just Like England: On the Liberal Institutions of the Circassians," *Comparative Studies in Society and History*, vol.51, no.3 (2009), 591.

the obligation of the yearly payment but could not be sold.[24] A retrospective, and

inevitably national or ethnicity-focused view on these tribes leads us see them as

cohesive and integral groups (in the face of Russian empire's encroachment that they ran

away from or Ottoman empire, which tried hard to absorb them) but from early on with

their arrival, there were clear indications that this was not the case. In most cases,

internal, minor disputes or offences that happened within the tribe were kept to the tribe,

although there were occasional cases of theft that were reported, which was partially due

to the fact that the refugees had to work against a language barrier, as in most cases they

did not know Turkish.[25] Aside from those, many of the conflicts that ended up with the

government authorities or legal institutions such as the local *Şer'i* courts, had to do with

the practice of slavery and the incoming refugees' slave status. Caught in a state of

uncertainty between the Ottoman state law and the "ancient customs/law" (*adat-ı kadime*)

of the tribal chieftains, these disputes also offer an insight into the internal power

dynamics of the transplanted tribal units.

As one slave petition submitted to the office of the Grand Vezir in 1859 made it

clear, the major cause for the slaves' discontent was the chieftains (who, in this particular

case, belonged to the Kabarda/Kabarta tribe) resorting to their "old customs" of selling

---

[24] BOA, ŞD 2872/30, 1289.Ra.7 (15 May 1872).

[25] See, for instance, BOA, MVL 620/84, 1278.B.20 (21 January 1862), for a case of murder that occurred between two brothers, recent immigrant-refugees from the Caucasus, for a passing note that their interrogation was conducted by the help of an interpreter. Also see Ömer Karakaş, " 19. Yüzyılda Anadolu'da Çerkes Göçmenlerinin İskânlari Sirasinda Karşilaştiklari Sorunlar: Uzunyayla Örneği," *Karadeniz Araştırmaları*, no. 36 (Kış 2013), 88–89. Karakaş mentions a rare debt dispute brought to the Şer'iyye court in Sivas in 1865. 36 numaralı Sivas Şer'iyye Sicili, can be accessed at BOA, MŞH.ŞSC.d 7729, page 115

the children of their slaves.[26] This particular complaint appeared in slave petitions recurrently, even during the early phases of the expulsion when most of the incoming chieftains were relatively wealthy. In another one from 1861, for instance, two enslaved men named Mehmed and Mustafa filed a petition, again with the office the Grand Vizier, to complain about their chieftains, Batuk, Babiç, and İshak, for putting them to work day and night, but more importantly, that in accordance with the old customs, "they were in the mind of selling" the former's daughters, saying that they were allowed to do so by the orders of the Sultan, even though the young girls were engaged and soon to be married.[27] Mehmed and Mustafa stated that if such an order indeed existed, they too were the subjects of the Sultan and moreover were, "all praise be to God," Muslims, indicating that they were ready to comply with the Ottoman sovereign's wishes. If not, however, they asked to be released from what they deemed illegitimate bonds of their so-called owners.[28] Later on, as the legal suits and procedures became more widespread and the legal language of slavery and freedom became more established, the parties debated over the contested notion of dominium (*kanun-i malikiye*), which the slave owners rooted again in the "ancient law," whereas the slaves asked for a new definition, both of slavery and ownership in general.[29] To be added to the disputes on the descriptions and limitations of slave ownership are the cases of apparent "blunders" by the slaves themselves. Slave flights, for one, were instances in which the *adat-ı kadime* were speedily transported into the Ottoman *Şer'i* and public law, by pushing the slave owners

---

[26] BOA, A.MKT.MHM176/37, 1276.B.09 (1 February 1860).

[27] BOA, A.MKT.DV 181/59, 1277.B.19 (31 January 1861).

[28] Ibid.

[29] BOA, ŞD 2872/30, 1289.Ra.7 (15 May 1872).

to appeal to and demand from the legal and governmental institutions to set its coercive measures against such "rebellious" behavior. Such was the case with Ömer, a slave owner from Şibu (possibly, Şabsu or Shapsug) tribe, for instance. When two male and three female slaves (referred to as *köle* and *cariye* respectively) of his ran away to Rhodes island in 1860, he petitioned the office of the Grand Vizier, requesting the recovery of the runaway slaves. The Grand Vezirate, for its turn, found the case to be the matter of the legal practice and ordered that it be heard at the Şer'iyye court and dealt with in accordance with the legal decision.[30] Besides the issue of in-kind payments pressed over the enslaved farming population by the chieftains (which put the slaves who were already trying very hard to dodge many hardships at once, in a desperate position), even more importantly than hard physical labor and torture (also frequently reported), the major conflict was a direct result of an ambiguous notion of ownership rights over people that referred to both customary and *Şer'i* law at once. This situation rendered, in a nutshell, the implementation of these laws the very source of problem itself.

The individual sale of family members and the breaking up of families produced violent resistance against the slave owners and caused closer appeal to the Ottoman government on the slaves' side. Cashing on his "transplanted" privileges, a certain chieftain named Kaspolat attempted to sell five of his slaves, Makval (or Markoval, 36 years old), his wife (35 years old) and their children (whose age ranged between 14 and 4 years), but met fierce resistance from the family, whose appeals stated that they would rather bring themselves to ruin and perish than seeing their family be broken, and

---

[30] BOA, A.MKT.MHM, 176/75, 1276.B.11 (3 February 1860).

themselves be removed from the remainder of their extended family and relatives.[31] Their

appeal found support from the district governor of Yanbolu (today's Yambol, Bulgaria),

who stated selling those over thirty years of age and those who had children would be

violating the notion of the family, and suggested that the sale should be halted.[32] Through

a decision by the Supreme Council of Judicial Ordinances (*Meclis- i Vâlâ- yı Ahkâm-ı*

Adliye), two legal systems and privileges came face to face to determine (or at least,

emphasize) the age limits as well as its legal implications within the practice of slavery.[33]

While the enslaved women bought and sold in urban areas (where most of the

sale/purchase deeds, receipts, etc. in the following chapter come from) were usually very

young (roughly between 10–14 years old, and rarely above 23–24 years old), the case

with slaves in the Circassian settlements was different. The composition of the age (as

well as social structure) of slaves in those settlements is best traced in what can be

defined as settlement logbooks or registers, that contained the records kept by *Muhacirin*

---

[31] BOA, MVL 991/62, 1281.M.13 (18 June 1864). Ehud Toledano argues that the established Caucasian customs were strongly in favor of maintaining the unity of slave families and it was the "hardships of emigration [which] eroded the old and established customs." Ehud Toledano, *The Ottoman Slave Trade and its Suppression: 1840–1890* (Princeton: Princeton University Press, 1982), 160. While it is true that the difficulties encountered during the expulsion and settlement process shifted the ethical boundaries of both the slave owners and traders (often one and the same), explaining these instances with "hardships of emigration," in the same as way as Um Mazed does in the introduction of this dissertation, is misguiding. Not only do the petitions written by the slaves themselves indicate that it was the prerogative of the chieftain to sell his slaves as he pleased, but also those customs rarely favored the slaves, especially the *abd-ı memluk*.

[32] The sale of the family was reportedly annulled, as an official notice sent by the Supreme Council to the Grand Vizier clarified. BOA, MVL 996/26, 1281.S.21 (26 July 1864).

[33] See BOA, MVL 991/39, 1280.Z.29 (5 June 1864), for a brief note on the extension of the age limit to all Circassian tribes. Written by the Supreme Council to the governor of Varna, the note stated that the condition (*mesağ*) of the permissibility/lawfulness of the sale of the tribe members relied upon the age limitations determined by the Supreme Council earlier.

Komisyonu, a commission that oversaw the settlement process,[34] as well as other agents, such as local government institutions or the police. Organized according to the households that constituted the tribes, these registers date back, in most cases, to the earlier episodes of the settlement process.[35] Settlement registers provide a good depiction as to how these groups were organized, the size of each family unit that constituted them, who owned slaves and who did not, and last but not the least, how these differed from one tribal group to another.

The first of these registers contained information on a Circassian tribe (*kabile*) named Anaçok, which came from the Caucasus in 1859 at the outset of expulsion, and contained 248 individuals in total, 54 of whom were slaves.[36] Broken down into families of different sizes, each entry began with a brief visual description (particularly of height and the shape and color of the beard), name and age of the head of the family followed by information on the remainder of the family members, starting with the wives and ending with the slaves that the family owned. The first entry in the book, in this case discernable as the chieftain's family, was the largest of all families that made up the clan, consisting of 44 members. The chieftain, named Pişmak Bey, was 50 years old, had two wives and six children. The remainder of his family consisted of his slaves (marked as *gulam*s in the list), their wives, and children, amounting to 34 individuals in total. Several of Pişmak

---

[34] For a comprehensive study for the scope and activities of the commission, see David Cameron Cuthell, "The Muhacirin Komisyonu: "An Agent in the Transformation of Ottoman Anatolia, 1860–1866" (Ph.D. Dissertation, Columbia University, 2005).

[35] It is common knowledge that the refugees were expelled from the Caucasus in groups, and came to the Ottoman Empire organized in such social units as tribes or clans, however, the composition of these units has hardly been touched upon.

[36] BOA, A.DVN 147/43, 1276.R.4 (31 October 1859).

Bey's *gulam*s were close to his age, indicating that he may in fact have inherited them from his family; a fact, as will be discussed below, that constituted the backbone of all of Circassian slave-owners' claims to slave-ownership, against the slaves' and abolitionists' call for emancipation.

A similar pattern can be observed in another register from the same period. Kupşak tribe[37] of Nogai people consisted of 64 households and 412 individuals in total, 49 of which were slaves. In this case, the chieftain's household was smaller in size, containing 24 individuals. 17 of those (that is, five *gulam*s and their families) had slave status. Out of 64 households, eleven owned slaves. A register for another Nogai tribe has a similar composition, in that it was composed of few large slave-owning households (and similarly, a low percentage of slaves to the total population), whereas two other registers for Besni and Abzakh tribes appear different,[38] as the percentage of both slave owning households and the total number of slaves are significantly higher than others. In the register for Abzakh, for instance, the households are much larger on average, with no apparent chieftain or prince. 18 out of 29 households owned slaves, particularly young female slaves, who seem unattached to a slave family, which makes the whole settlement seem like a slave market.

---

[37] The name of the tribe is noted as Kontak in the BOA catalog, although in the report itself it reads as Kubşak or Kupşak, possibly referring to Kıpçak people. A.DVN 147/27 1276.R.4 (31 October 1859).

[38] BOA, DH.MHC 1/60, 1277 (1860–61).

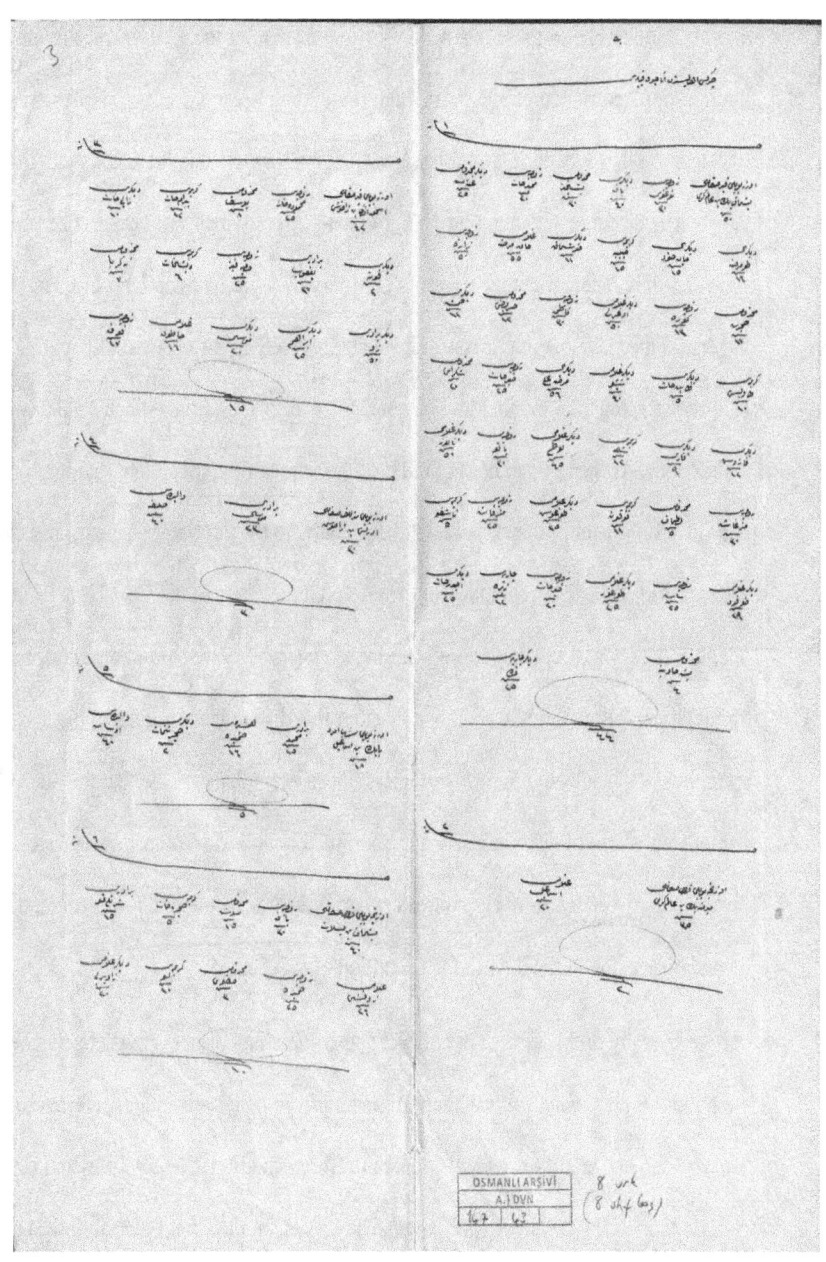

Image 2.1 The opening page of the settlement register for the Anaçok tribe, depicting the chieftain's household on the right side. BOA, A.DVN 147/43, 1276.R.4 (31 October 1859).

Another one of these registers, this time from after the second wave of the immigration , consisted of 336 individuals, excluding several deaths (possibly, en route), transfers to other locations, and four sales.[39] Again, the leading, that is, the chieftain's family was the largest, containing 15 individuals, 10 of which were slaves or members of slave families. There too, the larger the family (who were likely to be princes/nobles, or in general the slave owning classes), it was more likely to own slaves, although in the later register, the total number and percentage of the slaves seems much smaller than the earlier ones. As the register did not indicate the name of the tribe/clan, saying anything definitive on it is impossible, but it is likely that with the passage of time, nearly two decades after the expulsion, many of the enslaved members of the Circassian tribes did obtain some form of independence from their owners, or were sold in the slave markets of big cities. It is difficult to establish whether this difference is related to the tribal structures or changes in time. Nevertheless, these examples indicate that the main clashes within Caucasian tribes took place, and continued to do so in the ensuing decades, distinctly between the princely families and their slaves, as the remainder of the tribes owned only a few of them, with the exception of the Abzakh.

In many of these cases of conflict and complaints, the slave owners clutched to the notion of an "*adat-ı kadime*" that originated from their native lands referred to as "*vatan-ı asliye*," or simply as *Kuban* like the Nogai chieftain Canpolat Bey did in his petition that closed the previous chapter. The slaves, on the other hand, followed the legal developments generally more carefully, achieved some degree of knowledge and sense as to what their rights were, and acted, at times in an organized manner, to obtain or at least

---

[39] Taksim Atatürk Kütüphanesi, Belediye Yazmaları, BEL_Yz_B.000059, 1294 (1877–78).

claim them. Starting early on with the emigration process, the enslaved refugees were highly vocal in demanding change to their statuses, at times acting "rebelliously" (as per the descriptions by the slave owners went, such as above-mentioned Canpolat's), and potentially, mutinously. In the aftermath of their expulsion from Russia, where, as they themselves put it, they "left all that they owned, except for their poverty," the impoverished refugees were less likely to go into bloody conflicts within their community. Nevertheless, the instances of violent encounters did exist and both the possibility and fear of its frequency remained real.[40] Ehud Toledano depicts a case of violent clashes between slave owners and slaves as follows:

> On 9 September 1866 the governor of the *Vilâyet* of Edirne reported to the Grand Vezir that violent clashes had erupted in the village of Mandira between Circassian slave holders and their slaves. The issue was the slaves' status. A few policemen were sent to stop the fighting, but they were barred from entering the village. When the authorities learned about this, they immediately dispatched more policemen under the command of a *binbaşı* (equivalent rank of a major). This time the police managed to control the situation and put an end to the skirmish, but the dispute which had caused it still remained unresolved. The slaves demanded to be freed, and the slave holders refused to manumit them. The governor reported that he had sent to the village one of his staff officers to mediate between the factions. He was concerned, however, that with 400 households of immigrants—all armed—fighting could be resumed at any time. Therefore, the *Vâli* suggested that the villagers be disarmed, and he asked the Grand Vezir to authorize this move.[41]

---

[40] BOA, A.DVN 156/50, 1277.Ra.03 (19 September 1860).

[41] Toledano, *The Ottoman Slave Trade and its Suppression*, 162–163.

The Ottoman government was not there solely to appease these tensions, nor to

act as a judge to come to a mutual solution for the parties. It was also there to code the

slave owners' and slaves' behavior, to place them in the "grid of law" that it was

weaving. Such was the case with Listan, Yunus, and Zekeriya, three of the

Kabarda/Kabarta chieftain Makhar Ahmed's slaves, who took up rifles and shot at the

latter's house one night. In their interrogation, they said that they did so not with the

purpose of killing him, but rather to frighten him, so that he would forgo the cruel

treatments and torture he applied to his slaves.[42] Just like slave flights, these offences

sped up the process of legal assimilation of the slaves and often highlighted if not

imposed a uniform meaning of their slave status. In the case of Listan, Yunus, and

Zekeriya, for instance, their offence was brought to the local and eventually higher court

of Supreme Council, was determined to be a criminal offence perpetrators of which were

to be punished in accordance with the article 179 of the Ottoman Criminal Law that

called for imprisonment for the duration of one week to six months. But since these three

slaves (whose enslaved status was established with the very first question in the related

interrogation) committed the offence against their masters (*efendi*), their bold attempt was

found to be an aggravating factor, and their sentence was determined to be imprisonment

for the duration of a full year. Thus, by coding the slaves' act against their owners as

such, the Ottoman government, or its law administering institution helped define these

relationship as something above the ordinary and essentially unequal.

---

[42] BOA, MVL 698/20, 1281.L.13 (11 March 1865). BOA, A.MKT.UM 507/61. The armed
clashes between the chieftains/slave owning classes and slaves did occur especially in the
aftermath of the 1908 revolution, when the Circassians claimed full citizenship in the new,
constitutional order and when the government did give both the slaves and slave owners a
confusing message when it drafted enslaved men for the army.

While, judging by the age composition, many of the slaves who were recorded in the settlement registers were inherited and could be claimed ancestrally, the ancient law, "*adat-ı kadime*" was evoked not solely or necessarily to refer to ancestral rights to own slaves, whose enslavement took place during the tribes' days long-gone in the Caucasus mountains. In fact, "*adat-ı kadime*" did not only refer to the ownership of slaves, but also the means of enslavement, in accordance to these customs. In many instances, we see examples of crude expressions of power, when a land-holding Circassian man claimed the rights to the labor or sexual services of destitute members of their groups. In one such case, a Circassian man from Hatuqwai tribe named Dingozi and his seven friends petitioned the office of the Grand Vizier in 1859, and complained about a man named Hapuzi (or, Hapuji) for employing them forcefully and without payment. The petitioners asked the Grand Vizier to look into the matter or at least give them the permission to pursue the matter in accordance with the *Şer'i* legal formulations.[43] Another brief notice from 1865 reported on the enslavement of Receb and Bata Agurli by a man (possibly a chieftain) named Koç Çoseb.[44] As it would be reported many years later, in addition to those who came to the Ottoman Empire as slaves, many were enslaved en route to the Ottoman lands due to the harsh conditions of the journey that cost the lives of 200 to 300 people every day.[45] As chapter 4 explores, in the aftermath of the constitutional revolution in 1908, during which slave claims to freedom virtually exploded, many

---

[43] BOA, A.DVN 146/11, 1276.S.14 (12 September 1859).

[44] BOA, A.MKT.MHM 332/32, 1281.Z.21 (17 May 1865). Also see MVL 529/110, 1283.Z.29 (4 May 1867), in which 26 individuals were enslaved, reportedly with the simple promise of protection.

[45] Toledano, *The Ottoman Slave Trade and its Suppression,* 150–151.

stories of "unjust enslavement" during the Circassian expulsion came to the fore, especially to undo slaveholders' claims to ancestral slave ownership.[46]

Ehud Toledano has argued that it was the penalties not being strong enough for kidnapping and enslavement that allowed the traffic to go on unhindered throughout the remainder of the nineteenth and early twentieth centuries,[47] an argument that too readily assumes an uncontested universality of the newly adopted Ottoman criminal code, and the justice it promised. The penal code was not there to be simply and universally adopted by everyone, including the incoming Circassian refugees, whose justice system worked differently than both the Şer'i law that sought to maintain status quo above all, or penal code that aimed to reach a universal justice at all costs. It was there to be negotiated, by those who were also negotiating their participation and inclusion to the Ottoman Empire. The slave owners and slaves grasped it from different ends but they did negotiate both their understanding of the law (and such offenses as murder, theft, kidnapping, and enslavement), sovereignty, subjecthood or citizenship. From the Ottoman government's point of view, law had to be negotiated differently with the slave owners and slaves also. As Grattan Geary, the editor of *Times of India* put it in 1878, there was great benefit to the Ottoman government in recognizing "the authority of the Circassian chiefs over their followers," for they could, according to Geary, "keep their people in some sort of order if the government would empower them to do so:"

As it is, the law is too feeble a restraint, and the patriarchal rule of the chiefs

---

[46] For example, see DH.MKT 2891/97, 1327.B.17 (4 August 1909).

[47] Toledano, *The Ottoman Slave Trade and its Suppression*, 168.

being set aside the wild Circassian does whatever he pleases. His great physical strength and his perfect mastery over his weapons, of which he always carries a varied assortment, make him the most formidable of all the robbers in these parts. My experience was confined to those what had been taken into the Government service, and I found them to be very far the best in escort duty that I had on the whole journey. They were obliging, hearty, good-humored fellows never afraid of exertion or exposure and never inventing ingenious fictions as an excuse for coming to a premature halt. There is fine material in these Circassian settlers who have so unenviable reputation. Possibly in the reorganization of Asiatic Turkey, which cannot now be long delayed, they will be turned to good account.[48]

On the one hand, the Ottoman government had a lot at stake in empowering Circassian chieftains, to be able to implement/enforce the law which otherwise would be too feeble to have any use at all.[49] On the other hand, however (and this holds particularly true for the practice of slavery) endorsing the "*kanun-i kadim*" in perpetuating slavery, undermined the very law the Ottoman state wanted to implement.[50] Scholars of Ottoman

---

[48] Grattan Geary, *The Times*, Letters to the Editor, July 25, 1878 , 4.

[49] We know that the Ottoman government already favored Circassian chieftains in specific occasions. See, for instance, the petition by Şahin Giray Bey of Zodoh tribe, in which asked to be granted a military rank equivalent to that he had with Russian state before he departed for the Ottoman Empire, a request again deemed appropriate by the Ministry of War. BOA, A.MKT.MHM, 177/29, 1276.B.21 (13 February 1860). Similarly, Kasbolat Bey (the chieftain of the Altıkesek tribe) petitioned to the office of the Grand Vizier and asked for an "appropriate" amount of salary, and in case that it is unattainable, an administrative position at a government institution, a request deemed appropriate by the *Muhacirin Komisyonu*, BOA, MVL 434/79, 1280.Ş.03 (13 January 1864). For an elaborate discussion on the Ottoman policies of coopting the Caucasian and Crimean elites, see Cuthell, "The Muhacirin Komisyonu," 130–139. Cuthell argues that both the *Muhacirin Komisyonu* and the Ottoman government it represented "recognized and promoted continuity in the social structure common to both Crimean and Ottoman societies," 133.

[50] The Ottoman government was not always sure on what to do either. See, for instance, BOA, A.MKT.MHM 237/38, 1278.R. 7 (12 October 1861) and A.MKT.MHM 335/21, 1282.M.21 (16 June 1865) for cases where the office of the Grand Vizier is inquired about the procedure for slaves left behind from deceased chieftains and slave owners.

history have pointed out this dilemma, in which the Ottoman government was caught between its old habits of rule by coopting the local elites and the new political and legal order it aspired to implement.[51] Most recently, Janet Klein's study of the Hamidian era efforts to include the Kurdish region "into the Ottoman fold," and the government's extensive use and abuse of the local power networks (as much as regional conflicts) offers a good example of this dilemma. However, Klein's (and others') studies rarely go beyond the interactions between the Ottoman government and local power holders. Accordingly, law as the tracing paper of power appears to be negotiated only between these bodies whereas other, less privileged groups also took part in these negotiations whenever they could. This was especially (and transparently) so in the case of post-Circassian expulsion slavery in the Ottoman Empire. The following section looks into how slaves took part in these negotiations at a time when the legitimacy of slavery was highly contested throughout the world, which was increasingly more connected in the ways subjecthood and citizenship (and the notion of justice and equality that it was hypothetically contingent upon) were understood.

Freedom Suits

"With his faith in justice, he comes across as naive. Perhaps I do him an injustice. Perhaps it is an act. Or perhaps he is the stuff of which saints are made, unalloyed

---

[51] See Ussama Makdisi, *The Culture of Sectarianism: Community, History, and Violence in Nineteenth-century Ottoman Lebanon* (Berkeley: University of California Press, 2000).

innocence. But his story is classic: the man betrayed by justice."

Michael Taussig, *Law in a Lawless Land*[52]

"The universe of right and wrong is territorialized by a grid of laws," Michael

Taussig wrote, "and each law is numbered." However, those numbers never quite fit

reality, "neither the reality of the human condition nor the reality of the subtle

distinctions necessary to law. "[53] As we have seen in the section above, Caucasian slaves'

flight from their owners' estate, incidents of assault or other criminal acts hastily brought

them into the Ottoman "legal fold," where the distinctions between their status as *abd-ı*

hür and *abd-ı memluk* had collapsed and their relationship with their owners and Ottoman

society in general were defined anew. Slaves' legal pleas to freedom, which were literally

called freedom suits (*hürriyet davaları*) and began shortly after their arrival in the

Ottoman domains, came precisely at this juncture and embodied an effort, however naive

it may seem, to use the very same grid to thwart control of their owners over them on the

one hand and to claim full membership to Ottoman society on the other. When doing so,

they not only detached themselves from *adat-ı kadime* and question the legitimacy of

Şer'i law but also put the old mode of Ottoman rule, defined particularly by corporate

privileges, in competition with the new one, characterized by the fiction of equality

before the law.[54] Thus, the disputes between the Circassian chieftains and slaves, their

---

[52] Michael Taussig, *Law in a Lawless Land: Diary of a Limpieza in Colombia* (Chicago: The University of Chicago Press, 2005), 30.

[53] Ibid., 16.

[54] This argument is insightfully made by Dylan Penningroth in regards lineage systems in the American South and Africa: "... slavery in southern Gold Coast planted roots for a patrilineal system of inheritance and descent that tangled and competed with the matrilineal system. It was

usage of the same language of justice, yet with different meanings ascribed to it, were more than simple issues of ownership of a patch of land, an ox, or the plough. A foreign or transplanted law that enforced these descriptions of ownership was not the whole of it either. As Suraiya Farokhi put it, "the process of [slaves'] induction to Ottoman society was not simply a matter between slave owners and slaves," and the "state intervention went beyond simple tax collection and prevention of abuses."[55] "Acting in the name of religious law," Faroqhi argues, "the state also attempted to enforce general urban [or provincial] order, including the hierarchy between men and women, Muslims and non-Muslims."[56] Here we see that this involvement goes deeper than "acting in the name of religious law" or simply effecting the hierarchies in relation to what Madeline Zilfi called "the twin pillars of elite 'othering,'" that is of women and non-Muslims,[57] but all (and needless to say, shifting) subordinate groups. The Ottoman state mapped its subject-citizens primarily in accordance with the level of their subordination, and upheld (if not produced) the mechanisms that produced them. The Circassian slaves' claims to freedom, which meant in actuality no more than full ownership of their lands, ploughs, ox and daughters at that point, was one of the most significant attempts against these

---

the mirror image of slavery in British America, where legally enforced matrilineality set slaves apart and affirmed free men's authority over both property and their white and black "dependents." Comparing such innovations reminds us how contingent these kinship systems were, and how intertwined they were with slavery, not only in Africa but in the United States as well." Dylan C. Penningroth, "The Claims of Slaves and Ex-Slaves to Family and Property: A Transatlantic Comparison," *The American Historical Review*, vol. 112, no. 4 (Oct., 2007), 1051.

[55] Suraiya Faroqhi, "Quis Custodiet Custodes? Controlling Slave Identities and Slave Traders in Seventeenth and Eighteenth-century Istanbul," in *Stories of Ottoman Men and Women: Establishing Status, Establishing Control* (Istanbul: Eren Yayıncılık, 2002), 252.

[56] Faroqhi, "Quis Custodiet Custodes?," 252. This same argument constitutes the core argument of Madeline Zilfi's *Women and Slavery in the Late Ottoman Empire: The Design of Difference* (Cambridge: Cambridge University Press, 2010).

[57] Zilfi, *Women and Slavery in the Late Ottoman Empire*, 87.

mechanisms, one that was supported by a (trans)forming legal system by a government that promised to safeguard, at least in theory, the rights of all of its subject-citizens to life and property. From the beginning of the Circassian influx at the end of the 1850s, in attempts that the above-mentioned Nogai chieftain Canpolat described as "unruly behavior," slaves filed petitions or legal suits for their "freedom," and their rights to ownership of their possessions as well as their families. These petitions put the contradictions between the transplanted/old and the existing/new legal systems in writing and elucidated what slaves made of their new "homelands," in which they were as invested as their owners.

Dylan Penningroth argues that pluralistic legal orders, such as the imperial or colonial ones, "served a variety of powerful groups: ruling elites, male elders, and the colonial state itself," although other scholars pointed at the further complexities of this seemingly linear equation.[58] "Those groups' jostling assumptions and interests," Penningroth further argued, "often opened up space for ordinary people, and even slaves, to seize on legal institutions to pursue their interest."[59] In the Ottoman Empire, well-poised and often well-informed, slaves also framed their concerns and demands in reference to these assumptions and interests, beginning with the role of the Sultan and the Ottoman state itself. In their petitions, they put into words what sovereign power ought to mean and do, arguing that their position under the protection of and tax-payers to

---

[58] Penningroth, "The Claims of Slaves," 1057. See Lauren Benton and Lisa Ford, for instance, for an excellent account of how these groups related to each other in manipulating local legal practices and institutions. "Magistrates in Empire: Convicts, Slaves, and the Remaking of the Plural Legal order in the British Empire," in *Legal Pluralism and Empires, 1500–1850*, eds. Lauren Benton and Richard J. Ross (New York: New York University Press, 2013).

[59] Penningroth, "The Claims of Slaves," 1057.

Circassian chieftains not only caused their destitute state but also undermined the sovereignty of the Ottoman state itself.

While the slaves' claims to freedom began (or at least the news of it circulated) earlier, the first mention of its organized character was in 1863, a time when the expulsion was nearing its peak. In an official report written by the council of the province of Silistra for the office of the Grand Vizier, it was noted that an ongoing dispute among Circassian immigrants on the matter of slavery had been partially resolved when the slave owners and their slaves came to an agreement to travel to Istanbul with the purpose of mutually appealing to a judge or court hearing (*terafu'*) with the Supreme Council, but the latter reportedly changed their mind for no apparent reason.[60] Upon this, the owner of the mentioned slaves, a chieftain named Kobzik Zavir together with several other notables and elders (a total of thirty individuals), applied to the provincial court to file an official complaint about the "inappropriate" behavior of his slaves. Following the slave owners' official appeal, and in compliance with the local officials' suggestion that "one or two of the slaves with trustable judgment" should also be heard, a slave named Abrek was summoned to the provincial court of Silistre and stated (on behalf of other slaves in his village) that they could not and would not travel to Istanbul for the trial, as they were not slaves but free like other freeborn people. Thus, Abrek maintained, the plaintiffs had no right to claim ownership over them and even less to force them to trial (possibly to set the terms of bondage at this point), like the use of their agricultural land and equipment, sale, and resale of their family members. With rhetorical mastery, Abrek further stated that he and his enslaved colleagues migrated from their native lands in the Caucasus to

---

[60] BOA, MVL 964/64, 1280.M.18 (5 July 1663).

Ottoman domains with the hopes and desires of ridding themselves of Russian aggression and becoming farmers, worthy of service to the Ottoman sovereign. "Now, since all of us are slaves and subjects of our Padişah," he reportedly contended, "neither he, nor God would consent to [Kobzik Zavir] capture and hold us as slaves." Unless they were rounded and tied up and sent to Istanbul forcefully (which was not permissible, the council report clarified), they would not allow any one of them to be taken to Istanbul. They were not to be captured forcefully, yet plain talk did not suffice either, the provincial council complained to the Supreme Council of Judicial Ordinances (*Meclis-i Vâlâ-yı Ahkâm-ı Adliye*), where the case file eventually ended up. Here Abrek (as one man of sound judgment) appeared alone in the provincial court, and yet not as a plaintiff either, but representing a joint effort against the *adat-ı kadime*, the chieftains who claimed their ownership pertaining to that law, as well the Ottoman government, who was seeking to (re)define and enforce their status as slaves for the sake of public order and security.

These claims continued in the ensuing years and became more organized and collective in nature, producing actual petitions and lengthier arguments. In the meantime, however, both the slave owners and the Ottoman state developed their own (inter)related strategies and solutions. Convinced that manumitting slaves without the consent of their owners would bring on violent opposition and more clashes, the Council of Ministers suggested that self-purchase (*mükâtebe*) would be the best solution,[61] not only to appease the ongoing or future tensions but also to resolve the matter without deviating from the *Şer'i* law that governed all public and civil matters in the empire. *Mükâtebe*, an

---

[61] Toledano, *The Ottoman Slave Trade and its Suppression,* 164–165.

established *Şer'i* procedure, allowed the slaves and slave owners to mutually determine

the payment terms and to set the amount (often the equivalent of the slaves' sale price)

for manumission. Upon the completion of the full payment, the slave would be given a

manumission certificate and deemed free, while the owners themselves would receive a

fair amount of compensation at the same time.[62] One apparent problem with *mükâtebe*

was that exceedingly impoverished refugee-slaves, who were mere share-croppers on

their owners' land,[63] were not able to pay a slave's price, let alone pay for an entire

family. Moreover, legally speaking, it was a voluntary procedure and could not be

imposed upon slave owners, which was, as Ehud Toledano observed, a setback for the

slaves:[64]

> A *mükâtebe* could not be imposed on a slave owner who had not flagrantly
> mistreated his slave; it also gave greater leverage to the *Şerî* courts, before which
> such procedures were normally being conducted. Apparently, the government
> was unable to overcome the strong opposition of the Circassian slave holders, or
> simply preferred to avoid a direct, and undoubtedly bitter, confrontation with
> them. The readiness with which the *Şerî* courts were issuing orders supporting
> the position of slave owners against the claim of their slaves put the government
> in a different situation. [...] [t]he courts impeded the authorities' actions which
> were meant to benefit the slaves. This may be indicative of a general mood in
> religious circles, one which upheld the legality of slavery because it was
> sanctioned by Islam. The government, it should be stressed, was consistently
> careful in emphasizing the slavery, as distinct form of the slave trade, was not to

---

[62] Ibid.

[63] The initial land distribution among Circassian immigrant-refugees was reportedly not based on exceptions or princely prerogatives, and was done in accordance with household divisions. Since the slave families were attached to their owners' households, as has been discussed earlier, and that the land titles were registered with the owners' names, the slaves could not legally claim ownership of the land. See BOA, ŞD 2396/18, 1289.Ra.8 (16 May 1872), 8.

[64] Toledano, *The Ottoman Slave Trade and its Suppression,* 165–166.

be interfered with. The Persian Gulf *ferman* of 1847, the prohibition of the Circassian and Georgian slave trade in 1854, and the *ferman* of 1857 against the traffic in blacks come to mind in this context. It was only the institution of agricultural slavery among the Circassians that Porte was trying to dismantle, and that too—in the face of strong opposition—it did gradually, with great caution, somewhat diffidently.[65]

That the Ottoman government appeared more sympathetic to the cause and claims of the slaves than the *Şer'i* courts was not because it was inherently good-natured or benign. As has been argued above, the Ottoman government too favored the slave owners over slaves under most circumstances, but they did it more subtly and with a different set of obligations and priorities, particularly at the international level, in comparison to the *Şer'i* courts, which were exceedingly and purposefully local. First of these concerns was the return migration of the Caucasian refugees, which began almost immediately after their arrival, causing alarm with the Ottoman government over the potential "domestic chaos and foreign embarrassment."[66] Secondly, they had to comply or at least respond to Britain's intensifying efforts towards the wholesale abolition of slavery throughout the Ottoman domains. Having abolished the slave trade in 1808, and the institution itself as a whole in 1833, Britain concentrated its abolitionary efforts against the trade in the Atlantic and eastern Mediterranean, although often to enact or reinforce imperial hierarchies.[67] As the above quote suggests, starting with the 1847 Persian Gulf *ferman*,

---

[65] Ibid., 166.

[66] Cuthell, "The Muhacirin Komisyonu," 178.

[67] For a discussion on how these were mobilized in the eastern Mediterranean, see Alison Frank, "The Children of the Desert and the Laws of the Sea: Austria, Great Britain, the Ottoman Empire,

the Ottoman government issued imperial decrees that also functioned as pacts and treaties

between the Ottoman and other (specifically British) governments, which gave the latter

the right of search and seizure, as necessary.[68] Abolition of trade in Caucasian slaves in

1854, which was necessitated and forced upon the Ottoman government by the Crimean

War, and Africans in 1857 (an encompassing and carefully enforced ban, more a direct

product of Britain's worldwide abolitionary efforts) both had binding effects that brought

a close monitoring of the Ottoman sea and land routes by the British consular offices,

commercial agents, as well as naval forces in the Mediterranean. Unlike the issue of trade

in African slaves, the Ottoman government managed to dodge the British demands on

Circassian slavery to a great extent.[69] However, this did not mean that it was entirely

immune to British control, which occasionally pushed for measures against it as well.[70]

Moreover, the Ottoman government had domestic obligations, at least aspirations, in

providing a degree of equality before the law in the aftermath of the 1856 Reform Edict,

in compliance with the spread of the liberal ideals and liberalism as a "specific form of

governmentality."[71] Thus, the Şer'i legal institutions and the Ottoman government had

---

and the Mediterranean Slave Trade in the Nineteenth Century," The American Historical Review (2012) 117 (2).

[68] Hakan Erdem, *Slavery in the Ottoman Empire and its Demise, 1800–1909* (London: Palgrave Macmillan Limited, 1996), 99–100.

[69] Ibid., 113–114; Ehud R. Toledano, *Slavery and Abolition in the Ottoman Middle East* (Seattle: University of Washington Press, 1998), 113.

[70] Erdem, *Slavery in the Ottoman Empire and its Demise*, 114.

[71] For a discussion of liberalism not as "liberal politics, ideas or institution," but rather as a mode of govenmentality, see Patrick Joyce, *The Rule of Freedom: Liberalism and the Modern City* (London: Verso, 2003), especially the introduction. Although such *Tanzimat* era (1839–1876) intellectuals as Şinasi and Namık Kemal (two prominent figures in the Young Ottoman movement that culminated in the promulgation of the Constitution in 1876) are known to be well immersed in the liberal thought, there is no systematic study, to my knowledge, on liberalism as a mode of rule in the Ottoman Empire.

different positions in relation to slavery and abolition. *Mükâtebe* was a solution that supported both positions and favored the slave owners too, by "mak[ing] the application of the procedure contingent upon its acceptance by immigrants' leaders, most of whom were slave holders."[72]

The slave petitions and claims were presumably influenced by all these international developments and domestic aspirations, although they concerned themselves mostly with the definition of slavery, property ownership and sovereignty (Abrek, mentioned above, was one of the first to express it), making only rare references to the 1854 ban on Caucasian slave trade or the general prohibition in 1857 against trade in African slaves. One related note, written by the office of the Grand Vizier to the *Muhacirin Komisyonu*, pointed at the problem of the Ottoman governments' ambivalent position vis-à-vis Caucasian and African slavery and the possible discontentment it would cause among Caucasian slaves. While both the new importation and the sale and purchase of existing African slaves had already been banned throughout the empire, the note stated, the Caucasian ones were made exceptions and their previous statuses (determined by the *adat-ı kadime*) were upheld. The importation of slaves from immigrant settlements, and their sale ("openly, here and there" the note underlined) continued without much hindrance.[73] This ambivalence and discrepancy would became become one of the central arguments for the reformers (most notably the Ministry of Justice and Circassian intellectual organizations) demanding the wholesale abolition of slavery in the aftermath of the constitutional revolution of 1908. The semi-official

---

[72] Toledano, *The Ottoman Slave Trade and its Suppression,* 167.

[73] BOA, A.MKT.MVL 140/4, B.23.1278 (24 January 1862).

proclamation announced by the Ministry of Justice in late 1908 clearly stated the sale and purchase of Circassian slaves was prohibited, just as the trade in African slaves had been for a long time.[74] On a related note, the slave holders who claimed that their ownership of their slaves had a Şer'i basis (supported by numerous ayat and hadith, as they often clarified) found the abolition of trade in African slaves deployed against them as a claim-making strategy. As the chief of the Ottoman Parliament's Committee on Petitions articulated in 1909, even if the ownership of Circassian slaves was a Şer'i principle or right, had the African slaves not already been exempted from the jurisdiction of Şer'i law?[75] Similarly, the minister of justice Hasan Fehmi made an argument against slavery by pointing out that "slavery pertaining to the white race was already abolished by the Russian government in territories under their control" when Circassians emigrated to the Ottoman lands; a fact that rendered, according to the minister, the claims to slave ownership by Circassian notables unfounded.[76]

Neither the Azizian nor Hamidian-era Ottomans openly celebrated "freedom, equality, justice," as their counterparts did in the post-1908 constitutional revolution, but the idea that slavery was essentially incompatible with both the 1839 and 1856 edicts was in the making as early as the1860s, and Circassian slaves were instrumental in bringing that debate to the foreground. Their petitions did not mention the general ban of 1857 as one would expect them to do, since they would obviously benefit from it. There is no doubt that this was partially due to racial othering, as would be more clearly articulated,

---

[74] See İkdam, 17 Teşrinisani 1324 for an example of the announcement note.

[75] BOA, ŞD 2786/29, 1327.N.14 (29 September 1909), 66.

[76] Ibid.

often retrospectively, in the aftermath of the 1908 revolution.[77] What also figured in this absence was the Circassian slaves' predominantly rural character. They defined themselves as farmers and peasants in the service of the Ottoman sovereign and were removed from urban areas, where bonding with other slaves and learning about their experiences and sharing strategies would be easier. Most importantly, however, due to a variety of reasons, most significant of which was the difficulties encountered throughout the migration and settlement process, their protests were local ones, directed at a set of immediate problems and tangible items, such as the breaking up of their families and sale of their daughters or the ownership of their land and animals. In other words, theirs was not a moral or ethical quest against the "greater evil" of slavery, as was the case with abolitionists, reformers, or humanitarians, even though they made use of the same universal language of "freedom."

Such was the case described by a slave named Mehmed in his brief petition to the Council of State (*Şura-yı Devlet*) in July 1872.[78] Mehmed and other slaves from the town of Silivri brought legal action against their owners five years before the petition, that is, not long after their settlement in the area. While their first attempt was hastily suppressed by local legal bodies, they managed to bring the case to court in Istanbul and had been collectively residing there in the past year for what Mehmed called a freedom suit (*hürriyet davası*). While Mehmed and his colleagues were following a strictly legal path to claim their freedom, the slave owners were far from keeping within the "prescribed

---

[77] See, for instance, BOA, DH.MKT 2739/67, 1327.M. 25 (16 February 1909), 3.

[78] BOA, ŞD 2872/30, 1289.Ra.7 (15 May 1872). Branched off from the Supreme Council of Judicial Ordinances (*Meclis- i Vâlâ- yı Ahkâm- ı Adliye*) in 1868, the Council of State was a consultative assembly, where complex legal matters that could not be resolved or referred to by law was brought to.

98

boundaries" of the law, refused to wait for the result of the legal procedure, and restored

their violent means and tyrannized the remainder of the slave population in Silivri, with

the purpose of obtaining half of the grain that was recently harvested. These specific

instances of violence and abuse on the slave owners' side demanded a specific set of

responses. Moreover, at the core of the slaves' claim to freedom was the assertion of their

difference from the remainder of the slave population, particularly those employed in

domestic settings in the Ottoman center. Another, lengthier, petition filed by Haydar,

Osman, and Zoş to the Council of State in 1872 provides a more detailed depiction of this

particular point. Acting as representatives (*vekil*) on behalf of all those "who [were]

called slaves among the Circassian refugees that settled in Rumelia and Anatolia,"

Haydar, Osman, and Zoş, themselves also slaves, had been carrying out legal action of a

similar nature for the past several years. "It must be our poor command of the language

and the errors we made in expressing our intention thereof," they wrote in a sarcastic

tone, "that hindered and delayed the receipt of the answers and just solutions we have

been demanding in the last several years."[79] In their petition supplemented by a sixteen-

item fact list, theirs was not a discursive "double plea of humanity and international

right,"[80] but a response to a set of actual problems, concepts, and definitions, such as just

enslavement, property or sovereignty they grappled with in their everyday lives.

---

[79] BOA, ŞD 2396/18, 1289.Ra. 8 (16 May 1872), 21.

[80] This expression was used by the *The National Magazine* in the context of two Circassian chieftains, Hadji Hayden Hassan and Kustan Ogli Islam, visiting England and petitioning Foreign Secretary Earl Russel in 1863. That the Circassians, "a race who reach the highest perfection of human form," became a matter of ethical concern had to do with the security of Britain's Indian dominions. Here I borrow it to highlight the rhetorical character of such broad claims. "Our Dominions in India," *The National Magazine*, January 1863, 13, 75, 97–99.

The first of these concepts and definitions had to with the question of what it meant to be a citizen in relation to a sovereign power. In their native land of the "Circassian Mountain" (*Çerkestan Dağı*), the discussion went, they were not under the protection of any monarch, thus the stability and the order they needed (simple and vulnerable peasants as they were, they added) came from what they called "a few able swordsmen and those who had the "will to war."[81] Their present status as slaves originated within a specific context when their forefathers sought the protection of the chieftains and that their status in time was relegated from peasants to slaves. Even so, however, the root of the problem that afflicted them now had to do with the terminology rather than anything else: the word slave (*köle*) was understood only as those employed in domestic settings and sold at will (which was deemed incompatible with the *adat-ı kadime*, they clarified), but what they really ought to be called was peasants (*reaya*). The petition further clarified that this wrong usage of the word slave was devised by the Circassian chieftains, princes, and noblemen themselves, who were accustomed to act as the sovereign in their native lands but whose sovereignty was challenged by the Ottoman state upon their immigration to its domains.[82] Only by holding on to their slaves (and defining them as such, before all), the petitioners argued, the chieftains could hold on to or assert their princely qualities that they believed they had and guarantee their gains through in-kind payments they extorted from their slaves or simply by selling them.[83] This situation of being at the service of both the Ottoman state and the Circassian

---

[81] BOA, ŞD 2396/18, 1289.Ra.8 (16 May 1872), 19/1.

[82] Ibid., 19/2.

[83] Ibid., 21.

chieftains, which meant paying two separate taxes, was not only beyond the limit of their means but also impaired the authority of the Ottoman state itself. Moreover, their legal status as slaves exempted them from the military draft. While all other immigrants became eligible for the draft seven years after their arrival in the country, they were held back by their owners, which caused another harm to the Ottoman state.

In a long official letter, the Council of State agreed upon the rightfulness of Haydar, Osman, and Zoş's central claim. Like all other classes and groups of subjects, they wrote, they too became stakeholders in both *Şer'i* and civil laws upon their arrival to the Ottoman domains, which should have invalidated their status as slaves (*memlukiyet*).[84] But their enslaved status was due to an old and widespread custom (*itiyad*) among the Circassians, and the existence of it was acknowledged even by the slaves themselves.[85] Thus, the Council concluded, this long-established and acknowledged category could not retrospectively or automatically be undone by the simple fact that they migrated to another land. Ignoring, for the most part, the slaves' elaborate arguments on the meanings of citizenship, the Ottoman government in general and the Council of State in particular concerned themselves with finding a practical solution to the problem. They proposed the promotion of *mükâtebe* as a safe, just, and only option towards a wholesale abolition of slavery in the Ottoman domains. Fearing that the conflicts and fights between the two parties would get more violent and spread to

---

[84] Ibid., 9.

[85] Hakan Erdem mentions about a similar decision by Council of Ministers in 1867. Erdem, *Slavery in the Ottoman Empire and its Demise*, 118. That the Ottoman government's response remained unchanged during these five years, despite numerous legal suits and elaborate articulations by the slaves, indicates that its decisions was made independently from what slaves has written.

the rest of the society and turn into a general turmoil, the Council advised against any coercive measures against slaves or slave owners, but not without highlighting the importance of bringing limitations to both sides. According to those, slave owners were banned from breaking up families and selling each member separately. Moreover, age limitations were reiterated here, although a bit differently than when it was first brought up a decade earlier. The letter stated that the age of 45 and 35, for male and female slaves respectively, marked the end of their terms of service and rendered them free.[86] Yet, their freedom applied only to themselves and those of their children born after they obtained their freedom. With the consent of their owners, the remainder of their children could be subjected to *mükâtebe* also, whose fees would be determined by a special commission. In short, the Ottoman government opted for regulating and ameliorating the conditions of slavery, but eschewed an apparent intervention to achieve a wholesale abolition, even though it was aware of its undermining effects, which was discussed, "one by one, item by item" by the slaves in their claims to freedom. In fact, even the military draft was partially left to the slave owners' consent and will. The Council stated that those who were already in the process of *mükâtebe* could enter into army service, as a way of paying the self-purchase fee, but only with permission obtained from their owners.[87] In that, the Ottoman government undermined its power as the "holder of the sovereign decision," by tying it to the consent of another authority.[88] The Ottoman government failed to bring about an effective solution, and instead continued with half measures, that benefited in

---

[86] BOA, ŞD 2396/18, 1289.Ra.8, 12.

[87] Ibid., 16.

[88] Giorgio Agamben, *State of Exception* (Chicago: The University of Chicago Press, 2005).

most cases only the slave owners.[89] In other words, its justice betrayed the slaves who had the most faith in it. We know that these half measures as limitations and regulations were hardly enforced in the following decades also, as the Circassian settlements continued to supply the urban and provincial elite households with domestic slaves, as the following chapter will explore.

All in all, even the principal purpose of the Ottoman government's appeasement strategies failed, and the clashes between the slaves and slave owners continued in the ensuing years. A year after the Council's official communication, in 1873, a note written by the office of the Grand Vizier reported on the difficulties the slaves encountered in paying the self-purchase amounts that were previously decided on. Instead of the previous terms, the office suggested that the fee should be paid in kind, with whatever was left from the previous year's and half of the current year's crop.[90] The fee could also be paid in cash, by auctioning the crop, if the slaves preferred to do so. In almost an automated-sounding response, the Ottoman government reiterated that *mükâtebe* would protect and guarantee the *Şer'i* rights of both parties and help in doing away with the ongoing strife and for that reason, should be put into practice and the results be reported to the office of the Grand Vizier at once. Just as the Grand Vezirate issued this decision, an incidence of unrest was communicated from Canik, where armed slaves and slave owners reportedly assembled in the town square. The report explicated that there too, a group of slave representatives had been to Istanbul in pursuit of legal action to undo or get rid of their slave status. While there, the slaves and the slave owners came to an

---

[89] Erdem, *Slavery in the Ottoman Empire and its Demise*, 120.

[90] BOA, A.MKT.MHM 461/26, 1290.C.16 (11 August 1873).

agreement on the implementation of *mükâtebe* for the manumission of the slaves, but the latter retreated from the agreement and could not be persuaded in its implementation, even though they were given detailed explanations on the benefits of the solution. The parties were eventually calmed down through the local government's intervention, but given that the matter was left at a stalemate, it could be resumed any moment. Just as there were slave owners who refused to go into *mükâtebe* arrangements with their slaves, there were cases in which slaves rejected the idea of them paying for their manumission. A case from Çorlu from 1874 is told by Hakan Erdem as follows:[91]

> According to [the British Vice-consul in Edirne], the slaves asserted their freedom first, then the masters took up arms to compel them to return to their state of slavery unless they chose to purchase their liberty. It must immediately be observed that the masters were in fact willing for a *mükâtebe* but the slaves wanted to be free without paying for their manumission. [...] The local government assembled troops complete with field guns and 'informed the Circassian Beys of the Porte's instructions, threaten to abandon them to military.' The Beys had little option but to consent to the terms of the government. This was a radically different situation from that envisaged by the aforementioned decisions of the Council. The slaves were to be freed 'without money payments, the owners to receive as compensation the whole of the lands they hitherto held in common with the slaves.' The slaves, on the other hand, were to be dispersed 'among Turkish villages' and to have other land parcels. [The Vice-consul] added that there were some ninety Circassian chiefs connected with the late disturbances in the Edirne prisons.

---

[91] Erdem, *Slavery in the Ottoman Empire and its Demise*, 119.

Judging by the sizeable number of slaves petitioning with similar claims in the aftermath of the 1908 revolution, we know that *mükâtebe*, which the Ottoman government insisted upon, was far from bringing on a general or wholesale abolitionary solution. As already discussed above, it was after all a voluntary agreement, one that was at the slave owners' discretion. In that, it even failed to provide the means to secure public order that the Ottoman government valued most.

That the slaves were obliged to pay for their and their families' freedom aggravated the poverty of those who were already suffering the harsh circumstances of refugee life. "Add to that," Haydar, Osman, and Zoş stated in a rather angry tone, "the tools and things we owned or were given to us by the Ottoman state have been looted or broken by the slave owners," which made their condition even worse. And that was not all of it, either. Whenever they asked for what they rightfully owned (granted to them by the Ottoman state or its agents, such as the *Muhacirin Komisyonu*), they were beaten or even killed. In one instance, they further noted, a group of them were tied up together and thrown into a well, for being disobedient towards the chieftains. They maintained their ways, the slaves concluded, because they expected either a monetary gain by selling their slaves particularly in Istanbul, or forming alliances with high dignitaries or the Ottoman dynasty through slavery, which became common particularly among the Abkhaz chieftains in the late nineteenth and early twentieth centuries, a trait also explored in the following chapter. Consequently, the course of the Circassian expulsion as an elongated period of crisis created an overabundance of law that had to redefine its limits almost with each individual case, which gave Ottoman practice of slavery a highly arbitrary character. It continued to bent bend categorical limits until the dissolution of the empire,

105

creating ample discussion on who was entitled to emancipation (and indirectly,

citizenship) and who was not, along the way.

Conclusion

At about the same time as Haydar, Osman, and Zoş filed their petition and

articulated why they were indeed entitled to freedom, or as many others fought their

owners, refusing to pay for it, a brief report made its way to the Council of State. The

report concerned itself specifically with female Circassian slaves (referred to as *cariye*),

who had previously been under the ownership of a variety of people but managed to

obtain their freedom recently.[92] According to the report, these women, who were in most

cases vulnerable towards all kinds of intruders, were approached by certain men who

"drifted about as vagrants," who seduced them (*iğfalatına aldanarak*) with the promise of

marriage. These men, shortly after their marriage, divorced the women and caused their

destitution, which resulted in prostitution and "other kinds of disgrace." The report noted

that thirty or forty of these manumitted *cariye*s recently appealed to the *Muhacirin*

Komisyonu and obtained a daily salary of 6 piasters, but since the commission could not

afford such extra expenses, another arrangement, in accordance with the Council of

State's suggestions, was in order. The Council gave its opinion as to how these women

would be handled. Those who had tribal affiliations and whose free status was proved

were to be taken to their settlement at once. If they were not members of a tribe, the

women would be given the option of employment as maidservants and in case they did

---

[92] BOA, ŞD 2395/3, 1288.B.15 (30 September 1871).

not want to work as servants, they could also opt for marriage. Until a proper suitor came about, however, they would still have to be temporarily employed in service. These sorts of supportive or protective arrangements were in fact part of the manumission process, necessitated by law, but there were several obstacles foreseen for these women. Since they were divorced (and, implied here to have been engaged in prostitution), no household would be willing to accept them as servants. Even when they managed to find employment, the report asserted, the "traces of their former plight" would continue to cause problems and eventual aggravation of their situation. The commission was primarily responsible for close inspection of the women's suitors at all times and when marriage could not be arranged, to place them in appropriate places, in accordance with their kind, *cinsiyet*, understood here as an ethnic or linguistic group. In that sense, even though their names appeared in settlement registers or were often central to the claims in many slave petitions, the experience of slavery and freedom for women remained different from that of male slaves. The latter resisted conspicuously, either by pulling out weapons or bringing lawsuits against their owners. Women and young girls, whose flow especially towards Istanbul did not cease for at least another four decades, developed other sorts of relationships both with their owners and slavery as a practice. The following two chapters look at how slavery and freedom worked for them, in connection with what has been outlined in this chapter.

Chapter 3.
Slaver-Mistresses, Matchmakers, and Destitute Women

About a decade after the 1877–78 Russo-Turkish War ended, the Yıldız Palace

secretariat in Istanbul, where the second wave of Caucasian migration was still in

progress, received a report about a criminal case that involved three women and a number

of young girls that had been illegally appropriated and sold as slaves.[1] The perpetrators,

three women named Sıdıka, Şirin, and Kör (blind) Nadire, targeted the destitute families

in the Üsküdar district of Istanbul and in an ongoing scheme they went from door to door,

using a particular division of labor and narrative strategy to convince the families to give

or sell their daughters to them. In brief, they told the parents that they were from "inside"

(that is, one of the imperial harems), thus, they could present their daughters to the palace

to be sold as *cariye*s, a general term used for all types of enslaved harem inmates. In

return, they said, the parents themselves would receive money or gifts from the palace

and be rid of their poverty and misery. Besides, the girls would become *çirag* (literally,

apprentice) in eight years, be given in marriage to a *miralay* (colonel) or a *kaymakam*

(lieutenant colonel) and return home rich.

The families involved in the case were reportedly all refugees from Silistra,

forced to move to the Ottoman Empire in the aftermath of the 1877–78 Russo-Ottoman

---

[1] BOA, Y.PRK.BŞK 12/89, 1305.B.14 (27 March 1888). The file is exceptionally large and detailed in comparison to other files of similar content, containing three separate reports on the case providing different layers of information. It also contains long records of police interrogations, *istintakname*s, conducted by everyone involved in the case, except for the young girls Zekiye and Müzeyyen.

War.[2] In 1878, some 180,000 people (some of whom were Circassians, who were settled in the Balkans a decade earlier) were in Istanbul, waiting to be (re)settled by the Ottoman government.[3] In the 1880s, even in the early 1890s, there were still large numbers of refugees in Istanbul, either passing through the city to be settled in the provinces, or to stay, adding to the city's poor population,[4] all of whom were highly vulnerable to slave dealers in an environment where, as this chapter aims to demonstrate, practically anyone could become one at any time.

Among those refugee families who were targeted by Sıdıka, Şirin, and Kör Nadire was a woman from Silistra named Penbe, who told the police that she was widowed and came to Istanbul five months prior, with her four children, two of whom worked as porters at the dockside and one who sold candles. The fourth child was a girl named Müzeyyen. She was 12 years old and working as a servant for the monthly payment of 20 piasters at the time when her mother was approached by Sıdıka and Kör Nadire, with the promise of a post at the imperial harem and an upfront payment of 15 Ottoman liras (that is, 1500 piasters).[5] She had brown hair and hazel eyes with a "tint of blue," it was specified. Also a recent refugee from Silistra, Zehra was approached by the same group of women for her 8-year-old daughter Zekiye, who had "blond hair, hazel eyes." Both Müzeyyen and Zekiye were categorized as "Turkish," (here, to be understood as non-

---

[2] Roger Deal, "War Refugees and Violence in Hamidian Istanbul," *Middle Eastern Studies*, vol.49, no.2 (2013), 181. Overall, the war caused the dislocation of a million Muslim inhabitants of Serbia and Bulgaria.

[3] Deal, "War Refugees and Violence in Hamidian Istanbul," 181.

[4] Kemal Karpat, *Ottoman Population 1830–1914: Demographic and Social Characteristics* (Madison: University of Wisconsin Press, 1985), 86.

[5] BOA, Y.PRK.BŞK 12/89, 1305.B.14 (27 March 1888), 6.

Circassian, Muslim, and white) whose enslavement and sale were, under normal circumstances, strictly prohibited by law. The initial explanation that Sıdıka gave to the police, however, that she recently manumitted her slave and decided to adopt a young girl in her stead, made it seem like what she did was almost an act of benevolence.

Among the perpetrators of the incident, which touched virtually upon almost all "peculiarities" of the Ottoman practices of slavery, which will be discussed below, Sıdıka was specified as *Çerkes* (Circassian). She was a resident of the Tophane district in Istanbul, where the city port was located and many slavers resided. She was brought to Istanbul from *Çerkesistan* (Circassia), she told to the police, when she was eight years old, and like Zekiye she was recently appropriated. She served as an enslaved servant to the chief steward of Fatma Sultan (Sultan Abdülmecid's daughter) and was eventually freed and married off to a merchant from Egypt.[6]

Her close accomplice Şirin Kadın was also a manumitted slave. Specified as *Zenciye* (literally, Negress) in the report, she was the only slaver proper in the gang, and referred to as such. She also resided in Tophane and was well connected, not only to the captains of the slave ships that docked in her district but also the eunuchs and other palace officials who were authorized to buy slaves for the imperial harem. In fact, in one of her transactions, she claimed to have introduced the chief eunuch of the Beşiktaş harem to a captain, for "how else would they even know each other?" she claimed.[7] In short, save for Kör Nadire, Sıdıka and Şirin themselves constituted an earlier generation of slaves and were well entrenched in its culture and customs. For instance, they well

---

[6] Ibid., 3.

[7] Ibid., 14.

knew they had to account for the girls' fluent Turkish, hence they explained to their prospective buyers that the girls came to Istanbul many years ago and forgot their native tongues.[8] Part of the report also dealt with the recovery of the stolen girls, who were now the properties of such notable people as the chief eunuch of the imperial harem in Beşiktaş, Ferhad Ağa (who bought slaves on behalf of one of the *Kadın Effendi*s), as well as Sultan Abdülaziz's son, *şehzade* Mahmud Celaleddin Efendi. Since Şirin Kadın's close network also included her husband, a certain Baltacı Mustafa from Egypt, also a slaver by profession, she had several other girls dispatched there.

The division of labor among the three women was indicative of not only how the slave trade was organized, but how, as a whole, Ottoman society was hierarchized or compartmentalized along the lines of class, race, and ethnicity. The *dellal* (procurer) of the group, Kör Nadire, was from Gekbuze (Gebze), a town 30 miles east of Istanbul. During her interrogation, she claimed that she was brought to Istanbul when she was very young, implying that she had no ties to her native town, although later in the investigation, it became clear that Kör Nadire had been "recruiting" girls from her native town also, in addition to those she solicited in Üsküdar.[9] In fact, the report pointed out that she recently brought a Turkish girl (again, meaning non-Circassian, Muslim, and white) from her village, who was subsequently sent to Egypt and sold into slavery there. We do not know how she approached families in her native town, but it is likely that she allured them with the fact (possibly a made-up one) that she was married to a lieutenant. This was at least what she did when she approached Müzeyyen's mother in Üsküdar,

---

[8] Ibid., 4.

[9] Ibid., 3.

primarily to give her an impression of reliability but also to point at where she stood in the scale of women who had a stake in the slave trade, many of whom were ranked according to the profession of their husbands, as will be discussed in more detail below. She acted as a scout, locating the girls through her connections, making the initial contacts with the families and making informal appointments with them for Sıdıka to come in the following day. She was qualified to provide an "introduction" to the families and assess the girls at the same time, but it fell upon Sıdıka and her *saraylı* tag (used for all women who were or previously had been a member of the imperial harem) to convince the parents to hand their daughters over to her. What was started by Kör Nadire was continued by Sıdıka. She was the one who assured the parents that she had connections with the imperial harem and that she could have their daughters employed there as enslaved servants. Being once a slave herself, she knew exactly what the girls' mothers wanted to hear also. They could even see their daughters every six months, she assured them, on the condition that they did not disclose the fact that they were related to the girls. They just had to pretend that they were their previous owners. With this assurance, repeated several times in the interrogation records, she took the girls to bring them to her own household to observe their manners, good or bad habits. In short, anything that would effect the price, as the usual procedure went.

Both Kör Nadire and Sıdıka had ambiguous descriptions in terms of their involvement in the slave trade. The former procured not only slaves but also cooks, servants, or wet nurses. As it is well elaborated in Krikor Zohrab's story *Postal* with the *dellal* Hacı Dürük, this profession (not reserved to the Muslim population of the empire either) was a sound and sometimes the only means for especially poor women to make a good living. Like Kör Nadire, Hacı Dürük was depicted to have strong ties to her native village, where she took occasional trips to obtain young girls, in accordance with what was asked of her. She herself had worked as a servant, a wet nurse, a laundress, a cook, and as Zohrab described her, she "understood a lot from a few words."[10] The line between procuring servants and obtaining girls for sexual services was not clear-cut, so when Surpik Hanım, the wealthy Armenian woman from Kadıköy, asked Hacı Dürük to find her a "decent looking but shy young woman, not necessarily trained in housework," the latter knew that the girl was meant to be for Surpik Hanım's son.[11] As for Sıdıka, she declared that she sold slaves only once in her life, when she inherited three slaves from her deceased husband several years back. Other than that instance, she assured the police, she did not trade in slaves. But she did obtain *besleme*s or *ahretklik*s, she stated.

Şirin, on the other hand, made her living by buying and selling slaves, charging a 4% formal brokerage fee on each transaction.[12] Such details as her place of origin, when she came to Istanbul, or who she previously worked for are virtually nonexistent both in the police report and the interrogation records. She was questioned only on the details of the work she was doing. In line with the general versatility of slavers, Şirin was a resourceful businesswoman, at times lending decent sums of money to people in her circle. In fact, she stated in her interrogation that she had once lent Sıdıka 80 Ottoman liras, and she had been living in a house that belonged to her over the past five years, in

---

[10] Krikor Zohrab, "Postal," *Öyküler* (Istanbul: Aras Yayıncılık, 2001), 31.

[11] Ibid., 32.

[12] BOA, Y.PRK.BŞK 12/89, 1305.B.14 (27 March 1888), 14.

exchange for its interest.[13] In addition to the girls she sold in cooperation with Sıdıka and Kör Nadire, she also had her own resources. At the time of the interrogation, she was hosting in her house a 55-year-old woman named Emine, who was deported from Trabzon on prostitution charges.[14] Emine reportedly had three daughters she brought with her, one of whom was given to a towel merchant in marriage, another one who was sold to an undisclosed place, and the third sold to one of the *Kadın Effendi*s in the imperial harem, all arranged by Şirin.[15] The interrogator made a point that, being a professional slaver, Şirin should have known better than to sell "Turkish girls" to the imperial harems and that imperial harems did not employ "Turkish girls."[16] But what really mattered for Şirin was the consent given by the young girl's mother for the sale of the girl. In short, with flaxen hair, blue eyes and consent, any girl could be Circassian and would fetch a good price, too. Sıdıka's interrogation touched upon a similar point as well, in which being Turkish or Circassian seemed like arbitrary categories, which could easily change significance or meaning, especially when consent was given by the parents. Being well familiar with the process, Sıdıka managed to obtain a bill of sale for the 8-year-old Zekiye, signed and stamped by her parents, thus transferring her inalienable Turkish identity into an alienable Circassian one with relative ease. Once she captured them on paper as such, Sıdıka sold the girls "for commerce, to whoever wanted them," as she described it.

Taking place almost at the end of its long course, the incident embodied the

---

[13] Ibid., 13.

[14] Ibid., 11.

[15] Ibid., 11.

[16] Ibid., 14.

distinct features of the Ottoman practice of slavery: 1) its loose racial and ethnic perceptions which facilitated Sıdıka, Şirin, and Nadire's trade in freeborn children; 2) its traversing across different social classes which allowed manumitted slaves to own and trade in slaves as well as the permeability of class when slavery is taken into consideration; 3) its well-entrenched nature such that even at the height of abolitionist sentiments the Ottoman palace could still consider buying new slaves; 4) its peculiar relationship with the law that is made up of multiple legal systems; 5) the difficulty or even impossibility of detecting it, in the presence of slavery-like practices; 6) its linguistic dimension; 7) its demand for mobility; 8) and last but not least, that it involved, like the makers and victims of the above-mentioned scheme, mostly women. Taking this instance, which triggered a full criminal investigation as its point of departure, this chapter aims to explore the worlds of slave dealers, many of whom were women, who themselves had been slaves and exploited their "insider" position as well as their knowledge at great lengths. It also aims to explore how these worlds increasingly collided with the newly emerging international legal realm against slavery in the second half of the nineteenth century and the Ottoman state that pledged, at least in theory, to safeguard it.

Blue Eyes, Pockmarks and the Violence of Physical Categorization

When Kör Nadire roamed the streets of Üsküdar in search of young girls, she had a clear idea what she was looking for. She told in her interrogation that she saw several girls the day she found Zekiye, but she decided to make contacts with only two of them. Both the girls were reported to have clear white skin (one with a hint of freckles), blue or hazel eyes with a "tint of blue." These classifications were not due only to Nadire's or later on Sıdıka's liking but rather conventions of the slave trade network. At the other, higher, end of the scala, Pertevniyal Valide Sultan made similar choices. In close to a hundred notes of slave purchases, bills of sale, and related correspondence she wrote to various persons, primarily to her chief steward Hüseyin Efendi, her major concerns and preoccupations seem obvious and straightforward. With Circassian slaves—not only marked as "*Çerkes*" and "*beyaz*" (white) but often their ethnic or tribal affiliations, such as Abzakh, *Şabigh*, Hatuqwai, or Bzhedug were noted down on the bills of sale also,[17] it was primarily beauty or the lack of it: beauty as was seen, determined, and measured by Pertevniyal, the mother of the reigning sultan Abdülaziz and de facto head of the imperial harem. As in the case with Nadire and Sıdıka, this was a prospective form of beauty. The slaves presented to her were ordinarily between the ages of eight and fourteen, like Zekiye and Müzeyyen. The Valide Sultan gauged in these children's bodies an ideal womanhood, of "delicacy, gentility, and sexuality" as Walter Johnson described it for the slaves sold for sex in the 1850s American South.[18] To match the "blue eyes and flaxen

---

[17] Taksim Atatürk Kitaplığı (Library), Pertevniyal Valide Sultan Evrakı (papers), PVS_Evr_00967, 15 S.1281 (20 July 1864); PVS_Evr_00974, 20 Za. 1281 (16 April 1865). Pertevniyal Valide Sultan Evrakı was acquired by Taksim Atatürk Kitaplığı through purchase and was made available to researchers recently, although its source and the initial purpose of the collection remain unclear. Containing roughly around 5600 documents, most of which were written by Pertevniyal herself (or, possibly her scribes), the collection provides a somewhat continuous account on her financial, political, and daily life. Taksim Atatürk Kitaplığı, Fatma Aliye Hanım Evrakı, FA_Evr_000012-016, 7 Mart 1302 (19 March 1886). Also see Ehud Toledano, *As If Silent and Absent: Bonds of Enslavement in the Islamic Middle East* (New Haven: Yale University Press, 2007), 129–130 for similar classifications.

[18] Walter Johnson, "The Slave Trader, the White Slave, and the Politics of Racial Determination in the 1850s," *The Journal of American History*, Vol. 87, No. 1 (Jun., 2000), 18.

hair" of Alexina Morrison that both Johnson and Ariela Gross talked about,[19] Ottoman

slaves were depicted having "hazel eyes and flaxen hair" (*ela gözlü, lepiska saçlı*). Good

conduct, dexterity, and training, potential competence in excellent service, which

included both labor and sexual services, were all parts of this ideal womanhood and

accordingly emerged as major criteria in the decision-making process when purchasing

slaves for the imperial harem.[20] "Slaves had to be made," Walter Johnson asserted,

"sometimes violently, to enact the meaning slaveholders assigned to their bodies."[21] The

rules of this violent act (violent in physical terms during the slaves' capture and passage,

and particularly in terms of their categorizations and exclusions afterwards) were

determined, in part, by the Valide Sultan, as she stood at the top of a highly hierarchical

network of slave traders and slaveholders in the Ottoman Empire, and were reproduced

by practically anyone who took part in it.[22] As illustrated in many of her correspondences

pertaining to slave purchases, she provided specific details on the physical attributes of

the slaves (as Nadire and Sıdıka did), dismissing many on the basis that they were simply

not beautiful enough, at least not for the price asked for them. In some cases, whenever

---

[19] Ariela Gross, *What Blood Won't Tell: A History of Race on Trial in America* (Cambridge, MA: Harvard University Press, 2008), 1; Johnson, "The Slave Trader." By referring to Johnson and Gross' works here, I do not mean to imply that the Ottoman practices of slavery was comparable to the American South. In addition to drawing from Johnson and Gross' excellent analyses, bringing in Western cases of sexual slavery, in my contention, helps "de-exoticize" the overly-Orientalized case of Ottoman (also known as Islamic or harem) slavery.

[20] Virginity was also an important category when buying slaves. For pricing and sale strategies of non-virgin girls, see Ehud R. Toledano, "Slave Dealers, Women, Pregnancy, and Abortion: The Story of a Circassian Slave-girl in Mid-Nineteenth Century Cairo," *Slavery and Abolition*, vol.2, no.1 (May, 1981), 56.

[21] Johnson, "The Slave Trader," 19.

[22] It is difficult to ascertain whether the Valide Sultan defined these categories anew or that she was merely sustaining the existing conventions. I aim to point out here that, in either case, by defining them anew or upholding the existing categories, the Valide Sultan was instrumental in the "making" of slaves.

the girls were properly trained and had good conduct, "*rabıtalı*" as she called them, she ordered the purchase, despite the girls' stated lack of beauty.

Blackness was also important for the Valide Sultan as a category, but differently than whiteness and its different manifestations and appropriations which, in her perception, were more directly connected to her and her son's empowerment. The bills of sale for African slaves undersigned by her rarely provided any detail on their ethnic origins or physical attributes. In one of those rare cases, for instance, dated 27 Zilhicce 1283 (2 May 1867), it was noted that the enslaved girl who was subject to sale, approximately 14 years of age, was of Afno (possibly Hausa) origin. However, rather than giving any further information, the note quickly moved on, with formulaic language, to the conditions of the sale.[23] Other bills provided hardly any other information besides a generic "of black origin" (*siyah-ül-asl*) tag. African slaves were described in those notes more specifically in terms of the services they could provide for the harem as cooks, wet nurses, nannies, or servants. Just as the slaver Şirin was not asked by the police about her origins, Pertevniyal did not inquire the origins of the African slaves she bought.[24] In other instances too, their presence and value seem to be associated with the prosperity of a

---

[23] Taksim Atatürk Kitaplığı, Pertevniyal Valide Sultan Evrakı (papers), PVS_Evr_04771, 27 Z. 1283 (2 May 1867).

[24] It was not that this information could not be obtained, when necessary. An interesting case that took place in 1874 hints that tribal/linguistic affiliates could easily be summoned during an investigation. In this instance, a black woman from Alexandria was held at the customs with the suspicion that she was being illegally traded. After the police interrogation, it was found that she traveled to Istanbul as a newly employed servant at the Ecumenical Patriarchate, for she was Christian, a member of the Greek Orthodox Church. The interrogation then turned into questioning her possible conversion from Islam to Christianity. Eventually, the police brought in a certain Said Efendi, who recognized the markings on her nose and lips and confirmed that she was of Bano/Bono (?) tribe, which was of Christian origin. BOA, ZB 6/16, 1291.B.7 (20 August 1874).

household, whether it was the household of an aspiring bureaucrat or a notable. The wife of a powerful pasha at the time, whenever Melek Hanım wanted to express her occasional distress or impoverished state, she did so by saying that "her establishment was limited to an old woman and a black slave" or that "two black slaves formed [her] entire domestic establishment."[25] Similarly, the protagonist of Ahmet Midhat's story *Esaret*, described his misfortune and solitary situation by saying that his "harem was reduced to just himself and a black cook."[26]

While in appearance African slaves were sought and valued exclusively for their labor (*istihdam*), this did not exempt them from their owners' legal rights and claims over their sexual services (*istifraş*). Conditions of sale comprised, in more than one instance, clauses on pregnancy (see Image 1 below, for an example). However, this does not mean that an African slave's sexuality in the Ottoman Empire was categorically confined, to quote Monique Guillory, to "the mercy of her master's sexual appetites."[27] Drawing from Ellen Carol Dubois and Linda Gordon, Guillory demonstrated how it was the white abolitionist women's reluctance in acknowledging the possibility of willing sex between black slaves and white masters in antebellum America, which reduced black women's sexuality only to two possibilities, that of rape and prostitution.[28] While individual cases remain to be unearthed for the Ottoman case, it is safe to say that in practice, neither

---

[25] Melek Hanum, *Thirty Years in the Harem: or, the Autobiography of Melek-Hanum Wife of H.H. Kibrizli Mehemet-Pasha* (London: Chapman and Hall, 1872) 35, 54.

[26] Ahmed Midhat, "Esaret" in *Letâif-i Rivâyât*, volume I (Istanbul: Kırk Anbar Matbaası, 1315/1899–1900), 46.

[27] Monique Guillory, "Some Enchanted Evening on the Auction Block: The Cultural Legacy of the New Orleans Quadroon Balls," (Ph.D. Dissertation, New York University, 1999), 66.

[28] Ibid., 66–67.

black/white nor labor/sex divides should be understood as mutually exclusive categories.[29] Yet, in the Valide Sultan's perception of the world, as evinced in her correspondences, they had clearer boundaries. In other words, to refer to Ehud Toledano's expression of silence and absence, African slaves were absent neither in their masters' households nor in the ways such powerful figures as the Valide Sultan ordered their world. They were not so much silent, either, but silenced by the rigid racial categorizations, effected (or at best effectively perpetuated) by Valide Sultan and other slaveholders who reenacted these categories and traders who worked to match their expectations.

Walter Johnson argued that in the 1850s American South, the apparent physical differences, particularly those in skin tones, were formalized into racial categories on a daily basis in the market by slave traders who, according to Johnson, "were not only marketing race, but also making it."[30] The American practice of concubinage, known as *fancy trade* and *plaçage*, broke down what Johnson called "restless hybridity" into an "infinite variety of skin tone [...], into imagined degrees of black and white that, once measured, could be priced and sold."[31] Each of these varieties were then exploited separately and extensively, like selling the light-skinned women for sex in exchange of

---

[29] Madeline Zilfi proposes the labor/sex divide as a new foundational one to define Ottoman slavery in place of a black/white one proposed by Ehud Toledano. "Thoughts on Women and Slavery in the Ottoman Era and Historical Sources," in *Beyond the Exotic: Women's Histories in Islamic Societies*, ed. Amira El-Azhary Sonbol (Cairo: The American University in Cairo Press, 2006), 133–134. However, labor/sex was already an existing categorical divide in Islamic jurisprudence. The black/white divide, on the other hand, seems to have taken shape in the market, when setting prices.

[30] Johnson, "The Slave Trader," 16.

[31] Ibid., 17.

"heaps and piles of money," as described by Solomon Northup.[32] In essence, what Ottoman slaveholders (including the Valide Sultan herself) and traders were doing was no different than what the traders in the American South had been doing. They too meticulously categorized the enslaved bodies and put a price tag on each and every one.[33] Differently from the American case, however, they did so not always to sell them but instead circulated them for political purposes. In many occasions, they made gifts out of their slaves, as they sought favors from the palace or high-ranking bureaucrats. Whether they invested or traded in them "for commerce," or presented them as gifts, however, these women defined race, delineated beauty, and ideal womanhood.

---

[32] Solomon Northup, *Twelve Years a Slave*, quoted in ibid., 17.

[33] For an elaborate discussion on the complexities of racial categorization in slavery, see Johnson, "The Slave Trader," 16–20. Johnson argues that such specific categories as *griffe*, *mulatto* or *quadroon* were all products of "the alchemy by which skin tone and slavery were synthesized into race and profit..." 16. Also see Gross, *What Blood Won't Tell*, introduction, for a more extensive discussion on color line as "an effect of social convention and power," as Johnson put it.

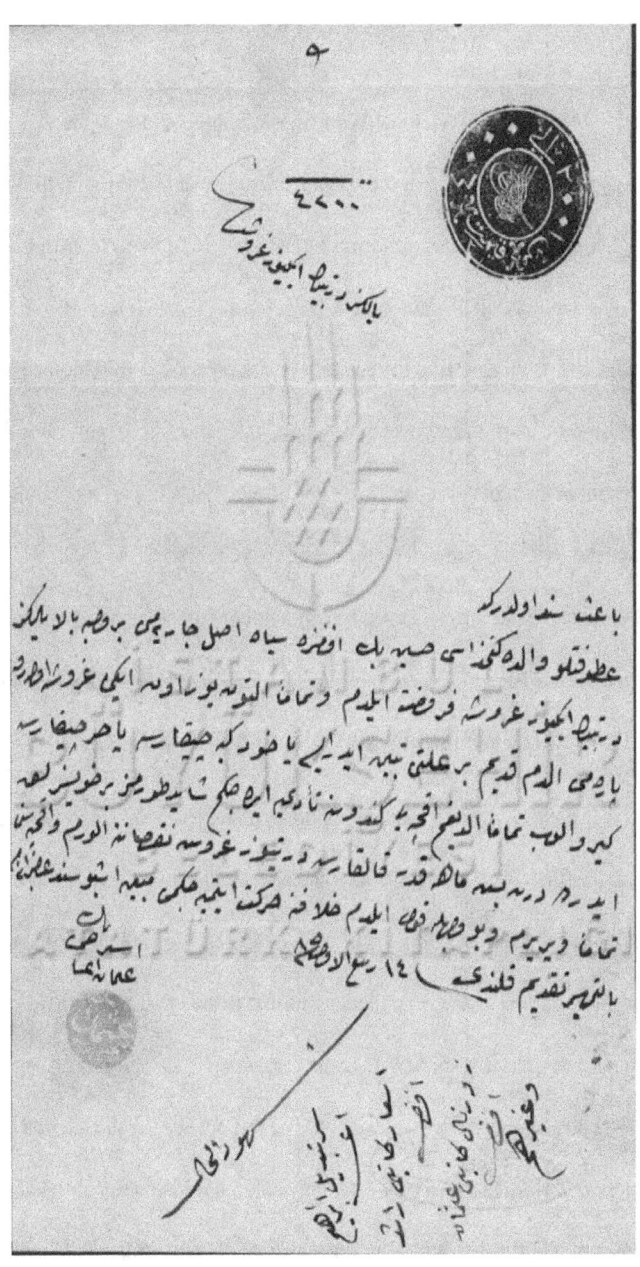

Image 1. Bill of sale for an African slave dated July 5, 1868. In addition to the usual sale conditions of preexisting diseases and free status (indicating unjust enslavement or illegal resale into slavery), the notice states that in the case of pregnancy, the seller accepted to take the slave back and pay the purchase amount in full. Taksim Atatürk Kitaplığı, Pertevniyal Valide Sultan Evrakı, PER_VAL_SUL_03396, 14 Ra. 1285 (5 July 1868).

Valide Sultan, Genteel Women and "Slaveholder Agency"

Pertevniyal's term as the Valide Sultan began in 1861 with the succession of her son Abdülaziz to the throne and was brought to an end by the constitutional intervention led by a small group of statesmen in 1876, a period that coincided with several different developments in regards to the course that slavery took in the Ottoman Middle East. The most significant of these developments was the Circassian expulsion which, as discussed at length in the previous chapter, created a legal chaos in the Ottoman Empire, in which the customary law observed by the Circassian nobility clashed with the public and *Şer'i* laws, which, in their turn intertwined with international law in complex ways. As the Ottoman state tried to sort out this mayhem, the chapter argued, it also found itself obliged to define more strictly what race and ethnicity meant for it.

That the Ottoman state was rethinking and reorganizing these categories did not mean that they were uniformly accepted and adopted by everyone throughout the empire. Slave traders and owners misinterpreted, deliberately or otherwise, the meanings of these categories as well as the legal regulations that related to them. Nor was it a simple task to define or determine who the "authentic Circassian" (*'an asl Çerkes*, as the tag went) was, or to explicate how African slaves could be left outside the jurisdiction of the *Şer'i* law, while the slave status of the Circassians, said to have been established by *āyāt* and *hadith*, were simultaneously deemed unchangeable. Such powerful and politically influential people as Pertevniyal could and often did act outside the law when obtaining slaves, whenever they deemed it crucial for the well-being of the imperial harem or an elite household. In fact, their understanding of political power meant at times being capable of acting outside the law. For one, in her obsession with the privileged access to incoming slaves, or rather potential slaves, Pertevniyal Valide Sultan gave recurrent orders to her steward Hüseyin, to closely scan Circassian ships for all eligible young girls and women. She even sent messages to the governor of Trabzon from firsthand (and possibly sent a palace representative to assist him, as well), to catch the ships in Trabzon port with the purpose of sparing "the good ones" for her. All this would have been alright, if the ships Pertevniyal meant were not those which carried Circassian refugees in the year 1862, at the height of the Circassian expulsion, which by then had already turned into an international humanitarian crisis.[34] As Eve Troutt Powell notes, foreign journalists and missionaries were reporting extensively at the time on the "destitution of the immigrants as they reached Cyprus, Samsun, or Istanbul"[35] and the issue was also widely known throughout the Ottoman Empire, as well. Nevertheless, for Pertevniyal Valide Sultan, both the crisis and the laws that aimed to regulate it seemed irrelevant. Her purchase of the above-mentioned African slave of Hausa origin also was made in illegal terms, as the sale took place a decade after the prohibition of trade in African slaves, enacted in 1857 throughout the Ottoman Empire.[36]

---

[34] As early as 1857, the Ministry of the External Affairs was obliged to take measures against the reported abuse and illegal trafficking of the Circassian refugees. For an example of a related note written by the Ministry of the External Affairs to caution the customs administration, see BOA, HR.MKT 180/61, 1273.B.13 (9 March 1857).

[35] Eve M. Troutt Powell, *Tell This in My Memory: Stories of Enslavement from Egypt, Sudan, and the Ottoman Empire* (Stanford: Stanford University Press, 2012), 127. Powell mentions *Times of London* article "The Circassian Exodus" as an example of international press coverage of the incident. *Tell This in My Memory*, 128.

[36] Taksim Atatürk Kitaplığı, Pertevniyal Valide Sultan Evrakı, PVS_Evr_04771, 27 Z. 1283 (2 May 1867).

For Pertevniyal Valide Sultan, the privileged access to sources of slaves, sometimes at the expense of law as can be glimpsed above, was just as important and accordingly accentuated a concern as the "hazel eyes and flaxen hair" of the girls she purchased. She was, after all, considered the most powerful woman in the country, and one that was closely responsible for the well-being of its sovereign. Valide Sultans did not necessarily determine the reproductive policies of the Ottoman dynasty, but they were the ones who supervised and strictly enforced them. Thus, Pertevniyal decided, like many Valide Sultans who came before her, who her son would take as wives and concubines, what qualities they would have, at times even limiting the number of offspring a concubine would have.[37] Early and privileged access to enslaved girls "just off the slave ship," meant that she could pick and choose them as she wanted, to "tame" them as she pleased. In practice, it also meant keeping many unwanted persons and parties away from this speculative market and protect her gains not only from professional traders but also from other "genteel women": the wives of high-ranking state or military officials and notables, who ordinarily sought to exploit the slave trade in ways that benefited them.

Ehud Toledano has written about the commonplaceness of "the *hope* of improving one's own social and economic status through slavery," while he simultaneously demonstrated, through the story of *Şemsigül*, how difficult that path actually was.[38] It is not certain how willing or eager the girls and their parents (say, *Şemsigül* and her mother) had been to sell themselves or their daughters into slavery.

---

[37] For an elaborate account on reproductive politics of the Ottoman dynasty, see Leslie Peirce, *The Imperial Harem: Women and Sovereignty in the Ottoman Empire* (Oxford: Oxford University Press, 1993). For the emergence of Valide Sultan as a political figure, see pages 109-112.

[38] Toledano, "Slave Dealers, Women, Pregnancy, and Abortion," 54.

There is an indication that slave "recruitments" were often carried out by palace officials, accompanied by an imperial order, at times leaving no option to the family.[39] Poverty, as it came to be discussed at length, particularly after the 1908 constitutional revolution, was another known fact that perpetuated the slave trade in Ottoman Anatolia.[40] On the other hand, we can talk about slave traders' and owners' *hopes* in improving their social and economic status through exploiting the slave trade network. My aim here is not to imply that slaves did not have "agency" in improving their lots within the practice of slavery. They did. However, what is crucial particularly for the purpose of this study is to point at the fact that, being well-equipped to implement brutal means in capturing slaves, having the economic means to trade in them, or present them as gifts, moreover having the power to decide what they should look like and how they should behave, the "slaveholder agency"[41] had the upper hand in determining not only the rules that pertained to the institution, but also indirectly delineating the laws that regulated state-citizen or inter-class relations in the Ottoman society. Moreover, I do not aim simply to reiterate what has already been said by the scholars of Ottoman and Middle Eastern slavery on the role of elite women in perpetuating the slave trade, either.[42] What I want to stress is that their involvement in slave trade was not detached from the political sphere. Far from it. Even

---

[39] See, for instance, BOA, BEO 3546/265908, 1327.R.21 (12 May 1909).

[40] For an example touching upon the class aspect of Ottoman slavery, see article entitled "Esir Ticareti" in *Sada-i Millet*, 8 Mart 1326 (21 March 1910).

[41] See Walter Johnson, "On Agency," *Journal of Social History*, vol.37, no.1 (Fall 2003), 113-114, note 4; Also see Johnson, *Soul by Soul: Life Inside the Antebellum Slave Market* (Cambridge, MA: Harvard University Press, 1999), the chapter entitled "Making a World Out of Slaves," 78-116.

[42] Although in most cases only in passing, this issue has been mentioned in the works of Ehud Toledano and Madeline Zilfi. Also see Nelly Hanna, "Sources for the Study of Slave Women and Concubines in Ottoman Egypt," in *Beyond the Exotic*, 122 on a note on how Mamluk households expanded and consolidated power in the eighteenth century Egypt.

126

though their influence in politics did not match those of the earlier centuries, their actions were nevertheless well engrained in, and in turn shaped, politics. In other words, Pertevniyal Valide Sultan may not have been Kösem or Turhan Sultan, who acted as regents on behalf of their minor sons and wielded great power and near full authority in politics, but she too held a significant amount of political power and the slave trade was one of the main outlets to sustain it.

"If any lady possess[ed] a pretty-looking slave," Melek Hanım wrote, "the fact soon would get known"[43] and ranks of elite women would start chasing her. In several of her correspondences, Pertevniyal appears to be frantic about the rumors pertaining to "pretty-looking slaves." In one of these cases, dated 23 Ramazan 1279 (14 March 1863), she wrote to her steward, in fact, almost begged that he arranged an occasion for her to take a look at a young girl—not even a slave but a *besleme*, and reportedly not for sale, either.[44] Note, for instance, the slave girl she bought about two weeks later, on 10 Şevval 1279 (31 March 1863), whom she felt obliged to buy, simply because she had good manners and that her eyes were beautiful.[45] Leyla Hanım (Saz) also mentioned the importance of what had been considered good physical features by the slave traders and owners and how easily each "bad feature," such as the absence of a tooth or flat feet could be expressed in terms of the slave's price.[46] Again, my aim here is not to state what is accepted to be the obvious, nor to dismantle what can be called the "hierarchies of

---

[43] Melek Hanum, *Thirty Years in the Harem*, 159–60.

[44] Taksim Kitaplığı, Pertevniyal Valide Sultan Evrakı, PER_VAL_SUL_03042, 23 N. 1279 (14 March 1863).

[45] Taksim Kitaplığı, Pertevniyal Valide Sultan Evrakı, PER_VAL_SUL_02969, 10 Ş. 1279 (31 January 1863).

[46] Leyla Hanum, quoted in Powell, *Tell This in My Memory*, 129.

beauty," but to point out that in the highly stratified and hierarchical organization of the Ottoman state, bureaucracy and society (which the organization of slave trade merely mimicked), such physical features as blue eyes, flaxen hair, or "unblemished" white skin, once captured, were made expressions of power that could also easily be translated into a price tag. A purchase receipt from 1899–90 illustrates this perhaps too well. The receipt (unsigned, with no sender/addressee information) lists the purchase of six female slaves, three of whom were categorized as "*büyük*" (here meaning older in age) and the other three as "*küçük*" (small, young). As can be traced in Pertevniyal's purchase orders and other correspondence, age was another major category in buying and pricing slaves. Buying a young slave meant several years of additional expenses on food, clothing, and most importantly, training. Thus, they were significantly cheaper than the older slaves with training (in housework such as sewing and embroidery, in Turkish language, and often in music, as well). The receipt accordingly lists the purchase prices for older slaves as 200 Ottoman liras (approximately 800 U.S. dollars at the time), whereas the price for younger ones was set as 100 Ottoman liras. However, the prices differed significantly for both old and young slaves, when physical attributes were taken into account. One of the older slaves, who was marked quite bluntly as "the ugly one," was priced as 150 Ottoman liras, while one of the younger slaves, who was marked as "the blue eyed one," sold for twice the amount as the other young slaves (see images 2, 3,4, and 5 below for examples).

It was not only the wives of bureaucrats or military officials that sought favors and exploited the slave network for their benefit. The palace women occasionally did so, as well. To refer to Melek Hanım once again, she recounted how she was called into the palace by one of the *Kadın Effendis*,[47] because the latter knew that Melek Hanım's husband was favored by "the then all-powerful Grand-Vezir," Mustafa Reşid Pasha (d. 1858). As Melek Hanım described it, *Kadın Effendi*'s invitation, which was not all that disinterested, "wished to secure [Melek Hanım's] services in behalf of Said-Pasha (Said Mehmed Pasha, *Damad-ı Şehriyari*, d. 1869), husband of her deceased daughter," who had reportedly been exiled at the time.[48] It should be noted that Melek Hanım did not miss the opportunity to take a Circassian slave girl and a eunuch with her, to present to the *Kadın Effendi*. All in all, whatever the immediate concerns were, holding and having privileged access to enslaved girls (particularly to those who had the tag "beautiful," whatever that signified in actuality) meant power, so much so that it was unacceptable for Pertevniyal that the palace and the imperial harem, the largest buyer of slaves, lagged behind even ordinary slavers in reaching ships coming from Circassia. In a note she wrote in 1862, she commanded that his steward be ready to dispatch his men to catch the ships in customs port (referred to as *Kavak iskelesi*) before they reached the city port in Tophane, the final destination of all commodities that came by sea, for other slavers would have "already picked and chosen" until they themselves had a chance to even peek

---

[47] There are more than a few factual errors and ambiguities in Melek Hanım's account. Here, it is not clearly identified which *Kadın Effendi* she is referring to. Melek Hanım mentions her being the mother of Merimah-Sultan, which makes her an *ikbal* (concubine), rather than one of the official wives.

[48] Melek Hanum, *Thirty Years in the Harem*, 164.

at the girls.[49] In another note she wrote a year later, she complained about the same matter, this time with a sharper tone. After reporting the arrival of a new Circassian ship in Trabzon, Pertevniyal complained that the moment the ship would arrive in Istanbul, people from all sides would be swarming to it, snatching and hiding the girls they took a fancy to, leaving behind barely anyone who was worthy to look at.[50] Thus, she ordered the governor of Trabzon to capture and reserve the girls for her, before showing them to anyone, for all "vanish[ed] as soon as the ship arrive[d] in the Bosphorus."[51]

---

[49] Taksim Atatürk Kitaplığı, Pertevniyal Valide Sultan Papers, PER_VAL_SUL_02885 (undated).

[50] Taksim Atatür Kitaplığı, Pertevniyal Valide Sultan Evrakı, PVS_Evr_02806, Şevval 1279 (March-April 1863)

[51] Ibid. In a brief undated note, there is an indication that the Trabzon governor did indeed comply with Valide Sultan's request. See PVS_Evr_05018 and PVS_Evr_05288.

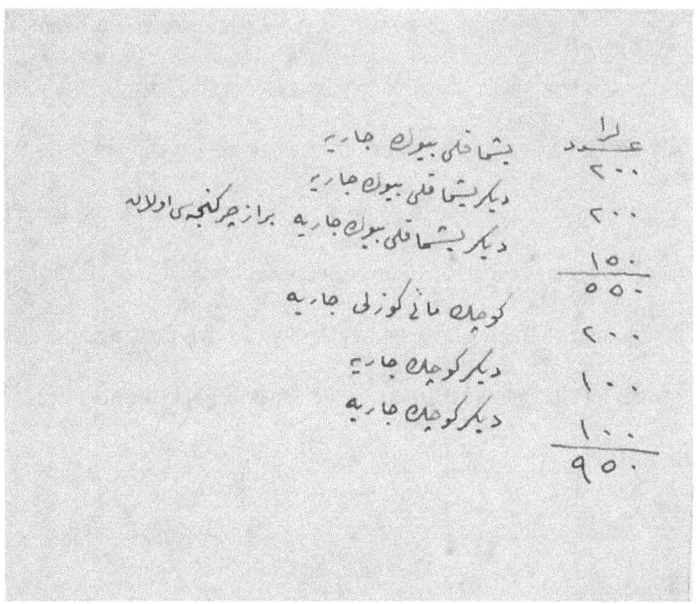

Image 3.2 A receipt for six girls purchased for the Yıldız Palace. The receipt lists the purchase prices with the following explanations: "The veiled older *cariye* 200 lira, the other veiled older *cariye* 200 lira, the other veiled older *cariye*, the uglier one 150 lira, the young blue-eyed *cariye* 200 lira, the other young *cariye* 100 lira, the other young *cariye* 100 lira."
BOA, Y.PRK.M 4/52, 1315 (1897–98).

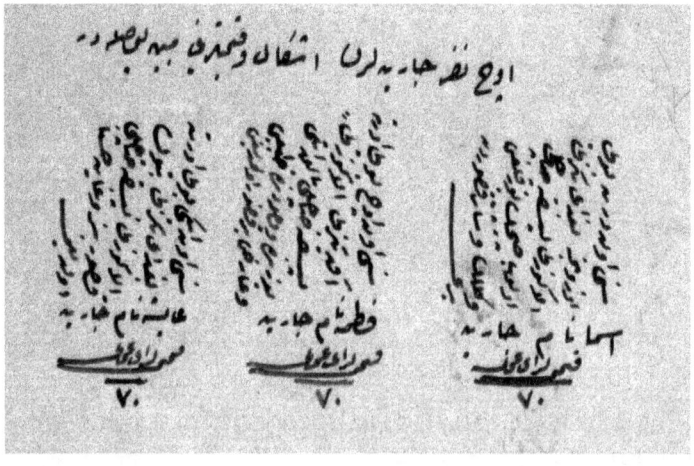

Image 3.3 A sheet that accompanied a bill of sale for Adviye Hanim, which contains physical descriptions, apparent "faults," and prices for three Circassian slaves, 12 to 14 years old.
BOA, Y..EE.. 142/292, 1327.R.6 (27 April 1909)

131

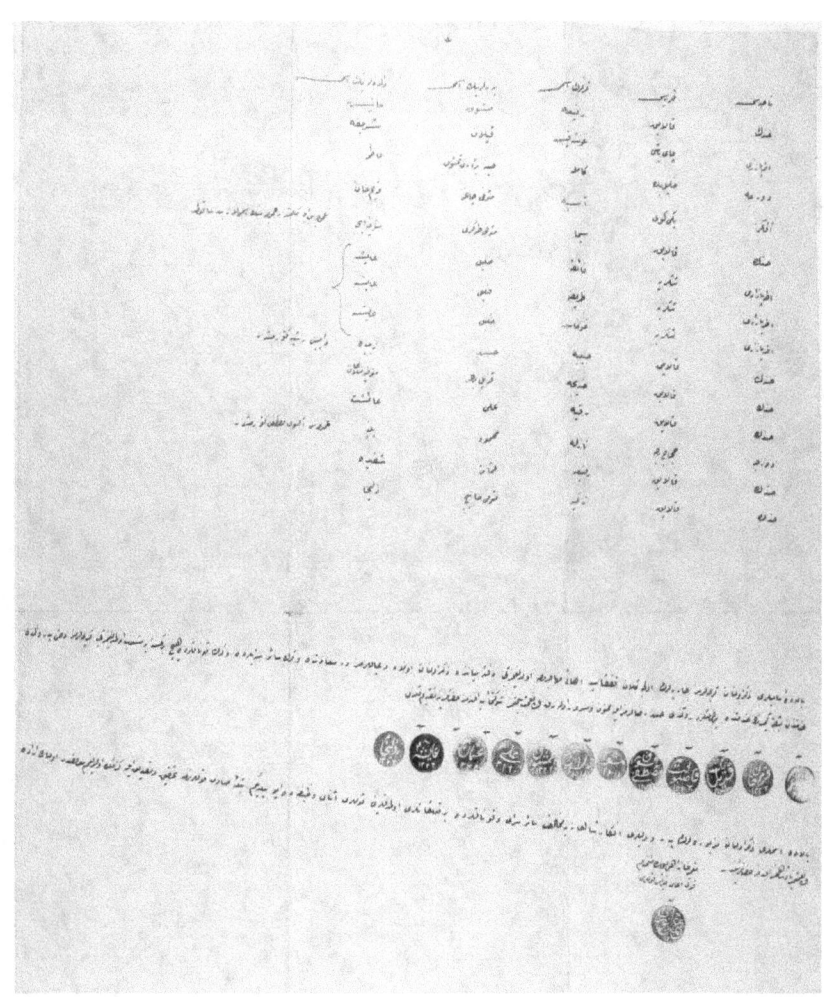

Image 3.4 While it does not indicate pricing, this bill of sale for 14 Circassian girls, signed and stamped by their families, reveal "not having served anyone but their parents" was one of the criteria that determined the initial price of the slaves.
Y.PRK.ASK 255/2, 1326.S.11 (15 March 1908).

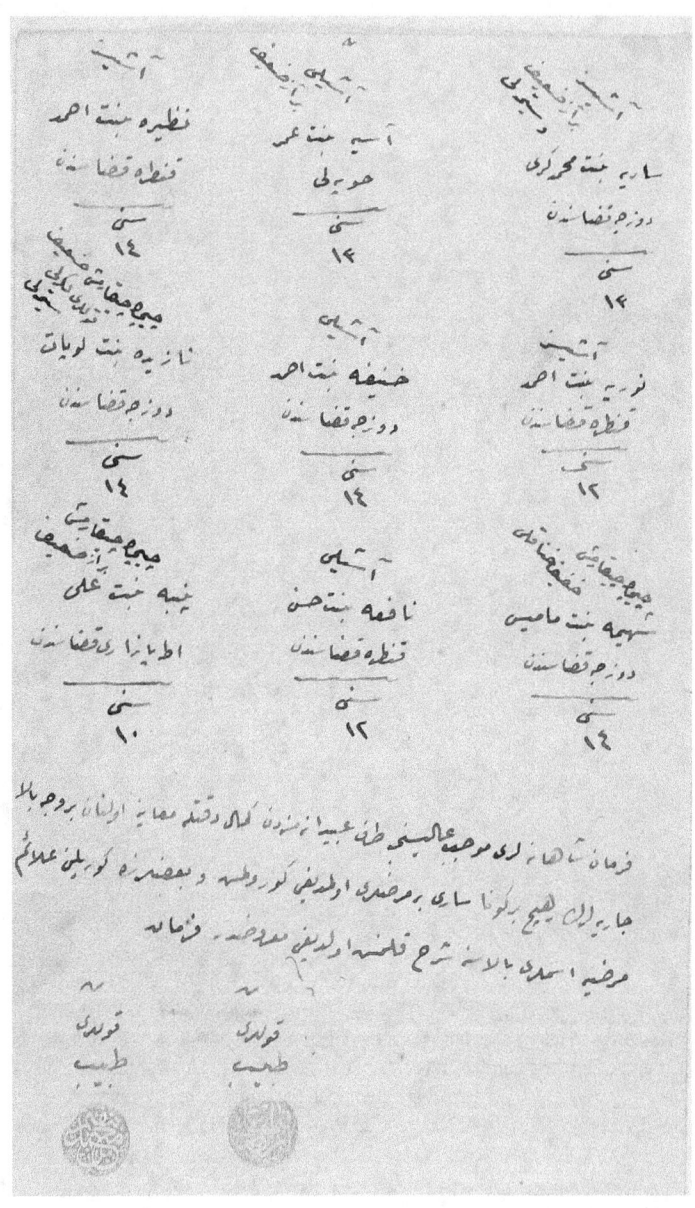

Image 3.5 This undated inspection report, performed and signed by two doctors for Yıldız Palace, indicate that existing and past diseases, body or facial marks such as those caused by chicken pox, body weight, and whether the girls were vaccinated or not all determined the acceptability of the slaves as well as their prices. BOA, Y.PRK.SGE 11/84, undated. Also see FO 195/946 for a note that a slave purchase was "often made conditional on a good medical certificate being obtained."

Matchmakers, Ordinary Marauders, and Versatile Businesspeople

"Wherever slaves were sold," Walter Johnson wrote in relation to the American South, "interstate traders were there to buy them."[52] Not unlike Johnson's traders in antebellum America, who ubiquitously attended sales "whether at court house estate sales, private sales on a slaveholder's land, or even in another trader's yard," traders of different varieties were everywhere, particularly in Istanbul, as already attested in Pertevniyal Valide Sultan's preoccupations. Istanbul had "the largest and busiest slave market in the Empire" until it was shut down in 1846, or as Ehud Toledano put it "reverted to the back alley," to be staged in the form of private sales at slavers' and buyers' homes or, as in one reported case, in coffeehouses located near the shut-down slave market.[53]

Both Ehud Toledano and Madeline Zilfi argued that most of the trade was carried out in the Tophane district in Istanbul, where the port was located and many of the slave traders resided. Madeline Zilfi even described Tophane as the main locale for "the larger and more lasting slave-selling enterprises that still stood in the 1860s."[54] In fact, Sami Paşazade Sezai's *Sergüzeşt*, the most famous of the abolitionist novels in the Ottoman Empire, opens up in Tophane. "When the Russian Company's ship from Batumi approached in front of Tophane," Sezai writes, "men waiting in their small boats out on

---

[52] Johnson, *Soul by Soul*, 48.

[53] Toledano, "Slave Dealers, Women, Pregnancy, and Abortion," 53; BOA, MVL 131/17 (1270/1853-54).

[54] Madeline Zilfi, *Women and Slavery in the Late Ottoman Empire: The design of Difference* (Cambridge: Cambridge University Press, 2010), 216.

134

the sea began climbing up the ship impatiently."[55] When one of these men, a slaver named Hacı Ömer agreed to "try" three girls for the night, he just walks them home, not far away from the dockside.[56] In Ahmed Midhat's *Felatun Bey ve Rakım Efendi*, Rakım Efendi found Canan, the enslaved beloved of the protagonist, as she was walking along a slaver to his home in the same district, in a similar manner described in *Sergüzeşt*. With her scruffy looks and inability to speak Turkish, Ahmed Midhat told his readers that Canan was one of the newcomers, freshly "recruited" from the "Circassian ship" that arrived in Tophane. In Hıfzı Topuz's semi-biographical novel *Meyyale*, when Pertevniyal Valide Sultan (she appears in the book as a character, too) wanted to purchase slave children to entertain her newborn grandson, she heads to Tophane, to take a look at the ships that brought Circassian refugees to the city.[57]

While found in great numbers in Tophane, slavers and the slaving businesses were not restricted there alone, but rather dispersed throughout the city. The examples are numerous. A slaver's house, reportedly burned down by a number of female slaves, was in Gedikpaşa, in intramural Istanbul.[58] The slaver woman Düriye Hanım (even though she was not called as such) in Ahmed Midhat's novella *Çingene* lived in a small seaside residence in a village along the Bosphorus.[59] There were others yet, who reportedly went on tour, most notably in the Balkan/European provinces of the Empire, bringing as many

---

[55] Sami Paşazade Sezai, *Sergüzeşt* (Istanbul: Kitaphane-i Sudi, 1340/1924). The book was originally printed in 1888.

[56] Ibid., 1–2.

[57] Hıfzı Topuz, *Meyyale* (Istanbul: Remzi Kitabevi, 2012), 19.

[58] BOA, A.MKT 99/78, 1263.11.17 (27 October 1847).

[59] Ahmed Midhat, *Çingene* (Istanbul: Kırk Anbar Matbaası, 1304/1887), 46.

as twelve slaves with them, to be sold or delivered particularly in such urban centers as Salonica.[60] What was different from the ubiquitous traders of the antebellum South was that professional traders constituted an indispensable yet only a small section of the slave trade in the Ottoman Empire. The majority of the trade was carried out by non-professional dealers.

Far from Toledano's assertion that the "dealers in white slaves were a highly esteemed lot," there was a certain stigma attached to all slavers, particularly drover-slavers known as *celeb*, transporters, and in general, non-elite slave holders and dealers.[61] Described in *Sergüzeşt*, they were deemed to be cruel, merciless men and women, "whose hearts bore no feelings," as the author expressed it, "and whose eyes looked like those of tigers." They were known to be concerned only with their personal gains, Sezai further asserted, and they cared about two things alone: first, the "progressive instrument" of their trade, the whip, and second, that each and every one of the poor girls who entered his household be orphans.[62] They were usually typified in plays as deceiving, unmoral men and women. In Recaizade Mahmut Ekrem's play *Vuslat*, which is about a slave girl with the same name, a slaver appears in disguise, as a woman seeking a bride for her son, with the purpose of obtaining a girl for little or no cost.[63] In one of the *Karagöz* plays (the traditional shadow theater, particularly popular at the time), *Sahte Esirci* (Fake slaver), the slaver appears as a trickster from Egypt and manages to "plant" a Circassian slave in

---

[60] BOA, A.MKT 187/1, 1265.5.7 (31 March 1849); A.MKT.MHM 151/194, 1275.B.3 (6 February 1859).

[61] Toledano, "Slave Dealers, Women, Pregnancy, and Abortion," 59.

[62] Sezai, *Sergüzeşt*, 1.

[63] Recaizade Mahmut Ekrem, *Vuslat yahut Süreksiz Sevinç: Üç Perde Tiyatro Oyunu* (Istanbul: Şark Matbaası, 1291/1874).

an affluent man's household, to burglarize it later on.[64] In fact, the stereotype was so well-entrenched that the notion of "Trebizon slaver" made it even to popular orientalist novels in mid-19th century America.[65]

The professional traders aside, many who dealt in slaves were ordinary people, who bought and sold slaves for practical reasons. In Ahmed Midhat's above-mentioned novella *Çingene*, Düriye Hanım took up slave dealing (or, matchmaking, as called in the book) out of necessity, when her husband became unable to work because of an illness and she was forced to provide for the household.[66] The arbitrariness of slave dealing or the thin line between the slave dealer and the matchmaker were not evident in literature alone but appear frequently in archival documents as well. In one such instance from the mid-nineteenth century, a Georgian man petitioning for the recovery of his slaves held at the island of Syra, told how he recently moved to Istanbul, converted to Islam, and took up slaving for no other purpose than to make ends meet. He was using his connections to procure Georgian children to sell in Istanbul or Cairo.[67] In another case, a certain Reşid Ağa entrusted his niece Zekiye (noted to be freeborn and of Circassian origin) to a slave-dealing woman named Hesna in Istanbul, and for the latter to arrange a marriage for her. Shortly after, another slave dealer named Süleyman took the young girl with the promise

---

[64] Abdurrezzak ve Katib Salih, *Sahte Esirci*, Taksim Kitaplığı, Belediye Yazmaları, Bel_Yz_K.001515/01. Similar cases appeared in archival sources as well. For an example, see BOA, A.MKT.MVL 143/68, 1278.L.6 (6 April 1862).

[65] Lieutenant Murray, *Turkish Slave: or, The Dumb Dwarf of Constantinople. A Story of the Eastern World* (Boston: Elliott, Thomas & Talbot, 1863), 14.

[66] Ahmed Midhat, *Çingene*, 46.

[67] BOA, A.DVN 66/84, 1267.4.3 (5 February 1851).

of marrying her to his own son, but instead took her to Egypt to sell her.[68] In another

instance, a certain Hüseyin haphazardly captured a boy while the latter was roaming in

the Sultan Mehmed district in Istanbul and sold him to a slave dealer in exchange of the

decent sum of 7,000 piasters.[69] In the case of Sıdıka, Şirin, and Nadire, discussed above,

Nadire took up slave procurement, exploiting her ties to her native village for the purpose

of getting medical care for her eyes that were going blind.[70] In a similar case of a criminal

nature, the wife of the governor of Bosnia took hold of two of her nieces upon the death

of their father, and casually sold them to a slaver named Ishak, who in turn sold them in

Istanbul.[71] Leyla Açba told of an uncle of hers, Kabasakal Mehmed Paşa of Circassian

origin, who recruited a *cariye* for Yıldız Palace, when he was on a business trip at the

coal mines in the Zonguldak region. According to Açba, he took the girl to the palace

rather as favor to the man who hosted him during his trip.[72] As already mentioned, the

wives of pashas and notables constituted a sizable chunk of the investors and traders in

slaves, some of whom had been described as the "embodiments of tyranny," such as the

wife of Süleyman Paşa, who reportedly provided the entire office of the Yıldız Palace

secretariat with enslaved women, specifically for sexual services (*istifraş*).[73] In short,

practically anyone could become a slave dealer at any time, if he or she had access to

sources of slaves and many did in fact get in and out of the profession, seemingly quite

---

[68] BOA, A.MKT.DV 183/39 1277.Ş.9 (20 February 1861). Illegal cases of enslaving and trading in freeborn women and children were numerous.

[69] BOA, A.MKT.MVL 59/93, 1269.R.3 (14 January 1853).

[70] BOA, Y.PRK.BŞK 12/89, 1305.B.14 (27 March 1888).

[71] BOA, A.MKT.NZD 173/81, 1272.R.5 (15 December 1855).

[72] Leyla Açba, *Bir Çerkes Prensesinin Harem Hatıraları* (Istanbul: Timaş Yayınları, 2010), 103–104.

[73] BOA, ŞD 2786/29, 1327.N.14 (29 September 1909).

easily and casually. Some declared (explicitly or otherwise) that they had no other choice, while others silently took advantage of their insider positions and knowledge.[74]

The scale of the business could be rather sizable, even when not performed professionally. In one case, for instance, a certain Hadice Hanım, the daughter of Rıdvanzade (presumably a government official) reportedly bought five Circassian slaves on a ninety-day credit in exchange of 13,500 piasters, secured by two sets of debenture bonds. In addition, Hadice bought two more slaves on credit, in exchange of 14,398 piasters and several others for an additional 4,000. Her debt amounted to the astounding sum of 31,898 piasters, which she has faulted by running away to Egypt, as reported by the guarantor in all of these transactions.[75] Another case hints at the fact that slavers were versatile businessmen and women. A tobacco dealer entrusted the slave dealer Fatma with 15,000 piaster-worth of tobacco, which the latter successfully managed to sell in its entirety, took the money and ran away, together with her husband.[76] That sort of versatility figures in other cases as well. In an earlier example, a certain man named Osman (profession not specified) gave a slave girl to a scarf merchant named Ahmed in exchange of 12,500 piaster worth of debenture bonds. Ahmed, for his turn, gave the girl to a tobacco merchant named Adem in exchange for his outstanding debt. Subsequently Adem sold the girl to the wife of a certain Tayyar Pasha, who eventually sent her to a

---

[74] A very similar pattern resurfaced recently, as already has been mentioned in the introduction, with the Syrian war refugees. In the case which opens this dissertation, a woman who calls herself a matchmaker arranged marriages for older Arab men from the Gulf and the Syrian girls they wanted—with white skin, blue or green eyes, and to be no older than sixteen—in exchange of huge sums of money. For an illustrative example, see Beth McLeod, "Syrian Refugees 'sold for marriage' in Jordan," BBC News, 10 May 2013, accessed online May 18, 2013.

[75] BOA, A.MKT 176/100, 1265.4.1; Hadice owed money to other people as well, A.DVN 117/82.

[76] BOA, A.MKT.DV 147/94, 1276.Ca.10 (5 December 1859).

prospective buyer's house, where the first owner of the slave, Osman, went and abducted the girl, as he never received the payment from Ahmed.[77]

The higher the rank of the women (rather, their husbands' rank within the organization of the Ottoman state), the bigger were the sums of money involved. In the seven months between March 1865 and November 1865, the total sum of money that Adviye Hanım, the wife of the esteemed Justice Minister and the author of *Mecelle* (the codified version of *Şer'i* law) Ahmed Cevdet Pasha, used in slave purchases and sales amounted to 50,000 piasters.[78] The manner of the transaction changed also, in line with the political nature of slave circulation among the elite women, which can be glimpsed in a correspondence between Adviye Hanım and the wife of the newly-appointed district governor of Yemen in 1873. Adviye Hanım had put (or rather, implied) an order for a eunuch with the governor's wife. After a long and persistent search, the latter managed to find a seven or eight-year-old boy named Selim ("nothing particularly to be proud of," she described him in her letter to Adviye Hanım) and sent him to Istanbul, presumably as a gift.[79] Judging by the number of letters that Adviye Hanım received from women asking for favors for their husbands, the governor's wife acted strategically,[80] possibly to secure a better post for her husband in his next appointment.

---

[77] BOA, MVL 92/3, 1266.L.13 (22 August 1850).

[78] BOA, Y..EE.. 142/292, 1327.R.06 (27 April 1909).

[79] BOA, Y..EE.. 142/173, 1287.S.29 (31 May 1870).

[80] See BOA, Y..EE.. 142, for examples of these letters.

Ottoman Slave Trade at the Juncture of Multiple Legalities

In all these cases, what is apparent is that the slave trade was so tenacious and deeply rooted in culture and society that those who took part in it do not seem to think capturing children by deception or by force whenever they could, selling them for a good profit to whomever they could, and giving them as gifts or better said, offering them as bribes in exchange for political favors, was in any ways problematic. People from across different ethnic or racial groups and classes seem to have collectively contributed to its perpetuation, as well. From the lowliest of haphazard traders, who literally "coveted his neighbor's wife," and eventually managed to capture and sell her into slavery, to the most deliberative ones, who traded in slaves for the well-being of the Ottoman dynasty and the empire's sovereign, all those who traded in slaves prospered due to several common factors, such as the peculiar relationship of the slave trade with the law and the multiple legal systems that governed it. More specifically, the slave trade was situated at the crossroads of customary, religious, public, and international laws, which made its control difficult for any particular law administering body, whereas it simultaneously made things easier for those who continued with the trade after its prohibition in 1854 and 1857, respectively for white and black slaves.[81] Moreover, as mentioned above, the extended Ottoman family, the palace as well as high-ranking state officials did not necessarily comply with the corresponding laws, as in the case of the Pertevniyal Valide Sultan's disregard of the laws pertaining to the prohibition of slavery in Circassian and African slaves and her persistence in obtaining slaves from the incoming Circassian ships

---

[81] Hakan Erdem, *Slavery in the Ottoman Empire and its Demise, 1800–1909* (London: Palgrave Macmillan Limited, 1996), 112–113.

at the midst of the Circassian refugee crisis in the early 1860s. Adviye Hanım and the governor's wife who did "business" with her were equally indifferent to the laws that banned the trade in African slaves, despite the international debates and enforcement against it at the time. In fact, when explaining the delay in finding a eunuch for Adviye Hanım, the governor's wife wrote nonchalantly that "whatever the reasons, they are very difficult to come by these days."[82] Ehud Toledano demonstrated that long after the 1857 prohibition of trade in African slaves, the Ottoman imperial harem still contained 194 eunuchs. Some of those were recent entries to the registry that Toledano reviews:

> One would expect that by the turn of the century, after almost 50 years of official prohibition against trading in African slaves, the number of eunuchs being entered into the Register should have declined, reflecting the gradual demise of the institution of harem-slavery. None the less, the picture is quite different: the more we approach the Register's closing date, the larger the number of eunuchs entered. Whereas between the years 1865 and 1875, only 17 eunuchs were registered, we note close to 50 fresh entries for the years 1880–1890. During the last ten years of registration (1893–1903), no less than 100 eunuchs were put on the Imperial payroll. The longest-serving eunuch was registered way back in 1849, and the last eunuchs presented to the Ottoman Family were registered in 1901. Of course, we have no indication of recruits effected past the closing date of the Register. This pattern clearly reflects the fact that the demand for eunuchs at the Palace survived into the twentieth century, and that it was possible to obtain African eunuchs as late as 1901, if not later.[83]

Although the 1854 trade ban in Circassian slaves, effected mostly as a response to the increased volume of slave traffic during the Crimean War was short-lived at the time, the

---

[82] BOA, Y..EE.. 142/173, 1287.S.29 (31 May 1870).

[83] Ehud Toledano, "The Imperial Eunuchs of Istanbul: From Africa to the Heart of Islam," *Middle Eastern Studies*, vol. 20, no. 3 (Jul., 1984), 385. Toledano also mentions that a significant number of the eunuchs in the imperial harem were not purchased, but rather were presented as gifts to the various members of the Ottoman household. Eunuchs who were presented as gifts were all received long after the 1857 prohibition. 386–387.

issue came up several times in the 1860s, most notably in 1864, with the prohibition of

trade in freeborn Circassians.[84] As Hakan Erdem asserted, the point here is not that the

Ottoman state banned what was already illegal according to Şer'i law, but it recognized

that slavery could easily percolate the world of the freeborn, if they were poor and

desperate enough.[85] Şirin, Sıdıka, and Nadire's disregard for legal categories as the

presence of consent and destitution, which was mentioned earlier, illustrates this well. At

the discursive level, there was an effort by the Ottoman state to banish Circassian slave

trade, as it was incompatibility with both the 1839 and 1856 edicts (that aimed to provide

a degree of equality before the law, for all of its citizens) was somewhat manifest. In

practice, on the other hand, the palace as well as the high-ranking state officials continued

with the trade, paving the way for others to follow.[86] Mind, for instance, the brief

ciphered note written in March 1900 that reported about a eunuch from the Yıldız Palace

named Abdülhamid Ağa, who recently "obtained six slave girls" in Adapazarı and was on

his way to Istanbul.[87] As can be observed in the above-mentioned bill of sale for fourteen

Circassian girls (Image 4), the recruitment carried out by a palace official named Çerkes

(Circassian) Osman on behalf of the Yıldız Palace took place rather late, in March

1908.[88]

---

[84] Erdem, *Slavery in the Ottoman Empire,* 106–107, 114–117.

[85] Ibid., 115.

[86] See Nelly Hanna, "Sources for the Study of Slave Women and Concubines in Ottoman Egypt," in *Beyond the Exotic*, 123 for a passing note on how "merchants and craftsmen, that is the members of the indigenous population who owned slave girls, followed the patterns of the military elite in some aspects."

[87] BOA, Y.PRK.ASK 159/65, 1317.Za.18 (20 March 1900).

[88] BOA, Y.PRK.ASK 255/2, 1326.S.11 (15 March 1908). The Yıldız fond contains many documents from the last two decades of Hamidian era, reporting on the palace officials sent out to

Such was the case with the elite households outside the palace as well. Adviye Hanım's daughter, the famous novelist Fatma Aliye Hanım, who is considered to be the first woman of letters and intellectual in the Ottoman Empire and hailed, for that particular reason, as the pioneer of feminist thought and action in the country, was also a known advocate of Ottoman slavery, particularly against the British and Western pressure to abolish it. She traded in slaves and maintained that being an enslaved servant or concubine were merely one among many different phases of womanhood.[89] The fact that she was fighting for women's rights or that she was involved in politics and conversant in law, did not make slavery problematic for Fatma Aliye and she kept on buying slaves well into the turn of the century. Moreover, one bill of sale that belonged to her showed that she bought a young enslaved woman named Perver, from the Hatuqwai-Bzhedug tribe, approximately 18 or 19 years of age, together with her newborn son Hasan.[90] As has been frequently argued, the sale of a slave who gave birth to a male child was strictly prohibited according to Şer'i law. The story of the slave herself is not in the file, nor mentioned in the bill of sale. Thus it is not clear who impregnated the woman, whether it was her master or not. It is not known who sold her to the slaver either but it is a known fact, as insightfully elaborated by Ehud Toledano, pregnant slave women caused alarm

---

Circassian settlements across the country to obtain slaves. For other examples, see BOA, Y.PRK.UM 17/6, 1307.L.5 (25 May 1890); BOA, Y.PRK.UM 17/11, 1307.L.11 (31 May 1890).

[89] Ehud Toledano, *Slavery and Abolition in the Ottoman Middle East* (Seattle: University of Washington Press, 1998), 130. In *Nisvan-ı Islam*, in which she had three long conversations with three foreign women and discussed the details of Ottoman slavery, she appears as a rather ardent defender of the institution as a definitive characteristic of the Ottoman culture. Fatma Aliye Hanım, *Nisvan-ı İslam: Bazı adat-ı İslamiye hakkında üç muhavereyi havidir* (Istanbul: Tercüman-ı Hakikat Matbaası, 1309/1891–92).

[90] Taksim Kitaplığı, Fatma Aliye Hanım Evrakı (papers), FA_Evr_000012-016, 7 Mart 1302 (19 March 1886).

for the wives of the masters, since the children born to concubines were legitimate heirs.[91] Intimate relations between concubines and the men of the household were kept under strict surveillance by the mistresses. Numerous examples can be found particularly in literary texts. Note that, for instance, the mistress in Recaizade Mahmud Ekrem's above-mentioned play *Vuslat*, who gave the slave girl Vuslat to a slaver in disguise, to keep her away from her son. In Sami Paşazade Sezai's *Sergüzeşt*, the ill-fated protagonist Dilber was sent away for similar reasons. In Nabizade Nazım's *Zehra*, it was the relationship that Suphi, Zehra's husband, had with the enslaved girl Sırrıcemal that pushed Zehra into a fit of jealousy with catastrophic consequences, particularly for the enslaved girl. In Halide Edib's *Sinekli Bakkal*, the newly purchased slave girl named Kanarya caused a fierce battle between the mistress of the household Sabiha and her slave-turned-daughter-in-law Dürnev. As a result, Kanarya was sent away as a gift. While it was highly likely that Perver was also sent away for similar reasons, by a cautious mother or a jealous wife, Fatma Aliye readily accepted the legality of the transaction without much questioning.

---

[91] Toledano, "Slave Dealers, Women, Pregnancy, and Abortion," 57.

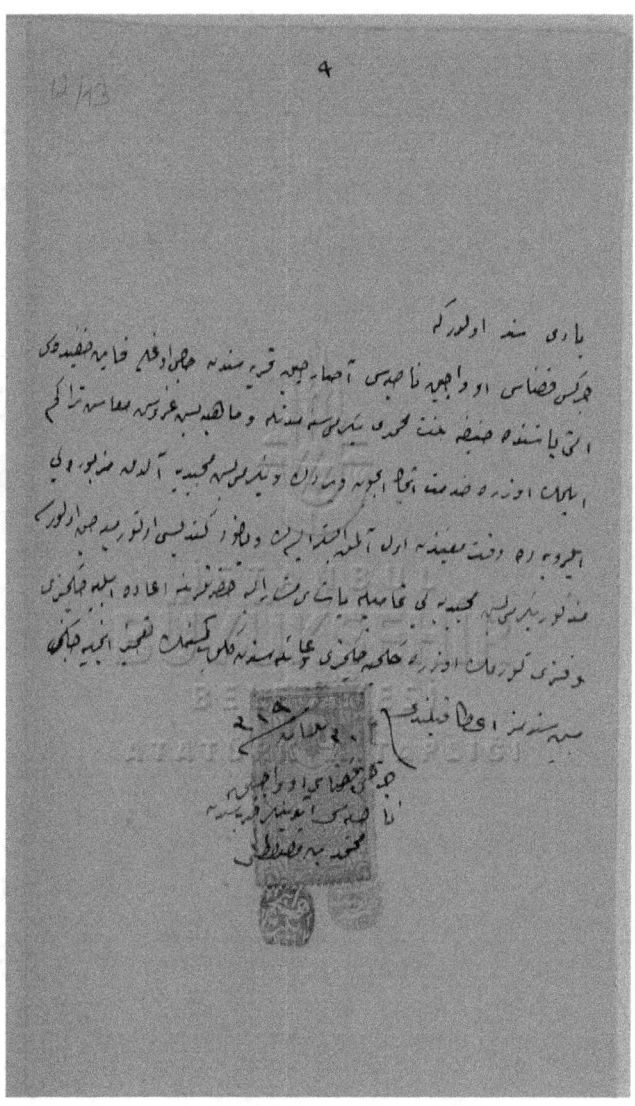

Image 6a. This indenture contract dated May 1903 states that Hanife bint Mehmed, 6 years old, is given to Faik Pasha's (Fatma Aliye's husband) household for a twenty year service term, in exchange of 25 *mecidiye* (500 piasters) paid up front. In addition, monthly amount of 5 piasters would be retained on behalf Hanife, to be given to her at the end of her term. Taksim Atatürk Kitaplığı, Fatma Aliye Hanım Evrakı, FA_Evr_000012-013, 21 Nisan 1319 (4 May 1903).

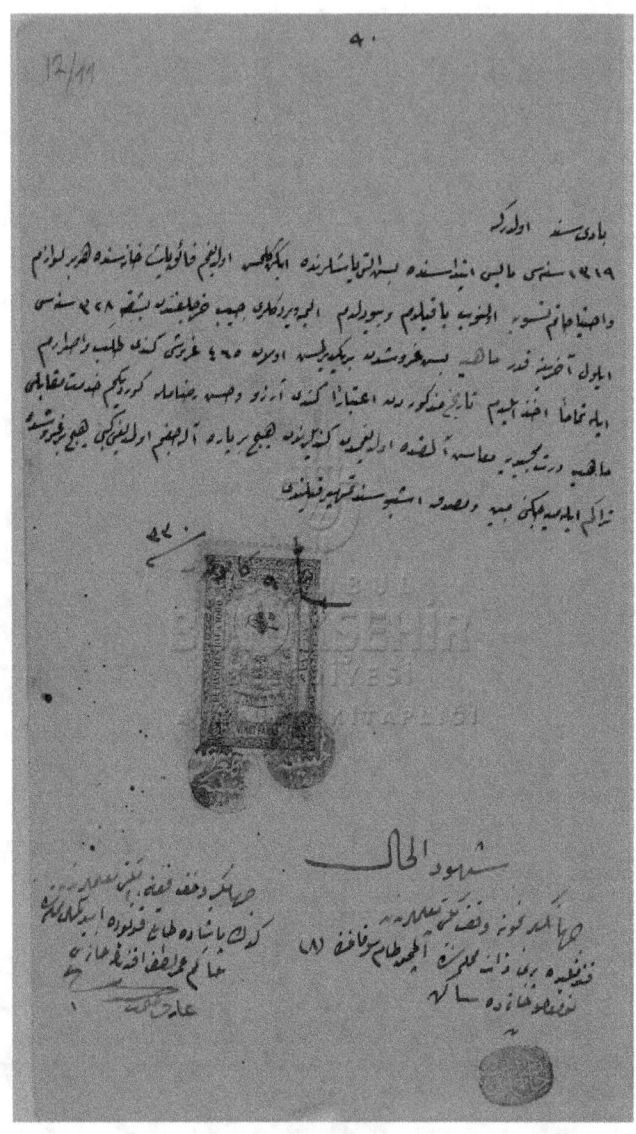

Image 6b. Addition to the previous one, this contract, written and signed by Hanife bint Mehmed in January 1915, roughly twelve years after the commencement of her services with Fatma Aliye, confirms both the ending of her term and that she received her earnings in full. Taksim Atatürk Kitaplığı, Fatma Aliye Hanım Evrakı, FA_Evr_000012-011, 9 Kanunusani 1330 (22 January 1915).

In all these cases, there is an implication that one could easily continue trading in slaves, despite the existence of laws and a significant amount of the international community against it, and for the most part, get away with it. Starting with the year of 1896/97, Fatma Aliye's slave purchases seemingly came to an end, or rather were replaced with indenture contracts, hinting at another aspect of Ottoman society which allowed slavery to flourish or at best go unnoticed; that is the prevalence of slavery-like practices, such as *evlatlık*, *beslemelik*, and *ahretlik*, all of which implicitly meant adoption for the purpose of servitude. Two or three indenture contracts among Fatma Aliye's papers do not constitute a sound documentary base to tell how they differed from the bills of slave sales, except for the obvious fact that they specified limitations for the durations of service. In addition, they seem to be concerned only with the labor of the indentured child as well as the initial and yearly payments made to or retained for the family (see Images 6a and 6b above, for an example). Despite their differences, as hinted in the indenture documents, *evlatlık*, *beslemelik*, and *ahretlik* practices all functioned at times as a safe harbor to those who traded in slaves "improperly." As might be recalled from chapter 1, a police investigation on an illegal sale of three Georgian girls by the aide-de-camp Çürüksulu Ali Pasha was thwarted when the girls' parents claimed that they gave away the girls as *evlatlık*.[92]

Conclusion

Sıdıka, Şirin and Kör Nadire merely reenacted what the women of the palace or

---

[92] BOA, Y.MTV 29/112, 1305.R.26 (11 January 1888).

the elite households had been doing: they exploited a slavery system that was governed by multiple (and at times, conflicting) legal systems, took advantage of the destitution and poverty caused by such socio-political upheavals as the Circassian expulsion or the 1877–78 Russo-Ottoman War, and hid their activities, when necessary, behind other slavery-like practices such as *evlatlık,* etc. They used their own tools of power, such as being a previous member of the imperial harem or being married to an army officer, when accessing sources of slaves. They carved out a space for themselves in the large and somewhat diffuse slave trade network, that effectively connected the provincial town of Gekbuze to the imperial harem in Istanbul. This vast network brought together a diverse groups of people, and it was so tightly-knit together that such people as Emine and her three daughters, deportees from Trabzon, could end up in Şirin's house in Istanbul, through a thick network of acquaintances or associates. With the discovery of the 8-year-old girl Zekiye as well, it was one of Sıdıka's acquaintances, a black woman named Fatma, who first alerted Sıdıka about the possibility of obtaining the girl for sale. Just as Pertevniyal, Adviye, or Fatma Aliye were protecting their positions and gains through the slave network, so did Fatma, Sıdıka, Şirin, or Kör Nadire, by forming alliances with whomever they thought necessary and amassing money for themselves as a form of a retirement plan for their approaching old age. The palace officials at the Beşiktaş and other imperial harems who readily purchased the girls from Şirin and Sıdıka, without much investigation, constituted the other half of the system that delineated the ethnic category of Circassianness as a somewhat arbitrary one, which was often tied strictly to class. As long as the girls or their families did not claim their free status, they could remain enslaved in and employed by the imperial harems.

Consequently, it was Müzeyyen's mother (who was relatively better off compared to Zehra or Emine) who notified the police and had Sıdıka, Şirin, and Nadire arrested. At the end of a long police investigation, which produced pages of interrogation records, they were found guilty for unlawfully capturing destitute Turkish refugee girls and deceitfully selling them into slavery "here and there, as if they were Circassians." For Sıdıka, Şirin, and Nadire, slavery could be extended to anyone who consented to be enslaved, even though that consent was induced by poverty, despair, and an overall destitution. For the Ottoman government, on the other hand, enslavement was tied, at least at the discursive level, to more strictly determined ethnic and racial categories and would not (and in fact, from its perspective, better not) extend to everyone who was sufficiently vulnerable. Not that the elites that constituted the Ottoman state personally did not breach these categories. As will be explored more fully in the following chapter, they in fact did, extensively. But the discourses of the state always developed with a degree of autonomy, independent from the people who took part in it. It was not that Sıdıka, Şirin, and Nadire were not aware that what they did was illegal, either. Their efforts to cover up their scheme with a series of lies hint at the fact that they were aware of the incompatibility of their actions with the law. But their customers at the palace made the matter more confusing for the three women, for if the palace could overlook the illegality of the matter and bought Turkish girls to be employed at the imperial harem, even possibly to be a concubine to one of the princes there, then what they have done was permissible, at least to a certain degree. What they did not understand was that the palace, despite the efforts of Sultan Abdülhamid to make it "the unquestioned center of power in the Ottoman Empire,"[93] did not carry the same significance as the state any longer, and that the latter was now under the obligation of not only transforming its internal legal order to effect a more encompassing criminal or civil law, but it also had to comply with the equally pressing international law, which ultimately rendered the imperial harems as utterly contradictive and thus contested institutions in the Ottoman Empire, as will also be explored in the following chapter. At the moment of the incident, the Ottoman Empire was already a signatory to several international agreements against the slave trade and was headed towards the more encompassing Brussels Conference Act, which would be signed a mere two years later. Thus, it could not turn a blind eye on such an offence.

In the end, with the stated purpose of making an exemplary case out of these women, the police, in cooperation with the municipal government and Yıldız Palace, deported Sıdıka, Şirin, and Nadire to Tripoli, where they stayed for at least half a decade.[94] Yet, as it was stated in the police report, the case was never brought to a court, and no official legal action was taken, since the "reputation of the palace and the imperial harem was at stake," the report explained. What can be discerned in the report is that the police held the imperial harem also responsible for the offence. Yet, the palace and the imperial harem were there to be respected and protected not to bring legal charges against. Hence, all was handled and resolved quietly. The three women were deported to Tripoli and the imperial harem continued with its customary practices for another two decades. It continued to buy slaves and receive them as gifts well until the constitutional

---

[93] Howard Eissenstat, "Metaphors of Race and Discourse of Nation: Racial Theory and State Nationalism in the First Decades of the Turkish Republic," in *Race and Nation: Ethnic Systems in the Modern World*, ed. Paul Spickard (New York: Routledge, 2005), 242.

[94] BOA, BEO 303/22678, 1311.R.20 (31 October 1893); BEO 587/43951, 1312.N.20 (17 March 1895).

revolution of 1908, which marked, among other things, the beginning of the dissolution of imperial harems in the Ottoman Empire. As will be discussed in more detail in chapter 5 below, the dissolution of the Yıldız harem and the mass manumission of several hundred enslaved servants triggered a host of debates on the slave trade and slavery, in conjunction with equality, justice, and citizenship. The four decades that preceded it, however, witnessed for the most part chaos, in which anyone who held some degree of power could become a slave dealer and everyone who was vulnerable enough could be enslaved.

Chapter 4.
The Uncertainties of Freedom

In September 1908, two months after the Young Turk Revolution and the
inauguration of the Second Constitutional Era in the Ottoman Empire, a female slave of
Circassian origin named Fatma Leman fled her mistress's house, taking refuge in the
Ministry of Justice in Istanbul. Her reasoning was straightforward: if this revolution,
under the slogans of "freedom, equality and justice," granted freedom to each and every
Ottoman individual, then she too was free like the rest of her compatriots.[1] Whether the
promulgation of the constitution guaranteed her freedom is another question, but her
conviction that she was now free and her decision to seek her rights at the Ministry of
Justice (which, in her view, was more closely associated with the new regime) instead of
the religious *Şer'i* courts (where manumission deeds were normally issued) led to an
institutional paralysis over the ensuing months. The Ministry of Justice, not knowing
what to do with the runaway slave and uncertain of its authority on the matter, responded
to the slave's appeal by not doing much more than writing an official communication and
sending her off to the Ministry of Police. The police did not know what to do with Fatma
Leman either. Finding themselves in a difficult position, in which they could not let the
enslaved girl go (as the issue of property rights was at stake) nor return her to her owner
(indicating that Fatma Leman's claim was at least partially valid) the police chose to

---

[1] BOA, DH.EUM.THR 32/34, 1328.R.26 (7 May 1910).

evade making any decision altogether and summoned the owner instead. For her part, the owner, whose faith in the old judicial order was intact and who had the means to employ an attorney, insisted that Fatma Leman be taken to the *Şer'i* court to "prove" her free status. The girl herself decided to wait for the reinstatement of the Parliament instead and make her appeal there. In the meanwhile, she was allegedly kidnapped from where she was waiting in hiding for the Parliament to convene, sold as a concubine to a high ranking provincial government officer, and eventually, when the Parliament urged the police to follow up on the case, was located in her native village living with her mother, unmarried but having given birth to a female child.[2]

What lay "beyond" slavery for Fatma Leman was analogous to her life as a slave, taking the usual course of slavery in the Ottoman Empire, as it would elsewhere such as in the Atlantic system. It comprised different forms of coercion such as kidnapping, rape or resale, touched by varying degrees of despair and vulnerability reflecting the lack of kin support, poverty, and conditions such as pregnancy and child bearing. What also lay in this "beyond," however, was what Frederick Cooper, Thomas Holt and Rebecca Scott called the "uncertainties of freedom," in which slavery simply dissolved into other forms of power and exploitation. As the legal and administrative institutions transformed or realigned themselves, or failed to do so for that matter, this uncertainty manifested itself in terms of ambiguities or contradictions in various social structures or arrangements, most notably the realm of citizenship.[3]

---

[2] Ibid.

[3] Frederick Cooper et al., *Beyond Slavery: Explorations of Race, Labor and Citizenship in Postemancipation Societies* (Chapel Hill: The University of North Carolina Press, 2000), 3.

The previous chapters traced not only the ways in which the Ottoman state positioned itself vis-à-vis slavery, but also how it defined itself and the limits of the new social and political order it aimed to establish, through slavery. The 1908 constitutional revolution was in many ways a culmination of these previous five decades, as the result of which a constitutional government claimed the ownership of the state power. Focusing on the immediate aftermath of the revolution, this chapter explores the ways in which the new regime's emancipatory efforts and failures determined the limits of citizenship in the Ottoman Empire. It probes the claims made by the slaves, who the very language of freedom, equality, and justice that the slave owners and the Ottoman state used, although they attributed different meanings to the words that this language comprised. These differences were not necessarily or solely due to slaves' needs, interests, or priorities, but were also shaped by their perceptions of what they thought was happening at the time: what sense they made out of the pillars of the revolution and the new regime; what they thought Ottoman citizenship meant; what they understood from emancipation (be it the emancipation from slavery or gaining equal rights as citizens); and last but not least, how they saw and ordered ethnic, religious, racial, and gender conflicts. Examining the (anti-) slavery idiom used by the Ottoman state, slave owners and slaves in distinct and often conflicting ways on the one hand and the perpetuated bifurcated nature of the Ottoman legal system on the other, I aim to offer a glimpse of the social and political conditions that determined who was entitled to claim freedom and who was not.[4]

---

[4] Eric Foner, *The Story of American Freedom* (New York: WW Norton & Company, 1998), xvi–xvii.

The "Spirit of the Constitution"

The revolution of 1908, often referred to by its contemporaries only as "freedom,"[5] was the culmination of a long battle between the absolutist rule of Abdülhamid II and a constitutionalist opposition that comprised statesmen, officers, members of clergy and intellectuals "who shared a common enemy, but not a common agenda."[6] Such efforts to introduce a constitutional regime were not unprecedented in the Ottoman Empire. Several decades prior to the 1908 revolution, a small cadre of bureaucrats led by Midhat Paşa and supported by a group of intellectuals who called themselves Young Ottomans, succeeded in deposing sultan Abdülaziz and bringing Abdülhamid II to power in his stead. The latter's accession to the throne was due to his declared allegiance to a prospective constitutional rule and his promise to promulgate a constitution. He did so only to suspend it merely a year later, which marked the beginning of a bitter struggle between his 33-year-long absolutist rule represented by Yıldız Palace, and the constitutionalist opposition, which intensified in the last decade of the nineteenth century and culminated in an army-led uprising and consequently the reinstatement of the suspended constitution in 1908. Viewed by some scholars as a complete rupture that subsequently transformed the Ottoman political culture "from a bureaucratically-run monarchist regime to a liberal democratic political system" and by others a mere (still, triumphant) restoration of an earlier interrupted revolution, it

---

[5] Michelle U. Campos, *Ottoman Brothers: Muslims, Christians, and Jews in Early Twentieth Century Palestine* (Stanford: Stanford University Press, 2011), 34–36

[6] Şükrü Hanioğlu, *A Brief History of the Late Ottoman Empire* (Princeton: Princeton University Press, 2008), 144.

nevertheless marked the beginning of an era that represented "a new experience in the way Ottoman subjects viewed their relations with the authorities."[7]

The series of events that sparked the 1908 revolution and eventually forced Abdülhamid II to restore the constitution was largely the making of ordinary soldiers and junior officers, all of whom were members of the Committee of Progress and Union, which at the time still a secret organization. Merely a sequence of local uprisings at the beginning, the news of the revolution reached the Istanbul public only after the constitution was reinstated, on July 24, 1908.[8] Once it was known however, "freedom" was embraced and celebrated with enthusiasm everywhere, regardless of the character of the revolution that brought it about, whether seen as a "well-planned army insurrection" or a "totally popular movement,"[9] which at times was emphasized by its contemporaries. For one, an almanac named "Almanac of Freedom," published in 1909, stressed that the "holy revolution" was not carried out by the Ottoman government but the very people themselves.[10] Aykut Kansu argued that the popular character of the revolution was already evident in the years leading up to it, in tax revolts throughout the empire, which

---

[7] Aykut Kansu, *The Revolution of 1908 in Turkey* (Leiden: Brill, 1997), p.25–26; Hanioğlu, *A Brief History*, 150–151; Vangelis Kechriotis, "The Second Constitutional Period of the Ottoman Empire: A Disputed Legacy," in *Istanbul as seen from a distance, Center and provinces in the Ottoman Empire*, Elisabeth Özdalga, M.Sait Özervali, Feryal Tansuğ (eds), (Istanbul: Swedish Research Institute In Istanbul, 2011), 33.

[8] Hanioğlu, *A Brief History*, 149.

[9] Ibid., 148; Kansu, *The Revolution of 1908*, 73.

[10] *Nevsal-i Hürriyet*, sahib ve naşiri: Memurin-i Hariciye'den Mehmed Ali (Istanbul: Vatan Matbaası, 1325/1908–1909), 73.

were largely popular uprisings, which broke out largely due to the "unequal levying of the tax."[11]

Not everyone, however, understood "freedom" the same way.[12] Like similar efforts at emancipation that accompanied sudden social and political change, the revolutionaries in the Ottoman Empire were unclear in their understanding and vision as to how "freedom, equality, and justice," were to be achieved.[13] It is not that the revolutionaries did not envision or desire a constitutional regime, representative democracy, freedom of press, or individual liberties. The representatives both in the Ayan and Mebusan assemblies continued debating these notions, plans, or visions in the subsequent years. Yet, like in all revolutions, the outcomes, as Şükrü Hanioğlu has put it, "differed markedly from the expectations of its true believers.[14] In that sense, they not only did not know how slavery would be abolished but were also unclear about the direct political consequences of the revolution itself; an ambiguity which had been attributed by some scholars to the suddenness of Abdülhamid II's capitulation that threw the country and its administrative institutions into utter confusion. The rapidity of change hindered the formation or transformation of legal and administrative institutions that would have facilitated the desired or envisioned change.[15] It may be that the revolution had a well-determined aim of creating "the modern secular Ottoman citizen whose loyalty was going

---

[11] Kansu, *The Revolution of 1908*, 38, 48, 73–75.

[12] For a striking set of examples, see Campos, *Ottoman Brothers*, 57–58.

[13] Pamela Scully, Diana Paton (eds.), *Gender and Slave Emancipation in the Atlantic World* (Durham: Duke University Press, 2005), 12.

[14] Hanioğlu, A Brief History, 150.

[15] Ibid.; Feroz Ahmad, *The Young Turks, the Committee of Union and Progress in Turkish politics, 1908–1914* (Oxford: Clarendon Press, 1969), 13.

158

to be to the state," as Bedross Der Matossian has argued, but the level of confusion attached to these concepts was astonishing.[16] For other historians, this difficulty stemmed not simply from confusion but the contradiction between being a constitutionalist and a revolutionary at the same time, as the former derived its "legitimacy from respect for the law, community consensus, stability, and continuity, while the other owed its legitimacy to itself—the act of revolution and its spirit, without which there would not have been a constitution."[17] In fact, the lack of a corresponding law or a law-enforcing institution often served as the basis for limiting the revolutionaries' claims to such rights as the right to assembly, freedom of the press, or individual liberties, such as freedom of movement.[18]

Moreover, the people were no less perplexed or contradicting than the revolutionaries either. The Sultan, after all, was the same monarch that kept them under virtual slavery for the preceding three decades, during which he revived the tradition of what Hakan Erdem called "rhetorical slavery" and once again made "the concept of loyalty to the person of the Sultan the cornerstone of the Ottoman sociopolitical system."[19] Drawing from Carter Findley, Hakan Erdem argued that this system, known to

---

[16] Bedross Der Matossian, *Shattered Dreams of Revolution: From Liberty to Violence in the Late Ottoman Empire* (Stanford: Stanford University Press, 2014), 94.

[17] Nader Sohrabi, *Revolution and Constitutionalism in the Ottoman Empire and Iran* (New York: Cambridge University Press, 2011), 18.

[18] See Meclisi Mebusan Zabıt Ceridesi (the registers of parliamentary proceedings, shortened MMZC), 18 Kanunuevvel 1324 (31 December 1908), 104 for a discussion on the uses, abuses and limitations of the notion of freedom; 18 Şubat 1324 (3 March 1909), 134 for a discussion on the freedom of assembly. For a lengthy discussion on the drawbacks of passports on freedom of movement, see 4 Teşrinisani 1326 (17 November 1910), 34–35. For a discussion directly related to slavery, see 18 Mayıs 1325 (31 May 1909), 222.

[19] Erdem, *Slavery in the Ottoman Empire*, 125–26; Campos, *Ottoman Brothers*, 43–44, 48.

the students of Ottoman history as the "system of loyalty," flourished particularly among officialdom. As indicated by the "oft-used appellation 'loyalty and slavery' (sadakat ve ubudiyet)," it was a "two-pronged system" in which "the quality of loyalty was supposed to stem from servility/slavery of the officials and they were expected to 'prove' it on suitable occasions."[20] Abdülhamid's choice of his sons in law, for instance, was also indicative of this tendency. "The deposed khan selected his sons in law himself," as Ahmet Mahir Efendi, a deputy from Kastamonu, reported "from among the orphaned, those without wealth or a cent, those who he deemed close to himself in thought and action."[21] Yet, except for the bendegan, which included the enslaved or indentured palace servants and eunuchs, only few of these officials were actually slaves or of slave origin. In addition, the suppression of the 1876 constitution, the subsequent dissolution of the Parliament and the failure to restore the constitutional regime throughout Abdülhamid II's long rule, backed up by the dissident voices of such intellectual and political groups as the Young Ottomans and Young Turks, brought to many subjects' minds a picture of the Ottoman subjects as slaves of Abdülhamid II; "the deposed khan," as one enslaved man called him in his petition in 1909, "who made the entire Ottoman nation moan under slavery for thirty three years."[22]

The historian Ehud Toledano has pointed out how the Young Ottomans (setting an example for later generations) "made more than occasional use of the idiom of slavery

[20] Erdem, *Slavery in the Ottoman Empire*, 125.

[21] MMZC, 17 Nisan 1326 (30 April 1910), 501.

[22] BOA, DH.MKT 2891/97, 1327.B.17 (4 August 1909).

as a metaphor in their writings about political and social freedom."[23] "Even the name of [Namık] Kemal and Ziya [Pasha]'s journal, Hürriyet (freedom)," Toledano has argued, "is the Islamic legal opposite of the term for slavery (rıkkiyet and esaret)."[24] Thus, a common binary of "freedom" and "slavery," as well as the violent nature of the latter, were already well established by the time the revolution took place. In fact, in the proceedings following the Parliament's reinstatement, deputies made frequent references to Hamidian rule and its strong-arm, violent traditions and procedures. In one instance, when the representatives were debating on the abolition of corporal punishment, the reasoning behind the change was directly connected to the slavery-freedom duality. "The spirit and the philosophy of the Constitution," Rifat Bey, a deputy from Aleppo, wrote in the proposal he submitted, "is based on mutual love, connection, compliance and understanding among persons," whereas the spirit and the philosophy of Abdülhamid's oppressive rule thrived upon fear, terror and hate. But with the inauguration of the Constitution, Rifat Bey contended, the people were released from their bonds of slavery and until their actions and manners in this new order are observed and considered, all old methods of physical punishment should be abolished altogether. For Rifat Bey, the stick, the whip or the bastinado (foot whipping) had no place in the courthouses of the era of freedom.[25]

Despite the frequent and common use of the slavery metaphor, particularly in reference to the Hamidian rule against which the revolutionaries explicitly positioned

---

[23] Ehud R. Toledano, "Late Ottoman Concepts of Slavery (1830s–1880s), *Poetics Today*, Vol.14, No.3, Cultural Processes in Muslim and Arab Societies: Modern Period I (Autumn, 1993), 491.

[24] Ibid.

[25] MMZC, 25 Mart 1325 (7 April 1909), 672.

themselves, the actual institution of slavery took almost an independent course from the current debates. In some references, it was even considered to have ceased altogether a long time ago. For example, when the Parliament was debating revisions to the Constitution, Yorgo Boşo Efendi, a deputy from Serfice (today's Sarvia, Greece) proposed an additional article to the constitution that would ban the sale and purchase of persons. Seyyit Bey, a deputy from Izmir, refused it altogether based on his conviction that in the Ottoman lands there was no one who was not free. When Yorgi Honeus Efendi, a deputy from Salonica, reminded him of "all those slave girls in Yıldız Palace," Seyyit Bey rebuffed it by saying that they were all manumitted and delivered back to their families, even though these manumissions were still in progress at that time and encompassed only the enslaved servants of deposed Abdülhamid II, not those of other members of the dynasty, nor notable households of Istanbul or the provinces.[26] In another debate on business enterprises and labor regulations about a year later, when the Finance Minister Mehmet Cavit Bey suggested an arrangement for workers which Kirkor Zohrap Efendi criticized for being "akin to slavery," the former refused it by saying that "humanity long left behind the age of slavery."[27]

As have been discussed in the previous chapters, operating within a global community regulated by international law, conventions, and agreements, as well as putative humanitarian concerns and efforts towards a wholesale emancipation, the Ottoman government found itself forced to push a policy against the practice of slavery. "Notwithstanding [the] revival of slavery rhetoric and regardless of the nature of

---

[26] MMZC, 27 Mayıs 1325 (9 June 1909), 222.

[27] MMZC, 12 Nisan 1326 (25 April 1910), 382.

Abdülhamid's rule," Hakan Erdem has argued, "the Ottoman government's policy against the actual institution of slavery persisted."[28] The Sultan did not always agree with the Porte on the anti-slavery measures and often caused long delays in securing his assent, rendering the issue of slavery a contested ground between the Palace and the Porte. In fact, the signs of this contention were already in place, according to Ali Haydar Midhat, the son of Midhat Paşa, the author of the 1876 constitution. Comparing the earlier drafts with the final text of the constitution, Ali Haydar Midhat observed omissions, even corruptions to Midhat Paşa's draft, one of which was related to slavery and Midhat Paşa's "idea of a manifesto," as Erdem called it, about anti-slavery measures to be taken in the Ottoman Empire with the onset of the first constitutional era:[29]

The buying and selling of slaves being contrary to the prescriptions of the Sacred Law (Cheri), We hereby enfranchise the slaves and eunuchs of Our Palace, and declare that henceforth all trade in slaves, whether purchase or sale, is hereby formally forbidden in Our Empire, and a date will be fixed for the gradual emancipation of all existing slaves, and special measures will be adopted to prevent any return to slavery.[30]

---

[28] Erdem, *Slavery in the Ottoman Empire*, 126.

[29] Ibid.

[30] Ali Haydar Midhat Bey, *The Life of Midhat Pasha: A Record of his Services, Political Reforms, Banishment, and Judicial Murder* (London: John Murray, 1903), 108, quoted in Erdem, *Slavery in the Ottoman Empire*, 126.

It is arguable whether Midhat Paşa expressed his provisions about slavery in these specific terms, especially in regards to the point that slave trade was against prescriptions of the Şer'i law (or, if he did, he really meant it) for a few years later, as reported by the British Consul of Jidda, he saw no fault in giving two female slaves as gifts to a religious official.[31] Nevertheless, furthering the process that started with the 1857 prohibition of trade in African slaves (to be renewed in 1877), Midhat Paşa not only revived earlier debates on abolition, highlighted the importance of such means as mükatebe (self-purchase) in order to achieve it, but also proposed, in an unprecedented way, to abolish palace slavery, convinced that it would set the example for the remainder of the Ottoman society. Following the dissolution of the constitution and subsequent arrest and extra-judicial killing of Midhat Paşa, the abolition of palace slavery was not be to debated again until after the 1908 revolution, but slavery and particularly its trade were subjected to a series of international arrangements in the subsequent years. The Anglo-Ottoman Convention for the Suppression of the Black Slave Trade in 1880 and the Brussels Act in 1890 rendered trade in African slaves illegal and made trade in Circassian slaves frowned upon to a certain extent, at least in theory, in the decades that followed.

Last but, not the least, the issue of slavery also had to be addressed at the local level, as it touched the essence of the definition of Ottoman citizenship, which was "inextricably linked" to the definition of constitutionalism, whose legitimacy was based unambiguously, at least in theory, in equality before law.[32] Thus, when Fatma Leman fled her mistress's house and claimed her freedom in September 1908, she was not only

---

[31] Erdem, *Slavery in the Ottoman Empire*, 131.

[32] Sohrabi, *Revolution and Constitutionalism*, 21.

capable of making a distinction between two legal systems (and judging what she believed to be their potential merits and dangers) but she was also aware of (or at least had been exposed to) the actual, rhetorical, local, perhaps even international usage of the words slavery and freedom. What she was less mindful of, perhaps, was that the ending of slavery for women and the freedom that came after it, worked differently for women than it did for men.

The Gendered Politics of Emancipation

The 1908 revolution, which also sparked the process of slave emancipation was largely militaristic in nature, particularly following the counter-revolution in April 1909, which was harshly suppressed by the army troops that marched from Salonica to Istanbul.[33] This had direct implications both on the gendered nature of the political environment that was shaped after the revolution and how emancipation affected men and women in the newly emerging social order, at times determining the hierarchies in which slavery was to be placed. For example, in the aftermath of the counter-revolution in May 1909, the Grand Vizier attempted to consult with Mahmud Şevket Paşa, the chief commander of the marching troops, on the dissolution of the deposed sultan's harem and the manumission of the cariyes. However, the latter responded in a stern manner that it was not appropriate, nor was it a time to busy the army with such trivial matters and that

---

[33] Ahmad, *The Young Turks*, 45.

165

these women should be transferred to Topkapı Palace and the matter be discussed and decided thereafter by the Ottoman state.[34]

Scholars of slavery and emancipation in the Atlantic world have stressed the explicit linkages between masculinity and citizenship, arguing that slave emancipation that resulted from armed struggle helped constructing a highly gendered political community in its aftermath.[35] The Ottoman constitution did not pronounce the limits of citizenship as clearly as its Haitian counterpart did roughly a century earlier, but implicit in its definition of state membership was the notion that no one was worthy of being an Ottoman "if he [was] not a good father, a good son, a good husband, and above all a good soldier."[36] Thus, emancipation meant, for enslaved women, the end of one hierarchical order and the beginning of another, in which existing gender relations were confirmed or disrupted, yet coercion, sexual vulnerability, and the gendered politics of public space remained.[37] "Despite the diversity of processes and outcomes in the Atlantic world," Pamela Scully and Diana Paton show, "slave emancipation everywhere took gendered forms, restructuring relationships between men and women, and making men's entitlement to leadership of a family a central feature of post- emancipation societies."[38] Women were to be released from slavery, but into a new kind of subordination and dependence. One of the older enslaved servants of the imperial harem, Sırrıcemal, who had been expelled from Yıldız Palace following Abdülhamid II's deposal, illustrated this

---

[34] BOA, BEO 3546/265908, 1327.R.21 (12 May 1909).

[35] Scully, et al., *Gender and Slave Emancipation*, 12.

[36] Ibid., 11.

[37] Ibid., 2.

[38] Ibid., 3.

in a written petition.[39] After sixty years of service, Sırrıcemal found herself on the street, penniless and with no family or friends, until a woman took pity on her and brought her home. "I think about my life in the past," she said in her petition asking for a pension "and of my future, I dread and get scared."[40] Sırrıcemal's personal connections as a former member of the palace, and the skills and training she acquired there, could not secure a professional means to earn a living. In fact, that option was not even addressed in any of the correspondences, but her efforts did gain her a pension. In another case, a young woman named Nazmiye, reportedly the slave of the former war minister Mehmed Rıza Pasha, also found herself and her 8-month-old child on the street, unmarried, with no friends or relatives and poverty-stricken.[41] Having no access to such organizational information as to whom to petition, or having skills and means to write a petition in the first place, Nazmiye and her child were found unsuitable even for the almshouse and were recommended to be admitted to a woman's hospital instead.[42]

Not the least important result of the new Turkish Constitution," the New York Times wrote shortly after the revolution, "will be the effect upon the inmates of the harem, who, it is admitted, measurably aided the Young Turks in their conspiracy against

---

[39] Ibid., 13. BOA, BEO 3636/272633, 1327.Ş.29 (15 September 1909); BEO, 3603/270220, 1327.B.5 (23 July 1909).

[40] BOA, BEO 3636/272633, 1327.Ş.29 (15 September 1909), "...mazideki hayatımı düşünüyorum, istikbalimden ürküp korkuyorum..."

[41] BOA, DH.MKT 2782/10, 1327.Ra.9 (31 March 1909).

[42] Ibid.; DH.MUI 126/26, 1328.Ş.25 (1 September 1910). Founded in 1869, Haseki women's hospital served as a detention center for needy women until the first decades of the twentieth century, when it gradually became a proper hospital. Some of the women in question here were not able to afford even the stamp duty required for submitting their petitions. For an illustrative example, see the *ilmühaber* attached to the file BOA, ŞD 3136/34, 1334.R.24 (29 February 1916), for the case of Makbule Hanım, also a deportee from Yıldız palace.

the former order of things." The paper noted that while "freedom, absolute freedom" was what Turkish women wanted, there were "convincing reasons" as to why they "may not at once enter into the full joys of it, since they were simply unable "to conduct themselves with decorum in the presence of the curious and fascinating glances of the opposite sex."[43] Yet for the women noted about—Fatma Leman, who was at the child-bearing age of 22 and recently subjected to resale, Nazmiye who was left alone with a newborn child out on the street, and Sırrıcemal, who was nearing age eighty and had no means, money, or personal belongings, and moreover, was all alone in Istanbul—what stood on the way to "freedom, absolute freedom" was more than being simply incapable of conducting themselves "with decorum in the presence of the curious and fascinating glances of the opposite sex." These obstacles included kidnapping, being recaptured and sold into slavery, being abandoned (or forced to relocate to their native villages, provided that they had one), and, in the case of Nazmiye, possibly rape. It was not that these women did not try to devise means to pursue their new lives. One enslaved woman named İspantiyar, who was expelled from Abdülhamid II's harem following its dissolution, allegedly found employment as the headmistress of an orphanage in Adana province. Nonetheless, it is doubtful that she performed this duty in an official capacity, for when the Ministry of Finance investigated the matter with the Ministry of Education concerning a pension-related issue, the latter found no record of İspantiyar's employment.[44] Fatma Leman, for her part, managed to produce an address of an old acquaintance, where she would reside while waiting for the parliament to convene,

---

[43] *New York Times*, "The Emancipation of Turkish Women," September 6, 1908.

[44] BOA, MF.MKT 1231/28, 1336.M.20 (5 November 1917).

worked at a mansion as a servant, and even took a room at a hotel when hiding became necessary. None of these actions could prevent her falling prey to slavery and eventually finding herself at her natal home "married to none and lamenting," as the report described it.[45]

It is true that male slaves too resorted to flight or demanded their freedom, but having been less marginalized than women, they had relatively easier access to work or to such institutions as the army. In two separate instances in Sivas province, bands of young enslaved men, driving off a few heads of horse and sheep, escaped from their masters' premises to Kayseri province nearby (the district governor of which had the reputation of being a guardian of fugitive slaves), where they eventually volunteered to be enlisted in the army as a means to claim their citizenship.[46] In the case of the enslaved male servants of the palace, the thirty nine eunuchs who were expelled from Yıldız Palace and subsequently exiled to Ta'if (in today's Saudi Arabia) were kept under virtual arrest there but were eventually provided with travel documents to seek employment elsewhere.[47] What made the women's case different than that of the men was the former's unchanged status as dependents of male benefactors, whether the Ottoman state, their male relatives or their husbands. The aim here, however, is not simply to reiterate how marginalized women were in the era of "freedom" but to point out their perpetually dependent state in which the discursive, ambiguous, or even contradictory nature of emancipation in the Ottoman Empire crystalized. After all, the Ottoman constitutional

---

[45] BOA, DH.EUM.THR 32/34, 1328.R.26 (7 May 1910).

[46] See BOA, ŞD 2786/29, 1327.N.14 (29 September 1909), pages 4, 8, 12, 24 and 27 for example.

[47] BOA, DH.MUI 3-3/25, 1328.M.27 (8 February 1910).

169

revolution too based itself on modern liberalism, which in turn hinged on, as Pamela

Haag points out, "the ideal of the masterless man." In the Ottoman case, not only were

the "masterless" women not assigned "the propriety, self-interested traits associated with

the market rendition of the individual," but the very notion of these women as

individuals, detached from an ethnic or religious claim to liberty and equality, was

questionable.[48] In that sense, Fatma Leman's and other enslaved women's stories were

both unique and exemplary at the same time, but not solely due to the degree of despair

or the sad endings they met in their respective experiences. Rather, they were indicative

of the limits of emancipation in the post-revolution Ottoman Empire; limits, as will be

discussed in the sections below, that can be traced through such underlying themes in

these stories as the singular faith placed on such overtly secular institutions as the

Ministry of Justice or the Parliament, as opposed to religious ones.

The Problem of the Bifurcated Legal System

Whether because of instinct or more informed decisions, Fatma Leman and other

slaves' faith in such secular institutions as the Ministry of Justice was not entirely

unfounded. Starting early on after the revolution, the ministry made a well-articulated

debate against slavery, highlighting particularly its corruptive effects and possible

dangers in undermining the constitutional order as a whole. In a note written to the

Ministry of Interior Affairs in November 1908, Justice Minister Hasan Fehmi reiterated

that the constitutional government assured, by definition and without exception, freedom

---

[48] Pamela Haag, *Consent: Sexual Rights and the Transformation of American Liberalism* (Ithaca: Cornell University Press, 1999), 9-10.

for each and every individual. Turning a blind eye now to the continuing sale and purchase of Circassian girls across the country and particularly in Istanbul not only harmed the reputation and legitimacy of the constitutional government but also gave way to the sale and purchase of free-born individuals, labeled Circassian under false pretenses, hence rendering everyone, at least in theory, susceptible to such offenses.[49] Both for the minister and the public prosecutor of Beyoğlu (who produced a similar note approximately ten days later, in response to the case of two fugitive slaves, one Circassian and the other African), the matter of the African slaves appeared clear and unambiguous, as the rules and regulations were already determined by international law. By contrast, the case of Circassians was complicated. When the "Circassians emigrated to the Ottoman lands" the minister noted, "slavery pertaining to the white race was already abolished by the Russian government in territories under their control," from where they had mostly emigrated; a fact that rendered, according to the minister, the claims to ancestral slave ownership by Circassian notables unfounded. Moreover, in Şer'i law, just enslavement was restricted to wartime only and bore no validity any longer. But even if it were valid, as the chief of the Ottoman parliament's Committee on Petitions articulated later on, wasn't it true that the African slaves were already exempted from the jurisdiction of Şer'i law?[50] Thus, for the Ministry of Justice, the continuing sale and purchase of Circassian girls was not only incompatible with the constitutional regime, which based itself first and foremost on the principle of political and legal equality, but no longer had a Şer'i basis either. Shortly after this official correspondence, the Ministry

---

[49] BOA, ŞD 2786/29, 1327.N.14 (29 September 1909), page 66.

[50] Ibid., page 13.

171

of Justice published a brief note in the newspapers announcing a ban on the sale and purchase of Circassian slaves, making its position against slavery public and open for the slaves who rightly favored it.[51] What was less apparent for the slaves was the position of the constitutional government, which was neither clear on the matter, nor immune from the notion of an obligation to maintain the existing hierarchies and privileges it inherited. What is more, the revolutionaries endorsed the old regime's corporate notion of modern citizenship, which was based on a particular form of representation rooted in the idea of ethnic-religious equality,[52] often at the expense of individual claims to freedom, equality, and justice.

The constitutional government, moreover, was not as comfortable disregarding *Şer'i* law as the Ministry of Justice was, at times overtly eschewing any modification of *Şer'i* law's area of influence. This position was indicative of the ambiguous relation of the Ottoman state to its two separate justice administering institutions. Bifurcation of the Ottoman legal system had its roots in the reform movements that began earlier in the nineteenth century, most notably with the *Gülhane* edict (that marked the beginning of the *Tanzimat* era), which had the declared aim of "guaranteeing personal rights and confirming equality between different religious and ethnic communities in the empire" as was described retrospectively in the inauguration speech of the 1908 Parliament.[53] As has already been discussed earlier, the first instances of the legal reforms consisted of mere codifications of the *Şer'i* provisions, which regulated almost all civil, commercial, and

---

[51]See *İkdam*, 17 Teşrinisani 1324 for an example of the note.

[52] Usama Makdisi, *The Culture of Sectarianism* (Berkeley: University of California Press, 2000), 6–7, 12.

[53] MMZC, 15 Kanunuevvel 1324 (28 December 1908), 65.

penal processes within the legal realm. With the adoption of the Imperial Ottoman Penal

Code in 1858, however, there emerged the first cases of intervention into Şer'i law by the

Ottoman state; interventions which sometimes by their nature resulted in the abrogation

of Şer'i law, particularly vis-à-vis the penal law.[54] Unlike penal law however, certain

segments of the civil law, particularly family law, marriage, inheritance, and laws that

regulated the domestic realm, of which slaves and slavery were part, remained under the

jurisdiction of Şer'i law until much later, although not without a constant threat of being

taken over by the Ministry of Justice. This was especially true after the 1908 revolution

and its promises of freedom, equality and justice for all citizens, a present danger, from

the viewpoint of the Şer'i law, that slavery too would fall outside of its jurisdiction.[55]

The first wholesale manumission of slaves in the Ottoman Empire took place in

1909, about three decades after Midhat Pasha's original suggestion. Overall, in the

months that followed the counter-revolution and the deposition of Abdülhamid, over two

hundred enslaved women were reportedly manumitted, 44 of whom were found to have

no families or relatives. The manumission process applied only to the enslaved servants

in Yıldız Palace, and was more a product of the unusual circumstances in which

Abdülhamid II was deposed and his harem dissolved than a specifically aimed or planned

emancipatory effort.[56] Throughout the disturbances during the counter-revolution, which

---

[54] Gabriel Baer, "The Transition from Traditional to Western Criminal Law in Turkey and Egypt," Studia Islamica, No. 45 (1977), 140.

[55] There were numerous debates in the Ottoman Parliament on the ambiguity of Şer'i law, particulary its codified form, Mecelle. See for instance MMZC, 11 Şubat 1324 (24 February 1909), 35, in which a group of 90 deputies undersigned a proposal to pen a comprehensive law, and use jurisprudence only for religious matters.

[56] Erdem, Slavery in the Ottoman Empire, 149.

took place between April 13th–24th, 1909, the inmates of Abdülhamid II's harem, according to the witnesses, were left to their own devices, with minimum access even to food and water and virtually no connection to the outside world.[57] Once the clashes between the groups supporting Abdülhamid II and the army ceased and the deposition of the Sultan was resolved in Parliament, the inmates of the palace had to face the police, the soldiers, the officials of the municipal government, and even a group of deputies from the Parliament, who collectively oversaw the dissolution process.[58] Associated with the old order, the enslaved women were handled less than gently, and the process of the dissolution of the palace property was, according to a firsthand witness to the events, nothing short of an act of looting.[59] Following days of thorough inspection to ensure that no valuable items (whether personal belongings or not) left the premises, the enslaved women were transferred to Tokapı Palace to be eventually manumitted. The office of *Şeyhülislam* (the chief religious official in the Ottoman Empire who also oversaw the religious courts) was asked to start the *Şer'i* procedure on the matter at once and thereby was named the highest authority on the matter. The slaves were to be delivered to their families (some of whom had been waiting outside Yıldız Palace for several weeks) but only after a proper decision, in accordance with *Şer'i* provisions, was made.[60] A brief note sent by the Ministry of Interior to the office of the Grand Vizier shortly after also emphasized the necessity of setting up a commission in order to handle the manumission

---

[57] Leyla Açba, *Bir Çerkes Prensesinin Harem Hatıraları*, Haz. Harun Açba (Istanbul: L&M Yayınları, 2004), 41.

[58] MMZC, 18 Nisan 1325 (1 May 1909), 139–41; 19 Nisan 1325 (2 May 1909), 148.

[59] Açba, *Bir Çerkes Prensesinin Harem Hatıraları*, 44.

[60] BOA, BEO 3546/265908, 1327.R.21 (12 May 1909).

process for the enslaved women. This commission, which was to be composed of representatives from the municipal government, the Ministry of Police and the Privy Purse was expected to accelerate the process and deliver the women back to their families as quickly as possible, but again, not before ensuring the *Şer'i* aspects of the procedure were properly carried out and completed.[61] In that sense, the revolutionaries who carried out both the constitutional revolution of 1908 and the suppression of the counter-revolution in 1909 and headed the government were not untouched by what the historian William Gervase Clarence-Smith calls "Ottoman conservatism."[62] They achieved their aim, "in a breach of the tradition" as Hakan Erdem puts it, not to keep the palace slaves enslaved any longer, but only in as much as it was allowed by the *Şer'i* interpretation on the matter, a condition that they would amend, only partially, in October 1909.[63] As Erdem points out, the revolutionary government also had to conform to the boundaries of the *Şer'i* law and insure that the "recognition of the legal status of slavery meant that there could be no wholesale abolition," but only cases to be individually decided by the *Şer'i* courts.[64]

Nourished by this ambiguous environment, claims to freedom and justice, which had already begun earlier, abounded. A Circassian man named Musa, who had been

---

[61] BOA, ZB 603/13, 1325.May.14 (27 Ma7 1909); DH.MKT 2823/66, 1327.Ca.4 (24 May 1909); ZB 377/4, 1325.May.16 (29 May 1909); ŞD 2786/29, 1327.N.14 (29 September 1909). In various other correspondences between different government institutions, this particular point is reiterated several other times.

[62] William Gervase Clarence-Smith, *Islam and the Abolition of Slavery* (Oxford: Oxford University Press, 2006), 140–41. On a different note, Michelle Campos states that the Ottoman revolution was a "deeply religious" one. See Campos, *Ottoman Brothers*, 49.

[63] Erdem, *Slavery in the Ottoman Empire*, 148.

[64] Ibid., 151.

forced by an imperial decree to hand over his daughter and niece to a palace officer four years prior, demanded the release of the two young women immediately, with the conviction that it was now the "age of freedom," although his relentless efforts for an entire month produced no results.[65] Among the same group was Kerim, who came to Istanbul and had been waiting outside the Yıldız Palace for fifteen days, to "rescue" his niece (who, save for him, had no other male relatives) and asked that she be set free promptly, "in the name of justice."[66] In a telegram message sent directly to the new sultan, three Circassian men demanded, on behalf of all "Circassians present in front of Yıldız Palace" that their daughters be freed immediately, a demand they made in the name of God and his prophet this time, indicating perhaps that they recognized the process of manumission still to be essentially a religious one.[67]

The mass manumission also set the example for other slaves from outside the place, one of whom demanded his freedom with the conviction that if the Ottoman state could manumit six hundred female slaves of the palace, it could easily undo his unlawful enslavement, as well.[68] In a petition sent to the Ministry of Interior dated January, 1909, a group of five Circassian slaves demanded their release from bondage, basing their claim on the "sun of freedom which bestowed emancipation on every individual who has ever settled in the imperial domains."[69] In another instance, Razdil Kalfa, a manumitted Circassian slave (whose name and title indicated her previous position as an enslaved

[65] BOA, BEO 3546/265908, 1327.R.21 (12 May 1909).

[66] Ibid.

[67] Ibid.

[68] BOA, DH.MKT 2891/97, 1327.B.17 (4 August 1909).

[69] BOA, DH.MKT 2723/41, 1327.M.7 (29 January 1909).

servant of the imperial harem) petitioned the Ministry of Interior Affairs in July, 1909 on

behalf of her enslaved family, with a clearly stated belief that "under the aegis of the

blessed constitution" any occurrence of slavery was simply not possible any longer.[70] In a

telegram message sent to the office of *Şeyhülislam*, also in July 1909, a male Circassian

slave named Ibrahim (on behalf of himself and other slaves in his district) demanded that,

at a time when everyone was celebrating together with zeal and joyfulness, "without

distinguishing one from another by race or religion," it was people's representatives' duty

in the Parliament, to put an end to trade in people.[71]

For the slave owners on the other hand, the "sun of freedom" looked different.

Objecting to the Ministry of Justice's announcement of a general ban several months

earlier, some articulated that such a move on the ministry's side not only meant the

approval of a wrongful interpretation of the meaning of freedom, but also violated public

law provisioned by the constitution, infringed on their personal rights and abrogated the

religious *Şer'i* law that sanctioned those rights. After all, their rights to their slaves' sale,

purchase, labor (*istihdam*), and sexual services (*istifraş*) were legitimate, in accordance

with *Şer'i* law. The constitution, which guaranteed both the right to life and property, had

to protect these rights as well for it to be legitimate. Moreover, there was no definitive

clause in the constitution that would banish slavery. So, if disobedient behavior did occur

among the slaves against their owners, it was not because of the constitution itself but

rather due to misinterpretations (consciously or otherwise) of the law. In a word-for-word

opposite of the Ministry of Justice's anti-slavery argument, they claimed that these rights

---

[70] BOA, DH.MKT 2891/97, 1327.B.17 (4 August 1909).

[71] Ibid.

had been passed down from their ancestors and were firmly established by numerous *āyāt* (verses of the Quran) and *hadith* (deeds and sayings of the prophet Muhammad). If such lawful property cannot even be litigated or claimed at the court, they asked, what is the use of legal justice or the *Şer'i* provisions?[72] Fatma Leman's mistress, Hatice Berriye, expressed her ownership rights over her fugitive slave in similar terms. For Hatice Berriye, her ownership of the slave was a *Şer'i* principle that could not be abrogated. It was the police officers' (who, Hatice Berriye asserted, "acted in the name of freedom") incompetence, not the mutability of *Şer'i* law, which caused her to lose a slave and go back home empty-handed.[73] Moreover, as a group of Circassian chiefs articulated it, the slaves' unruly behavior, supported and often times outright provoked by such government officials as the Kayseri district governor, or groups like the Armenian Revolutionary Federation (referred to as *Taşnaksutyun*) was a direct intervention to the internal policies of the empire.[74] Hence, it was a duty of grave importance for the government to punish disobedient slaves and stop those whose motive was to harm the Islamic community (*ehl-i Islam*).[75] In sum, slaves, slave owners, and the Ottoman state used in their claims the very same language of freedom, equality, and justice, but they attributed different meanings to the words that this language embraced. These different interpretations helped sharpen both the definition of Circassianness and the content of

---

[72] For examples of petitions by slave owners see BOA, ŞD 2786/29, 1327.N.14 (29 September 1909), pages 3, 13, 16, 30/1 and 34; BEO 3565/267343, 1327.Ca.14 (3 June 1909); BEO 3839/287906, 1328.Z.27 (30 December 1910).

[73] BOA, DH.EUM.THR 32/34, 1328.R.26 (7 May 1910).

[74] BOA, BEO 3565/267343, 1327.Ca.14 (3 June 1909); ŞD 2786/29, 1327.N.14 (29 September 1909), page 13.

[75] BOA, BEO 3565/267343, 1327.Ca.14 (3 June 1909).

Circassians' claims to freedom, equality and justice, now strategically woven together with ethnic-national ones, as my last sections shows.

"The Pitiable Daughters of the Pitiable Caucasus Lands"

The few years that followed the 1908 revolution in the Ottoman Empire brought about a social upheaval in which discourses of citizenship were not only used by those who claimed rights and liberties in the new political order but mobilized "to enact hierarchies, to institute registers of difference along lines of gender and race, ethnicity, or marital status."[76] "The promise of emancipation was," Pamela Scully et al. have argued, "to some extent, a gendered one: that is, men were promised the entitlement of masculinity, of being head of household," and women, on the other hand, "were liberated into dependence," most notably through marriage.[77] Marriage has always been a common promise to emancipation for female slaves in the Ottoman Empire also, particularly for palace slaves. A police interrogation with a slave dealer indicates that the term of service of an enslaved young girl, which ideally ended with marrying her off (a process known as *çırağ/çırak çıkmak*) by the owner, was part of the bargain that took place in the slave procurement or recruitment process. When the above-mentioned dealer tried to convince a young girl's parents to hand their daughter over to her, she described the whole process as an 8-year-long contract term, after which their daughter would be married off to "a *kaymakam* or a *miralay*" (colonel or a lieutenant) and the parents themselves in the

---

[76] Kathleen Canning, Sonya O. Rose (editors), *Gender, Citizenship and Subjectivities* (Oxford: Blackwell Publishing, 2002), 7.

[77] Scully et al., *Gender and Slave Emancipation in the Atlantic World*, 17.

179

meanwhile would get rid of their poverty and misery.[78] Marrying off slaves, *çırağ*
çıkarmak, was one of the few details, along with death and salary arrangements, deemed
important to be marked on the harem registers.[79] The importance attached to
çırağlık/çıraklık (that is, the status of being married off, apprenticeship) was primarily
due, as explored previously in chapter three, to the fact that it almost bore the same
significance of the marriage of a relative, especially in forming ties between persons or
households. For one, in her memoirs, Halide Edip Adıvar used the term *çıraklı* more than
once, to refer to former slaves that came out of specific households.[80] *Çırağ/çırak*
çıkarmak did not necessarily involve marriage, as veteran *cariyes* also could be sent to
live outside the palace, either in someone else's household or in a new one set up by the
owners, but the term and the practice itself applied, more often than not, to younger
slaves completing their term of service and being emancipated, cementing bonds among
households, or extending the influence of a household through a larger network, along the
way. With the reinstitution of the constitutional regime and the coming of "freedom"
however, the ties between slavery, marriage, *çırağlık/çıraklık*, freedom, and emancipation
began assuming a different character and a new level of significance.

The period that spanned roughly from 1908 until the onset, in 1912, of a series of
wars that resulted in the collapse of the empire, constituted a moment when the "dynastic
legitimacy and state sovereignty within clearly defined borders" was abruptly shifting
towards what Eric D. Weitz called the Paris system, a move from traditional diplomacy

---

[78] BOA, Y.PRK.BŞK 12/89, 1305.B.14 (27 March 1888).

[79] For an example, see BOA, Y.EE.d 891. The date is not given but the register is presumably
from early twentieth century.

[80] Halide Edip Adıvar, *Mor Salkımlı Ev* (Istanbul: Can Yayınları, 2014). See pages 25, 48, 55.

"to the handling of entire population groups categorized by ethnicity, nationality, or race, or some combination thereof."[81] Despite the ongoing debates on the "ominous trade in Circassian girls" and its dangers of undermining the constitutional order, or contemporaries' assertions that the elite households in Istanbul were filled with slaves, slavery did not become central to the debates on freedom, equality, constitution or citizenship.[82] The more immediate and pressing concerns were related, at least at the discursive level, almost always to "the awakening of national sentiments" of "the Circassian, the Arab, the Kurd, the Greek, the Armenian."[83] In all slaves' claims to freedom and justice there was an effort to delineate Ottoman citizenship as civic citizenship in terms of rights and liberties, which worked against a simultaneous fear that such claims would eventually lead to religious or ethnic-based ones. It was on this fractured ground also that the defenders of slavery, mainly slave-holding Muslim elites, strategically conflated slaves' claims to freedom and equality with an attack on Islamic order itself. For their turn, opponents of slavery did not shun strategic usage of ethnic-national designations either, occasionally turning slaves' claims to freedom, justice and equality into a corporate claim to Circassian emancipation. This is not to say that it was the abolitionists, Circassian intellectuals, or slaves themselves who invented this particular ethnic designation. On the contrary, as the earlier chapters tried to demonstrate, Circassianness as a term that denoted a variety of Caucasian ethno-linguistic groups was

---

[81] Eric D. Weitz, "From the Vienna to the Paris System: International Politics and the Entangled Histories of Human Rights, Forced Deportations, and Civilizing Missions," *The American Historical Review*, vol.113, no.5 (December 2008), 1314.

[82] BOA, DH.EUM.THR 32/34, 1328.R.26 (7 May 1910).

[83] Hasan Amca, *Doğmayan Hürriyet* (Istanbul, Akım Yayınları, 1958), 12.

a mere construction, at times even used to legitimize destitute people's entry to slavery. Nevertheless, despite its fictive character, it was a category used to determine enslavability. In fact, a report issued by the Council of State (*Şura-yı Devlet*) in 1912 stated that in the parlance of *Şer'i* law, there was no such thing as a non-Circassian slave, since all other ethnic groups were considered inalienable, hence indicating that, in view of slavery, Circassianness was not only an existing category but also an exclusive one.[84] What happened in the aftermath of the revolution, through the abolitionists' or Circassian intellectuals' claims was that the existing and exclusive category of Circassianness became attached to an ethnic-national identity and pride, which described itself, among other things, through the chastity of its women.

"A great number of young girls," an article that appeared in the women's magazine *Kadın* (Woman) in early 1909 stated, "who are the hearts of the motherland, hope of the society, and sisters of free and thinking humanity: they are enslaved and helpless."[85]

> These are so neglected and thought unworthy of attention and investigation
> ... Ah my poor sisters, who have neither a mother nor a family, who have no
> one! What a deep animosity, resentment and anger I feel towards those of
> your fellow sisters, who do not bother to consider, even for a fraction of a
> moment, to defend, take back and grant you your civil/personal freedom.
> Here I am, having been waiting and aching, becoming more and more grief
> stricken every day in the past six months [...] Recently, when the Ministry
> of Justice [whose name and the vastness of its meaning, as well as the

---

[84] BOA, ŞD 3104/42, 1330.B.19 (7 July 1912), page 6.

[85] "Esaret Var!!! Halayıklara Dair," *Kadın*, no.15, 19 Kanunusani 1324, 2–4. Published in Salonica, the revolution's de facto center, *Kadın* was an important forum in which the revolutionaries debated women's issues at length.

182

expansiveness of the area of its activities, admittedly caused perplexity for the author] announced through a circular, the abolition of trade in slaves, I gave much thought about those who remained as slaves, whether or not they too deserved a decision in favor of freedom, whether undoing their fetters would suit the time and place we are living in [...] How could I not think about it, how could I not make a legal comparison? We, thirty million Ottomans acting as one, have been thinking, trying to procure and recover one and only one thing: with all its meanings, inclusiveness and comprehension: Freedom![86]

It was a grave contradiction, for the author of the article too, to talk about freedom, when the number of enslaved women (made into "cold and lifeless decorations of the palaces" as the article described them) exceeded thousands. That these enslaved women were exploited as mere ornaments was unacceptable to the consciousness of the free Ottomans, for they were chaste and virtuous Circassian orphans, who deserved, as much as anyone else in the empire, to become free and happy mothers whose sons "would shine like the sun in the Ottoman cities, and like clusters of stars in its periphery."[87]

> Not thousands but even hundred sons... Do you not know that Ottomans unleashed utmost fear and terror in Rumelia by no more than forty men? Perhaps your elders would remember, in grief-stricken Caucasus lands, when our forefathers raided over the peaks and hills like thunder unto the enemy their numbers did not count that many either. [...]
>
> Leave slavery aside; in those pompous rooms you are confined and dragged along, what do they teach you on humanity? Instead of womanly honor and personal dignity, [they teach you] slavery and servility [...] In a great nation

---

[86] Ibid., 2.

[87] Ibid., 3.

183

[like ours], who is free and esteems freedom above life, how can we allow thousands of individuals, especially women to be enslaved and confined?

The "pitiable daughters of the pitiable Caucasus lands" had the right to claim their freedom too, and the ongoing formulations would have to take shape everywhere: the Ottoman parliament, the public, as well as the recently founded *Çerkes İttihad ve Teavün Cemiyeti* (Circassian Unity and Mutual Aid Society),[88] the latter already having been a claimant in numerous petitions and other correspondences made with the Ottoman government on behalf of Circassian slaves.

Hakan Erdem has argued that, besides the old motive of the wholesale manumission of the palace slaves and setting an example for the remainder of the society, the constitutional regime also had the aim of winning the "goodwill of the Circassians at least some of whom had come to loathe the employment of their kin as slaves in the increasingly Western-oriented atmosphere of the early twentieth century."[89] Even when Deli Fuat Pasha, a prominent Circassian statesman (and president of the above mentioned Circassian Mutual Aid Society) had reservations on the issue of abolition "on the ground that the Circassian girls would be worse off," Erdem has argued, other Circassian men of influence mostly asserted that "this was a matter of national pride and, as such, should be pushed ahead."[90] Mehmed Fetgeri Şuenu, a Circassian intellectual and the co-founder of the Circassian Mutual Aid Society asserted that Circassians were a people with a glorious

---

[88] Ibid., 4.

[89] Erdem, *Slavery in the Ottoman Empire*, 149–50.

[90] Ibid., 148.

184

past, weakened over time by a twist of fate and since then they have come to be known as the "wretched people, dealers in young girls, who go as far as bringing up their own daughters to quench the lustful desires of lascivious masters"[91]:

> Africa's negroes, America's 'peaux-rouges' ['redskins'], Caucasus's miserable girls; they were all subjected, from time to time, to this greedy madness of humanity... By means of the civil law promulgated by the West[ern states] 'peaux-rouges' obtained—even though partial—their freedom; those negro *lala*s [high-ranking manservants of the palace] and eunuchs from the Sudan and Abyssinia who were deprived of their manhood for this contemptible grandeur... Even they rid themselves off of slavery. But the misfortunate children of the Caucasus still carry the burden of this shameful trade [...] The same way the lazy majesty of the East had objected to abolition of black slaves when it became obvious that he would lose the means to his grandeur, he is now resisting the loss of his white slaves from the Caucasus... Because they are his means to satisfy his despicable lust.[92]

Circassian intellectuals made slavery, particularly women's slavery, their focus, as they tried to formulate ways of doing away with what they called the "blemish" on the Circassian "nation," prevent the "gates of hate and hostility" ever to open and cause strife between the Turks and the Circassians, and along the way, rethink, reformulate, and reconcile ways of being Ottoman and Circassian at once.[93] For some, this issue also had a personal dimension. Mehmet Fetgeri Şuenu, for example, noted the memory of his mother's pain and misery when his sister was taken away to become an enslaved palace

---

[91] Mehmed Fetgeri Şuenu, *Osmanlı Alem-i İçtimaisinde Çerkes Kadınları* (Istanbul: Zarafet Matbaası, 1330/1914), 8, 11–12, 16.

[92] Ibid., 27.

[93] Ibid., 11.

servant. In Şuenu's highly romantic depiction, his mother exclaimed: "there, your sister, in that dungeon called the palace, weeping and moaning, in front of a stranger's hearth," and supposedly urged Şuenu to work hard to put an end to this matter in which "the [Circassian] 'nation's life and womanhood was subjected to satisfy the desires of lustful and immoral people."

At the time Mehmed Fetgeri Şuenu wrote his book on Circassian women, the trade in Circassian slaves ("theft and sale of the Circassian girls and presenting them [as gifts] to others" as Şuenu described it) still continued in an unofficial, semi-secretive way. Mingled with these claims to national honor, however, there was again the pronounced complexity of the ongoing slave trade with the "July 10 Constitution" (as Şuenu called the 1908 revolution) and the European Civil Law that went into effect before it.[94] At a time when even animal rights were protected, Şuenu argued, the current status of Circassian slaves, by law, was compliant neither with "sublimely distinctive religion of Islam" nor the spirit of the Constitution.[95] This pronounced contradiction, backed up by claims to national honor and occasionally by more encompassing debates on class,[96] shaped and determined the ways in which the Circassian intellectuals and the Circassian Society they founded constructed their claims to freedom, justice, equality and citizenship on behalf of Circassian slaves.

---

[94] Ibid., 35.

[95] BOA, BEO, 3710/278209, 1328.S.17 (28 February 1910).

[96] See article titled "Esir Ticareti" in *Sada-i Millet*, 8 Mart 1326 (21 March 1910), for a discussion on the connections between poverty and the perpetuation of slave trade in Ottoman Anatolia.

One among many similar organizations that emerged in the immediate aftermath of the revolution, the Circassian Mutual Aid Society was founded in early November 1908 and served as a hub, providing support and information to both slaves and slave families on legal procedures, composing and following up on petitions and other official correspondence as well as discussing the matter publicly, especially after the Society's journal *Gûâze*, began publishing in April 1911.[97] With a clear aim to navigate the bifurcated legal system and efforts to reconcile slaves' and slave owners' demands, who at times inextricably referred to the same article in the constitution for their respective rights and claims,[98] they repeatedly stressed the indispensability of government action on the matter and demanded, through a number of petitions and other official correspondence that slavery be abolished and prohibited by law once and for all.[99]

While the Circassian Society's involvement and efforts in resolving the issue of slavery started early on, a clear formulation of their claims and demands began taking shape only later. In a tangible manner, the Society formulated its demands in a petition that it sent to the *Ayan Meclisi* in February 1910. These demands were elucidated in a list of six items, the first of which, in an inclusive way, demanded from the Ottoman administration that it announce once and for all, the practice of slavery was abolished and prohibited by law. Reviving an earlier debate, the society also suggested the implementation and encouragement of *mükatebe* (self-purchase) as a means to abolition.

---

[97] For a detailed account on the Circassian Mutual Aid Society, see Elmas Zeynep Aksoy Arslan, "Circassian Organizations in the Ottoman Empire (1908–1923)," M.A. Thesis, Boğaziçi University, 2008.

[98] BOA, ŞD 2786/29, 1327.N.14 (29 September 1909), page 22.

[99] BOA, BEO 3710/278209, 1328.S.17 (28 February 1910).

187

Yet, since the great majority of these enslaved men and women were devoid of any personal wealth, it insisted that the state should determine a set amount and consider lending money to the slaves, to facilitate their emancipation, cutting their ties to their owners at once.[100]

In the following months, the society made several similar attempts, some of which were discussed in the journal *Ğûâze*. In fact, the article "Against Slavery" in the first issue of the journal was rather a summary of the society's efforts in the preceding months. Providing an overview of the events in the aftermath of the revolution, the article stated that, following the reinstatement of the constitution and the rights and liberties of the Ottoman public were restored, there emerged two separate points of view among Circassian intellectuals. First of these was a belief that these right and liberties would extend to Circassian slaves, abolishing slavery among their ranks unconditionally. The second view argued that the constitution could be no more than a motive to abolish Circassian slavery, which was sustained by the slave classes within Circassian community and the *Şer'i* law that sanctioned it. As the current situation confirmed, the Society argued, without resolving this complex system of slavery, which exploited two distinct systems at once, slavery could not be abolished in the Ottoman domains.

The society submitted its first petition both to the government and the Parliament, requesting the method of self-purchase to be promoted by the Ottoman state and that the self-purchase amount be paid by the state treasury, demanding a corresponding bill that would also banish the sale and purchase of individuals, to prevent unlawful enslavement

---

[100] Ibid.

of, often too vulnerable, manumitted slaves.[101] These demands were reiterated by the society numerous times in the years that followed the revolution, only to be disregarded by the government. Occasional responses from the office of the Şeyhülislam, which, with opaque language, repeated that the basic principle in the lands of Islam was not slavery but freedom, yet maintained that the approval of enslavement by Şer'i law could still apply, if special [religious, yet undisclosed] conditions were met by the owners.[102] Not content with what they called the "dubious results" of their attempts, the Society "regrettably confessed" that they were not sure if their voice was even heard by the Ottoman government. "Not only are we not able to have our voice heard" the article further asserted "but we are not even able to tell from our correspondences, nor from the reports drawn up by different state institutions, nor the imperial decree or the bill, in what mind the government is, in regards to abolishing slavery, hence we are forced to halt in utter astonishment in our expectations of action against it."[103]

That slavery was "prohibited by law and the prohibition was confirmed by the constitution," as the bill stated, was already known to everyone, the article maintained, asking "who would argue that the sanction of enslavement is not subject to special conditions and regulations?" For the society, the Ottoman state agreed to abolish Circassian slavery, but this was so only in appearance. Had this been not the case, why

---

[101] "Ayan ve Mebusan-ı Kirama 1: Kölelik Aleyhinde," *Gûâze*, sene 1, numara 1, 21 Mart 1327 (2 April 1911), 2.

[102] Ibid. The date for the corresponding imperial decree is given as 15 Şevval 1327 (30 October 1909). Also see Düstur, Tertib II, Cilt 1, 831–32; Erdem, *Slavery in the Ottoman Empire and its Demise*, 150–51.

[103] "Ayan ve Mebusan-ı Kirama 1: Kölelik Aleyhinde," *Gûâze*, 2.

would they weaken the very law they promulgated, by adding a *Şer'i* clause confirming

the owners' right to bring legal charges against suspected slaves.[104]

> While in a free country, bringing legal charges against the members of a free
> people, whose freedom has been proven, could be assumed to imply and result in
> freedom, the society expected the Ottoman state to have more lucidity and
> precision on such crucial matters as personal rights and liberties.

> What we demanded [from the Ottoman state] was a clarification of the
> procedures, of what comes after a so and so court decision. Let's say the court
> came to a decision in favor of freedom... Then, what comes next, what should be
> done, we wonder. The government did not provide the method or points [of
> clarification] that we demanded. Let's assume that in Aziziye the şeri' court
> upheld the sanction on someone's slave status, would that person maintain his or
> her status as slave? That is, would he or she remain as a slave or not? We have
> been trying to secure [the conditions] that they would not remain as such.[105]

Baffled but unyielding, the society took up the issue of slavery once again in the

second issue of *Ğûâze*, this time pointing at a different aspect of it. A letter received from

above mentioned Aziziye district (one of the largest Circassian settlements in the

country) of Sivas province, written by a certain Dumanişzade Mahmud, informed the

society about the crisis escalating in the region and warned about the danger of a possible

mutiny among the slaves against their masters.[106] In fact such news of an anticipated

mutiny was already in circulation much earlier. In a note sent from the Ottoman

parliament to the Ministry of Interior on 25 Kanunusani 1324 (7 February 1909), several

---

[104] Ibid.

[105] Ibid., 3.

[106] "2: Kölelik Aleyhinde," *Ğûâze*, sene 1, numara 2, 28 Mart 1327 (10 April 1911), 6.

Circassian slave owners, certain Bekir and Mehmed Arif and their six colleagues, were said to have sent a telegram to the Parliament to warn about an unrest, which might be caused by the slaves. The telegram (a copy of which was attached to the correspondence) stated that even though their ownership of their slaves and *cariyes* were legitimated firmly and indisputably by various verses from the Koran, prophet's deeds, as well as a *fetva* given by the office of the *Şeyhülislam* and an imperial decree, the slaves, who were reportedly encouraged by a recent declaration by the Ministry of Justice in regards to a ban on slave trade, began claiming their freedom. The telegram requested that it be known by the Ottoman parliament, that these slaves were "capable of villainy" and in complete disobedience, they already began obtaining arms. Hence, the article concluded, it was them who should be held responsible for any bloodshed that might occur.[107] Written almost about two years later, the article in *Ĝûâze* talked about the same danger, yet it held the Ottoman government responsible for it, for not taking necessary precautions on the matter, not acting in both party's interest and thus causing them (slaves and their owners) to form two opposing groups, and not to make a legal arrangement to mitigate the increasing tension, which the article maintained, could be done only by the government.[108]

The Society continued with its claims and abolitionary efforts throughout the subsequent year, most of which continued to be discussed in *Ĝûâze*. An article that appeared several issues later, it was noted that the society submitted another petition, yet

---

[107] BOA, DH.MKT 2739/67, 1327.M.25 (16 February 1909).

[108] "2: Kölelik Aleyhinde," *Ĝûâze*, 6.

failed to obtain any tangible results.[109] The Parliament had reportedly decided that the slaves in the Aziziye and Canik districts were to be settled outside their masters' estates, with the financial support from the Ottoman state,[110] a development the society found insufficient, as they believed the core of the problem laid elsewhere. Several weeks later, the journal published an article dispatched from Aziziye, which highlighted the general negligence of the press (with the exception of *Ğûâze*) about the issue of slavery, despite the fact that the crisis was going through a critical phase at the moment, in which new occurrences of violence were taking place. In the preceding weeks, as a consequence of a rather perplexing measure taken by the Ottoman state (namely conscription from among the enslaved), reportedly a fight broke out between a group of slaves and their owners, leaving one slave dead and six others injured.[111] Under these circumstances, the article argued, the slackness of the press, which ought to be the "interpreter of the thoughts and opinions of the peoples, defender of the rights, facts, and truths" was inexplicable, in the face of slavery, which was a threat to personal freedom and even a danger for the Constitution.[112]

Contrary to what the Society has been pushing for until then, however, the article argued that among Circassians, there were no legitimate (*meşru'*) slaves, *'abd*, that complied with the status of slavery as delineated by *Şer'i* law. After all, the practice of slavery and methods of enslavement among Circassians were historical developments

---

[109] "4: Kölelik Aleyhinde," *Ğûâze*, sene 1, numara 7, 5 Mayıs 1327 (10 April 1911), 1–2.

[110] For the 1407 slaves living in Aziziye, the parliament consented to provide 911,800 piasters for their housing and immediate needs. The number of slaves settle in Canik is not given in the article, the total amount provided is 570,000 piasters.

[111] Untitled, *Ğûâze*, sene 1, numara 9, 19 Mayıs 1327 (1 Haziran 1911), 5.

[112] Ibid.

192

different than what *Şer'i* law recognized, and largely endemic to the Caucasus.[113] Thus,

setting the *Şer'i* law as the barrier to abolition and causing this tension between the slaves

and their owners, the Ottoman state was responsible for the escalation of crisis.

Moreover, the "illustrious" *Şer'i* law was discredited by such actions as well. "What

precautions the government is considering to take against these saddening events, we do

not know," the article concluded, "what is certain is that the Ottoman government is not

taking the matter seriously, giving the due importance that it deserves [...] if a solution is

delayed any further, regrettable events are likely to reoccur." From the viewpoint of the

society, the Ottoman government acted only on paper, as if it was merely expressing a

wish.[114] A year later in 1912, the government finally consented to pass a bill in regards to

self-purchase, yet declined to pay the purchase amount from the state treasury.[115]

Consequently, the following year, an official communiqué written by the Ministry of

Interior proposed that the Bank of Agriculture provide the credit for slaves for their self-

purchase (the amount to be determined by the Ottoman government), on 10–15 year

terms, which turned abolition's on-paper existence, after almost a four-year struggle on

the slaves' side, to a practical reality, although freedom, equality, and justice presumably

came to the slaves in the form of a bank loan and debt.[116]

---

[113] Ibid.

[114] Ibid.

[115] Untitled, *Gûâze*, sene 1, no.31, 9 Şubat 1327 (22 February 1912), 2.

[116] BOA, DH.HMŞ 10/62, 1331.3.24 (6 April 1915); DH.I.UM E-84/15, 1336.Z.25 (1 October 1918).

Conclusion

That the issue of abolition met such setbacks in the Ottoman Empire was due to several different factors that comprised, as discussed above, contradictory meanings attributed to the words freedom, equality, and justice, the complexities of the bifurcated legal system, as well as the new regime's corporate notion of citizenship. However, neither the new government's particular interpretation of freedom and equality, nor its unwilling, or at best deliberative stance against abrogating *Şer'i* law, help to explain the general negligence of the deputies in the Parliament when debating the issues of slavery and freedom. To go back to the above-mentioned debate that took place in the Ottoman parliament in June 1909, when Yorgo Boşo Efendi suggested with a formal proposal that the Ottoman constitution, like its European equivalents, should include an item that would ban the sale and purchase of individuals, Seyyit Bey found it improper and unnecessary on the basis that *Mecelle* already prohibited the sale of persons, making it illicit and unlawful.[117] Likewise, Mehmet Tevfik Efendi from Kengırı, Salim Efendi from Konya, also in support of Seyyit Bey, argued that all Ottomans were already in full possession of their freedom, and any violation to that effect was punishable by law, as indicated in *Mecelle*.[118] For Manastır, Ankara, and Istanbul deputies Trayan Nali, Mahir Sait, and Kozmidi Efendis, however, this was an issue of grave importance, to be regulated directly by the constitution itself, rather than by penal or ordinary law, for even though such clauses had existed in *Mecelle* for a long time, the sale and purchase of slaves, "such as Circassian girls," Trayan Nali Efendi specified, continued in the

---

[117] MMZC, 27 Mayıs 1325 (9 Haziran 1909), 222–224.
[118] Ibid.

mansions of the ministers as well as the palace, all this time. Thus, Kozmidi Efendi argued, it was necessary to tie this to a more encompassing law, which would apply even to the Sultan himself. In the end, Yorgo Boşo Efendi's proposal met more objection than support and was eventually rejected by the majority of the parliamentarians, most of whom believed that slavery no longer existed in the Ottoman Empire, and if did, it was merely due to a violation of the penal and *Şer'i* law. Even when Kigem, Muradyan Hamparsum and Vartkes Efendis tried to demonstrate that there were occurrences of sale and purchase of Armenian peasants in the Eastern Provinces, they were rebuked on the basis that such practices remained in the old regime, and did not exist in the age of freedom and constitution.[119]

Scholars of constitutionalism have argued in the case of the United States that those who said they were acting in the name of all Americans "formally consulted propertyless white men only rarely and consulted neither black men nor any women, whatever their race or class."[120] In the Ottoman Empire too, the emancipation of the "subordinate elements of [Ottoman] society," was deemed "unnatural," and to be "upsetting the moral order" of the society.[121] Hence, the emancipation efforts after the revolution produced two different layers of results: in the first layer were the truly vulnerable women, who lacked financial means, or family and kin support like Fatma Leman. She did not claim her Circassianness or seek help from the Circassian Society,

---

[119] Ibid.

[120] Linda Kerber, "The Paradox of Women's Citizenship in the Early Republic: The Case of *Martin vs. Massachusetts,* 1805" *American Historical Review,* vol.97, no.2 (Apr.,1992), 350.

[121] Keith David Watenpaugh, "The League of Nations' Rescue of Armenian Genocide Survivors and the Making of Modern Humanitarianism, 1920–1927," *American Historical Review,* Vol. 115, no. 5 (Dec., 2010), 1329.

and could still be sold as a concubine after the revolution. In the second layer were those who received recognition and support, and who had partial rights as "free and happy mothers" but in a loophole, insofar as they were Circassian women.

When Mehmet Fetgeri Şuenu reported about the persistence of sale and purchase of Circassian slaves in 1914, he attributed it to the rich men's, the elites' fancy of slave women, and their belief that they could not live without them.[122] "Just like the slavers of the old days" Şuenu asserted, "many a butcher and monster, who took up slaving as their profession, are still making profit out of it."[123] Merely a year later after Şuenu's assertion, following the Armenian genocide, there emerged a new source of poor, orphaned, alienable girls who were appropriated as slaves with ease. The movement for their rescue, according to Keith Watenpaugh, sheds light "on the degree to which Ottoman reform efforts of the previous century, which incorporated the extension of rights of equality and emancipation as part of a larger modernization schema, had taken root within Ottoman society and could withstand the multiple and existential crises and widespread social and economic dislocation of the war years."[124] What humanitarian efforts found in the post-1915 Ottoman Empire was not only the decades-long ethnic strife between the Turks, Kurds, Circassians, and Armenians that chronically surfaced with catastrophic consequences in 1895, later in 1909 and finally in 1915, nor the war. They also found a long-standing practice of slavery, perpetuated, in ways discussed above, by the duality of the legal system that regulated it; the laxness, negligence, or sometimes outright denial by

---

[122] Şuenu, *Osmanlı Alem-i İçtimaisinde Çerkes Kadınları*, 45.

[123] Ibid.

[124] Watenpaugh, "The League of Nations' Rescue of Armenian Genocide Survivors," 1322.

the constitutional regime in taking measures against it; and by the "magic but elusive"

nature of the word freedom.[125]

---

[125] Foner, *The Story of American Freedom*, xiv.

Chapter 5.
The Relics of an Unwanted Ottoman Past

The March 1924 issue of the journal *Resimli Ay*[1] came with what would have

been a scandalous headline a decade earlier. Hinting at a shift in the significance of the

imperial harem as a political institution, the article stated, quite bluntly, that the "imperial

harem had been a source of prostitution and disgrace, which hid thousands of enslaved

young women in its bosom." Corresponding with the abolition of the caliphate and the

exile of the Ottoman dynasty, the article drew parallels between the extravagant life led

by the Ottoman sultans, their families, and no less, their concubines on the one hand and

the poverty and misery of the Turkish peasants who had to pay for all of that

extravagance with their taxes on the other. "Until the people came to this final decision

[of exiling the Ottoman dynasty]" the article stated, "the palace housed 1500 *cariyes* and

150 eunuchs," all of whom were employed to sustain the decadent lifestyle of the royal

family. "Today's distresses and disasters" it further exclaimed, "are the fruits of

yesterday's excesses."[2] Described in the style of a fairy tale, these excesses included

items of clothing, jewelry, or food served on golden plates, as well as lavish orgies that

took place in lush palace gardens, "ornamented with jasmines, honeysuckles, and flowers

of every color." Appearing ambiguously both as subjects and objects of this

---

[1] *Resimli Ay Mecmuası*, Sayı:2, Cilt:1, Mart 1340 (March 1924). Edited by two of the most esteemed intellectuals of the early Republican Era, Zekeriya and Sabiha Sertel, *Resimli Ay* began publishing earlier in 1924, largely as an illustrated popular magazine and evolved into a significant left-wing literary journal within several years.

[2] Ibid., 20.

extravagance, enslaved concubines figured prominently in all these depictions. "In avenues that lay between flowerbeds," one description went, "the *cariyes* lined up, all naked, resembling white lilies" and continued, in a highly Orientalized tone as follows:

> Both [the princes and the *cariyes*] would then begin bustling and rushing about under the sweet and dreamy light emanating from the lanterns that hanged down from the green branches [...] Reared up with lust, the princes would race after the girls they sought after, with a burning desire to reach them, to clutch their arms around their slender waists, to push their lips against their burning lips. Finally, once they seized their prey, they would vanish into the dark corners of the garden, trampling the flowerbeds, knocking down silver trays left over from the feast [earlier in the evening].[3]

In addition to these lavish orgiastic ceremonies, there were what *Resimli Ay* called "pool orgies" in which the senior stewardesses of the palace would take a number of these young women to the pool and prepare them for the sultan, by stripping them naked, clothing them only with a piece of silk wrap. Then the sultan would come, place himself on his throne in the garden and entertain himself watching the girls bathe, who giggled with occasional coquettish screams.[4] This tradition too, the article noted, continued until the very last of the Ottoman sultans, who customarily gathered beautiful girls in their harems to "quench their lustful appetite, keeping over a thousand of them to this day"[5]

> Neither the court nor its disgraces have been fully erased yet. The dynasty is no more. The sultans, who blotted and stained our history with blood have now

---

[3] Ibid., 21.

[4] Ibid., 23.

[5] Ibid., 23.

become history themselves. However, they left behind a burdensome inheritance for the people: the palace and the palace inmates. The sultanate had been toppled over, but the palace remains. The sultans all passed on and away but the palace inmates stayed. [...] A palace in the republican order, how could such a contradiction be allowed?[6]

About a decade and a half earlier, following the constitutional revolution of 1908, the imperial harem began to be referred to as merely an outdated institution and its inmates as victims, but it was still dealt with as a legitimate institution. When the constitutional government tried to redefine its administrative and legal institutions in the aftermath of the revolution, especially following the dethronement of Abdülhamid II in 1909, it employed brutal means when handling the palace property and its harem inmates, particularly those in Yıldız Palace, but it did so strictly on the basis of politics, as it viewed both the institution and its inmates as political actors, associated with the old regime.[7] What was new with this new conception, which the *Resimli Ay* article exemplified, was not only that it implied those particular sorts of brutal means; violent storming of the palace premises by the republican army or the police, appropriation and confiscation of royal property "by the people and for the use of the people." It also pointed at an effort to disengage the palace in general and the imperial harems in particular, from the political milieu they had so long been a part of. An institution that had traditionally been a hub where long-lasting patronage relationships (with great

---

[6] Ibid., 24.

[7] See Leyla Açba, *Bir Çerkes Prensesinin Harem Hatıraları* (Istanbul: Timaş Yayınları, 2010), 208 or Şadiye Sultan binti Abdülhamid Han, *Hayatımın Acı ve Tatlı Günleri* (Istanbul: Bedir Yayınevi, 2000), 32–33 for two of harem inmates' accounts of Abdülhamid's dethronement.

political implications) were cemented[8] was now depicted as a setting for a *One Thousand and One Nights*-style fairy tale, in which women appeared only as highly sexualized objects; as "white lilies," "pleasure fairies," or "white winged angels" who flew here and there in the "heavenly garden" of the imperial harem, whose delicate and fragile bodies were no more than vulnerable targets to the sultans' lecherous advances, or the princes' sexual assaults.[9]

Irvin Cemil Schick argues that the use of sexual imagery, particularly of sexual violence, as a political metaphor, "performed double duty" and helped in reproducing gender roles.[10] This held for the Turkish Republic as well, where one of its leading intellectual journals highlighted sexuality and sexual excesses as the essence of the imperial order and its relics, such as palace slavery, to channel the public opinion of its readers in favor of the republican measures taken against the Ottoman dynasty. At the same time, this depiction also helped "objectifying women and portraying them as natural objects of appropriation and targets of violation," and for the case at hand, exploitation.[11] Bringing forth the sexual content effectively helped demonize an enemy, namely "an unwanted past," that was marked with, as Lerna Ekmekcioglu argued, "heterogeneity, outside intervention, and European chastisement of Ottoman Turks for Islamic

---

[8] Betül İpşirli Argıt, "Manumitted Female Slaves of the Ottoman Imperial Harem (*Sarayîs*) in Eighteenth-Century Istanbul," (Ph.D. dissertation, Boğaziçi University, 2009), 20–33.

[9] Resimli Ay Mecmuası, Sayı:2, Cilt:1, Mart 1340 (Mart 1924), 21.

[10] Irvin Cemil Schick, "Christian Maidens, Turkish Ravishers: The Sexualization of National Conflict in the Late Ottoman Period," in *Women in the Ottoman Balkans: Gender, Culture and History*, ed. Irvin Cemil Schick and Amila Buturovic (London: I.B. Tauris, 2007), 296.

[11] Ibid., 296.

backwardness, even barbarity."[12] *Resimli Ay* was surely aware that only a small number

of enslaved palace servants served, in their expression, to the "lecheries of the sultan and

his sons." The great many that constituted this "burdensome inheritance" were low-

ranking enslaved servants who were, as was partially explored in the previous chapter,

left to their own devices after the exile of the Ottoman family.[13] They were stripped of

what they deemed to be their personal property and faced poverty, survival marriages,

forced relocations that ended, in some cases, with suicide. Moreover, there were other

slaves in this inheritance too, manumitted before the inauguration of the republic, who

had been on the imperial payroll since then.[14] By the same token, there was the legal

status of slavery, as well as other legal "laxities," such as polygamy, that went with it.

The republican order had to come to terms with its own "twin relics," retrospectively

condemned as backwardness if not barbarism that came directly from its immediate

past.[15]

---

[12] Lerna Ekmekcioglu, "Republic of Paradox: The League of Nations Minority Protection Regime and the New Turkey's Step-Citizens," *International Journal of Middle East Studies*, vol. 46, no.4, Special Issue: World War I (November 2014), 660. Ekmekcioglu here draws parallels between the republican regime's policies towards the non-Muslim minorities and their measures against the Ottoman dynasty, arguing that the latter was easier to execute by simply exiling all members of the Ottoman family. As this chapter aims to demonstrate, getting rid of the "burdensome inheritance" of the *Ancien Régime* was not an easy process either and necessitated the deployment of similar narrative strategies that Ekmekcioglu mentions.

[13] See for instance Başbakanlık Republican Archives (BCA) 30.18.1.1 14.39.7, 132–23 (1925) for a note on 30 enslaved men and women expelled from the palace, now employed as servants in various institutions. Other contemporaries noted that many of the enslaved women both from the imperial harems and the households of other dynasty members were eventually sent to the Ottoman state almshouse, *Darülaceze*. In a later example, two eunuchs named Zülkefil and Said, expelled from the Yıldız Palace in 1909, had been reportedly living in a shanty house since then. "Yıldız Sarayından Kısıklıda gecekonduya," *Cumhuriyet*, January 28, 1952.

[14] For an example, see parliamentary minutes of Grand National Assembly of Turkey (Türkiye Büyük Millet Meclisi Zabıt Ceridesi, TBMMZC henceforth), 25.2.1340 (1924), 345.

[15] See "Medeni Kanun: Tarihi 17 seneyi bulan büyük içtimai inkılabın kıymeti," in *Cumhuriyet*, February 17, 1940 for a note on these "twin relics" of backwardness.

قدر گلچیمدن مردّد مزّکردی . کلده خجلید اولرله بلطاود صر ابچبد فندرلك عابا
قدر بیجیدده مردّد مزّکردی . کلده خجلید ایچبدد صدر ابجتد فندرلك عابا
دشمزکد قازندن قرطام داربابعلدی صر اسمردك اند درگند آندد بعد اگنبزدی .

Image 5.1 *Resimli Ay*'s visual depiction of the 'pool orgies' that it describes. *Resimli Ay Mecmuası*, Sayı:2, Cilt:1, Mart 1340 (March 1924).

Last but not least, there was the long line of women as political actors, who did not have an easy place in the republican political order that was now claimed by a group of men who called themselves, above all, "comrades in arms." Just as everything else in relation with the Ottoman polity changed, the significance of these women's political participation also had to change. This chapter explores, first and foremost, the "republicanization" of the imperial harems, and what the successive constitutional and republican orders and its takeover meant particularly to the palace inmates and their material world in the Ottoman Empire. As has already been discussed in the previous chapters, the palace slaves constituted only a small portion of the slaves in the empire. However, not only was there a sizeable industry attached to this small group of people but also the enslaved women themselves were closely and intimately tied to the larger political realm, as explored particularly in the third chapter. Moreover, their emancipation was deemed to have set the example for the rest of the enslaved population of the Ottoman Empire. Especially in the aftermath of the 1908 revolution, agricultural slaves in the provinces made specific references to the mass manumission of Abdülhamid II's *cariye*s, when they made their own claims to "freedom, equality, and justice."[16] In that sense, the palace slaves and the imperial harem embodied the "twin relics" of the unwanted Ottoman past. In this specific context, this chapter follows how the republican "project of regulated amnesia,"[17] dealt with the physical disposal of items found in the palaces and imperial harems, along with ideas and discourses attached to them. In that, it aims to trace the ways in which the mode of women's political participation changed in

---

[16] See Chapter 4, for a discussion on this matter.

[17] Murat Ergin, "'Is the Turk a White Man?' Towards a Theoretical Framework for Race in the Making of Turkishness," Middle Eastern Studies, 44:6 (2008), 837.

the republican order, which now belonged almost entirely to the veterans of the National Resistance.[18]

The past three chapters explored, from different perspectives, the ways in which slavery confronted the new governmental order that was taking shape in the Ottoman domains from the mid-nineteenth century on. In these chapters, I argued that the Ottoman government, which pledged to safeguard equality for all of its citizen-subjects before the law, especially after the 1856 Reform Edict, found itself increasingly more entangled with the problem of slavery and freedom in both domestic and international contexts. To invoke Dylan Penningroth's observation once again, the "jostling assumptions and interests" of such intellectual groups as the Young Ottomans (or statesmen like Midhat Pasha)[19] "often opened up space for ordinary people, and even slaves, to seize on legal institutions to pursue their interest."[20] In that the above-mentioned entanglement took place in a widespread manner within the (trans)forming legal realm, rendering the debate on slavery and freedom an indispensable part of the eventual, however delayed, reform in civil law (particularly, family law). The amendment process began in 1917 but then was interrupted by World War I and the collapse of the Ottoman Empire, followed by the

---

[18] Ekmekcioglu, "Republic of Paradox," 662.

[19] For a comprehensive discussion on how slavery and freedom were understood by the Ottoman intellectuals and statesmen during the *Tanzimat* era, see Ehud Toledano, "Late Ottoman Concepts of Slavery (1830s–1880s)," *Poetics Today*, Vol. 14, No. 3, Cultural Processes in Muslim and Arab Societies: Modern Period I (Autumn, 1993); Toledano, *Slavery and Abolition in the Ottoman Middle East* (Seattle: University of Washington Press, 1998), chapter 4. Toledano demonstrates that while these intellectuals and statesmen, including Midhat Pasha, advocated a wholesale abolition of slavery, used the metaphor of slavery and freedom extensively in their political writings, or were contributors to the abolitionist literature, they were often slaveholders themselves at the same time.

[20] Penningroth, "The Claims of Slaves," 1057.

National Resistance. Nevertheless, when the matter was eventually taken up again in 1926 with the enactment of a new, comprehensive civil law, slavery as an institution or practice in and of itself was virtually nonexistent in the parliamentary debates. Rather, it appeared as an unidentified segment of a larger problem of law, expressed both in terms of the inadequacies of codification efforts pertaining to the *Şer'i* law and the conflicts that were concomitant with the bifurcated nature of the Ottoman legal order. Slavery did not appear in parliamentary debates until June 5, 1933. When it was brought up, it was treated as an international problem, rather than an intrinsic issue that resulted from the social, cultural, and legal peculiarities of the Ottoman practice. This chapter also aims to provide an overview of this legal (trans)formation that took place between the years of 1917 and 1933, and explore the ways in which the state-citizen relations changed within this process, offering a glimpse of how the Ottoman "relics" were dealt with within the legal realm.

The Problem of Slaves as Imperial Property

The debates on the ownership of imperial property and its public and private character first emerged in 1909, with the dissolution of Yıldız Palace in general, and Abdülhamid II's personal wealth and his harem, in particular. Both the removal of the harem inmates and the assessment of the harem's content were overseen by a commission, which was drawn up by the newly established parliament and comprised of

206

representatives from different government institutions.[21] Starting from May 1st, 1909, the

handling of palace property was discussed at the parliament over a number of long

sessions during which a small group of deputies suggested the formation of the above-

mentioned committee to supervise inspections that had been implemented by the local

government.[22] The debates following this suggestion partly dealt with, not unlike the

parallel debates on the manumission of the enslaved harem servants at the time,

determining the institutions responsible for or legally entitled to carry out the process. For

instance, Sinop deputy Hasan Fehmi Efendi suggested that the matter could not be left to

Municipal Government (*Şehremaneti*), as the primary responsible institution in the

process had to be the Treasury or the Ministry of Finance.[23] Nafi Pasha from Aleppo

suggested that since palace property was considered *beyt-ül mal*,[24] its inspection was also

a *Şer'i* matter, to be supervised by the office of the *Şeyhülislam* (chief religious official in

the Ottoman Empire, one that overlooked the Islamic *Şer'i* courts, as well). Hiristo Dalçef

Efendi from Siroz (Sérres in today's Greece) pointed out that this inspection and

confiscation could not be left to the municipal government alone, as the wealth of Yıldız

Palace did not belong only to Istanbul, but to the entire country. Zohrab Efendi, from

---

[21] The initial committee, that aimed to oversee particularly the cash, valuables and important documents reportedly comprised the mayor of Istanbul, two members from the Municipal Council, the district mayor of Beşiktaş and two army officers. Meclisi Mebusan Zabıt Ceridesi (MMZC), 24 Haziran 1325 (7 July 1909), 213.

[22] MMZC, 18 Nisan 1325 (1 May 1909), 139–141.

[23] Roughly about three years later, any lost or stolen item from any of these premises were determined to be subject to Treasury Law, not to be debated in the parliament but directly handled by the Ministy of Finance, although even then the issue was not all that clear to deputies, either. MMZC, 11 Temmuz 1328 (24 July 1912), 416.

[24] Literally meaning "house of wealth," *beyt-ül mal* (*bayt al-mal* in Arabic original) denotes royal treasury in Islamic jurisprudence and was strictly regulated in accordance with Islamic (*Şer'i*) law.

Istanbul, stated that what was subject to inspection and takeover was not solely the wealth in Yıldız Palace, but also documents, particularly informant records known as *jurnal*s, collected there in the previous three decades, that concerned specifically such political actors as themselves. For Antalya deputy Ebüzziya Tevfik Bey, the Ottoman law commended that all this wealth and documents were to be transferred to the new sultan, and no government institution was entitled to inspect or confiscate them.[25] Similar to (and in fact, indicative of) the debates on the manumission of the harem inmates, neither the legislature nor the executive branch of the government had a clear idea on the procedure as to how the palace property would be handled, and more than one legal and administrative body were deemed entitled to supervise this process. In the meantime, however, the Third Army Corps had reportedly removed all the cash and some of the valuable items from Yıldız Palace and secured them in the vaults at their headquarters.[26]

The critical questions came when the sorting out began. What exactly was subject to proposed (and subsequently carried out) inspection and confiscation? Was it only Sultan Abdülhamid's personal wealth and if so, where did his person end? Did his wealth include his extended family's also?[27] Were palace slaves to be considered part of the

---

[25] MMZC, 18 Nisan 1325 (1 May 1909), 139–141; Also see MMZC, 3 Mayıs 1325 (16 May 1909), 415–417, for Menteşe deputy Halil Bey's proposal for close guarding of the informant reports (*jurnal*) found in Yıldız Palace, accumulated over 33 years. During the course of long debates, there were other deputies who stated that every object within the palace premises had a monumental value and suggested that Yıldız Palace be turned into a museum to be entitled *Museum of Ottoman History* (*Târîhi Osmânî müzehanesi*). See, for example, Sivas deputy Nazaret Dagavaryan's proposal in MMZC, 23 Mayıs 1325 (5 June 1909), 144 and Arif İsmet Bey's related concerns in MMZC, 16 Haziran 1325 (29 June 1909), 76. For a debate on the extraordinary case of *Hareket Ordusu*, see MMZC, 24 Haziran 1325 (7 July 1909), 215–216.

[26] MMZC, 19 Nisan 1325 (2 May 1909), 148–149; MMZC, 28 Mayıs 1325 (10 June 1909), 293.

[27] MMZC, 21 Nisan 1325 (4 May 1909), 206–210. The parliament debated the necessity of a restrictive order, particularly in relation to bank accounts of all members of the Ottoman dynasty.

Ottoman dynasty by association or were they considered property? When it came to the physical removal of the harem inmates from Yıldız Palace, questions pertaining to the property rights of the enslaved inmates also came to the fore. Consequently, the palace inmates themselves were determined to be persons rather than property, and their manumission, which began soon after their removal from Yıldız Palace, was finalized after a long and, for the most part, ambiguous process, as explored in the previous chapter.[28] Nevertheless, because of their association with the old regime, their belongings could not be sorted out that easily. As the archival sources, parliamentary records, and particularly memoirs indicate, strict inspection was in order during the assessment process, which Leyla Açba described as follows:

> On Wednesday, 28th of April [1909], the ravenous rebels, who decided to remove all inmates and officials from the palace, were letting the women out only after a strict inspection. They did not let the palace women to take even a small purse with them. They gathered all of us in the *Küçük Mabeyn* [one of the offices used by the palace secretariat] [...] In the meanwhile, the wives of police officers were brought in [to assist with further inspection]. They took groups of five women into a room, where they checked them to their underwear, to make sure that they were not hiding jewelry or other valuable items under their clothes.[29]

The same session also hosted a debate on legal means to effect any confiscation, deciding consequently looking into the international law and practices on the matter, 209. Also see MMZC, 25 Nisan 1325 (8 May 1909), 272 and MMZC, 3 Mayıs 1325 (16 May 1909), 417–418.

[28] MMZC, 19 Nisan 1325 (2 May 1909), 160–161. "...aslı nesli malum olmayarak, abd ve cariye halinde bilcümle saraylarda istihdam edilmekte bulunan kesandan rıkkiyetleri sabit olanların i'takı ve olmayanların ıtlak ve tahliyesi..." Also see BOA, DH.MUI 37-2/23, 1328.Ş.23 (30 August 1910), for a later note written by the Grand Vizier that explicated the handling of the objects and documents by imperial treasury, among other institutions. This ambiguous process constitutes the core of the fourth chapter of this dissertation.

[29] Açba, *Bir Çerkes Prensesinin Harem Hatıraları*, 208. Born in 1898 in Istanbul, Leyla Açba was from a noble Abkhaz family, whose female members had prominent positions in Abdülhamid II's harem. Her maternal aunt Peyveste Hanım and her paternal cousin Fatma Pesend Hanım were two of Abdülhamid's wives. Leyla Açba spent her childhood in the Yıldız Palace,

When Leyla Açba was in the inspection room, an officer forcefully pulled down her

aunt's headgear (*hotoz*), while another one told them to take all of their clothes off, which

Açba recounted in astonishment. Following the inspection, Açba wrote, they left the

palace and conjoined together with the other *cariye*s who were let out earlier and had

been waiting outside. As they were walking through the crowd that gathered in front of

the palace, they were surrounded by a group of young (and, as Açba specified, evil-

looking) men. Açba's mother and aunt asked the men to let them pass, which the latter

complied only after the women handed their earrings to them.[30] After the inmates were

removed from the palace, Leyla Açba further reported, the main gate to the harem was

broken open and a group of soldiers entered and looted the place with the slogans of

"freedom!"[31] As reported later on by Sazkar Hanımefendi to Leyla Açba, not only their

savings and jewelry were taken away, but the soldiers even looted the furniture. "Even

the curtains, the stoves!" were taken away Sazkar Hanımefendi exclaimed, not sparing a

---

and officially became the *cariye* of Sultan Vahideddin's first wife Nazikeda Kadınefendi quite late, in 1919.

[30] Açba, *Bir Çerkes Prensesinin Harem Hatıraları*, 208.

[31] Açba, *Bir Çerkes Prensesinin Harem Hatıraları*, 217. Açba notes that the authority to loot the harem premises was given to the Army by the Parliament, although the latter did not hold such power during the incident, and took part in the process only to produce reports of it, as evinced in the debates. The parliamentary minutes indicate, however, that the Third Army Corps did go into the palace and as noted above, took away the valuables to secure them at the military headquarters, although it is safe to assume that some items were appropriated for personal purposes. Açba also mentions that the Parliament strictly ordered the Army not to touch the palace women, and hence any incidence of rape could be avoided, although no such order was issued by the Parliament.

large mirror that belonged to Abdülhamid, which the soldiers broke into pieces, as they tried to remove it from his bedroom.[32]

As the Parliament, Army, and other state institutions tried to determine the limits of private and public property,[33] the primary question the harem inmates faced was a more personal and urgent one. Those who were removed from Yıldız Palace knew that their lives as *sarayi*s have been brought to an end.[34] When she was brought to Topkapı Palace, İşvezad Hanım knew that she would never be able to return to Yıldız Palace again but she was less certain as to what she would do to sustain her living or where she would go or reside. It took several weeks until she was sought after by her father Özbek Maan, who took İşvezad Hanım to her native village.[35] Among the women who were transferred to Topkapı Palace and had no relatives was Layık Seza, who ran a tenacious campaign to recover her "mahogany colored" piano after her expulsion from Yıldız Palace in 1909. Roughly about six months after her removal from Yıldız Palace, she petitioned the office

---

[32] Açba, *Bir Çerkes Prensesinin Harem Hatıraları*, 219.

[33] The parliament also tried to determine their own work description as the members of the national legislature. See MMZC, 24 Haziran 1325 (7 July 1909), 214 for an interesting discussion, in which the parrots found at the imperial gardens are defined to be the responsibility of the executive branch, not the legislature.

[34] Literally meaning palace dweller, the word *sarayi* signifies all enslaved women who received palace education and served at the harem, even after they were manumitted and left the palace. For an elaborate account on the *sarayi*s as components of the extended Ottoman court, see İpşirli Argıt, "Manumitted Female Slaves."

[35] Açba, *Bir Çerkes Prensesinin Harem Hatıraları*, 219. Özbek Maan's related petition can be found at BOA, DH.MKT 2816/32, 1327.R.27 (18 May 1909). Leyla Açba's memoire here reads almost exactly the same as the Ottoman archival files which describe the procedure. It states that following the girls' transfer to Topkapı Palace, the municipal government set up a commission, headed by the chief police commissioner Şevki Efendi who oversaw the manumission and placement of the girls with their families, except for the forty four, who did not have families. It may be that this was common and widely known news at the time, especially among those who had stake in it, like Leyla Açba herself. It may also mean, however, that this information was added to the memoire later on by its subsequent editors.

of the Grand Vezir, urging them to search and locate the piano as quickly as possible. Layık Seza, who was described by Mislimelek Hanım as a "tall, graceful young woman," was known to be close to Abdülhamid.[36] Although it is not specified in the related accounts, it is likely that the piano was given to her as a present by the sultan himself and for that reason deemed valuable by Layık Seza in a specific way during her time in the palace. Following her removal however and after she subsequently became a servant to one of the concubines (*ikbal*) of a navy lieutenant named Tahir Efendi, the meaning and value of the piano changed.[37] Like many other harem inmates, especially those who lacked kin support, she relied mostly on her own resources to sort out her life outside the palace. Until a small amount of a pension was granted to her about a year later,[38] the recovery of her piano (either for sale or for other reasons) might have been Layık Seza's only way to make a living.[39] Apart from the items accumulated in the palace, in rare instances women possessed items that they brought with them to the harem. Such was the case with Mislimelek Hanım (who came to the harem as an enslaved young girl), who had in her possession an ornamented wooden box given to her by her (then deceased) grandfather. Like all other furniture in her room, the box was lost during the chaos of the 1909 events. Mislimelek later on pursued the matter with the new sultan, Reşad, but

---

[36] Mislimelek Abdülkadir, *Haremden Sürgüne Bir Osmanlı Prensesi: II Abdülhamit'in gelini Mislimelek Hanım, istibdat döneminin bilinmeyenlerini* (Istanbul: İnkılap Kitabevi, 2011),105.

[37] BOA, BEO 3636/272633, 1327.Ş.29 (15 September 1909); DH.MUI 40-1/49, 1327.Z.5 (18 December 1909).

[38] MMZC, 13 Kanunuevvel 1326 (26 December 1910), 629.

[39] Note, for instance, how two of Naciye Neyyal's enslaved servants sold some of their valuable items given to them as gifts by their owner, to buy a house after their manumission. Ressam Naciye Neyyal, *Mutlakiyet, Meşrutiyet ve Cumhuriyet Anılarım* (Istanbul: Pınar Yayınları, 2000), 55.

failed to recover the box, despite her efforts.[40] Layık Seza and Mislimelek were not alone in pursuing their belongings with the officials who oversaw the dissolution of Abdülhamid II's harem or the successor sultan. One of the chief eunuchs of the Yıldız Palace, Nadir Ağa among others, also petitioned to recover his binoculars and complained about not achieving any results in his pursuit almost a year after the dissolution of the Yıldız harem.[41]

While harem inmates and members of the Ottoman dynasty were in pursuit of recovering their belongings, the government debated how the cash, bonds, stock, valuables, and antiques were to be put in use for the "people." In one such debate in parliament, which followed the proposal given by the head of the Hijaz Railroad Commission, the deputies discussed whether or not the government had the authority to transfer a sum confiscated at Yıldız Palace to the construction and maintenance of the railroad.[42] Apart from these large-scale projects, however, the immediate concern was largely about the (re)usable items, particularly in the harem section. One such example

---

[40] Mislimelek Abdülkadir, *Haremden Sürgüne Bir Osmanlı Prensesi*, 137.

[41] BOA, DH.MUI 79-1/28, 1328.Ra.18 (30 March 1910). These efforts were not particular to the manumitted slaves, either. Ayşe Sultan, one of Abdülhamid's daughters, for one, was worried about her parrots and petitioned for their recovery. Şehzade Burhaneddin, one his sons, pursued his photography development equipment, in addition to an electric chandelier. On a different note, in an official inquiry, the office of the Grand Vezir asked the Ministry of the Interior on how the foreign medals/decorations that belonged to the deceased sultans, particularly of Abdülmecid and Abdülaziz, would be handled. Involving several different institutions, including the two above-mentioned offices and the palace secretariat, it was decided that these medals were to be sent to the imperial treasury, in compliance with the ancient customs (*teamül-ü kadime*). None of these cases, however, carried the tone of urgency that Layık Seza's petition had, which hinted at, among other things, an ample degree of despair.

[42] MMZC, 4 Mayıs 1325 (17 May 1909), 480–482. The proposal was strongly objected by some deputies, on the basis of its illegitimacy, as the mentioned money belonged to the people and could not be utilized arbitrarily, 482.

concerned the transfer of bedframes and copperware in Yıldız Palace to the newly established Cerrahpaşa Hospital.[43] Having been informed about these items, stacked up and idly waiting at the palace, the Directorate General for Health and Public Assistance (*Müessesât-ı Hayriye-i Sıhhiye Riyaseti*) requested their donation from the municipal government who for its turn, asked the Ministry of the Interior for their transfer, but not without a number of justifications for its request. These requested items included no more than a few iron bedframes, copper pots and pans, and straw matrasses and did not hold any value, the deputy mayor Tevfik specified. Moreover, they were left there unused, to rust and decay whereas they could be of the utmost use, serving the sick people of the city instead. The Municipal Government had no money, the letter stated, yet the hospital had urgency, thus these items would ease the financial burden on the former.[44] In another instance, during the debates on budgetary planning, the deputies voted in favor of donating various tools and instruments in Yıldız Palace's observatory to a newly established meteorological station.[45] Consequently, all valuable items, particularly jewelry, were priced in accordance with expert assessments and reports and sold, bringing a decent sum of 3 million francs to the Treasury. In the following months, the furniture and other items were partially restored to what was deemed to be their original locations in other palaces, and others were given away particularly to the Ministry of Education, to be utilized in schools.[46] Despite these examples, the handling of Yıldız

---

[43] BOA, DH.MUI 65/55, 1328.Ra.5 (17 March 1910).

[44] BOA, DH.MUI 65/55, 1328.Ra.5 (17 March 1910). Even with such reasoning, however, the Ministry of Interior found this request unacceptable, until the Grand Vezir Hakkı Pasha's involvement and the new sultan's approval of their transfer.

[45] MMZC, 28 Temmuz 1325 (10 August 1909), 307.

[46] MMZC, 12 Nisan 1326 (25 April 1910), 370.

Palace and its harem was largely untouched by the ideological effect of the regime change, as evinced in the parliamentary debates, in which the primary effort seems to be about figuring out what it meant for the "people" to own property, as well as determining the institutional and legal basis of the process of the take-over. The wealth of the sultan (a specific one, Abdülhamid II, rather than all sultans), who was deemed to have accumulated it by "enslaving" the people, was now defined as his "debt to the people," legally, literally and metaphorically. All in all, because the constitutional regime concerned itself only with toppling Abdülhamid's reign, and not the absolutist rule itself, the pressing question of what it meant for "the people" to possess Yıldız Palace (or any other imperial property, including all movable items found at the palace premises) was also shaped by a particular sense of retribution, from which the enslaved palace women and their material world were not spared.[47]

---

[47] That Yıldız Palace was chosen by the constitutional regime as the place where the first year anniversary of the revolution would be celebrated is indicative of this. MMZC, 8 Temmuz 1325 (21 July 1909), 473.

Images 5.2 - "Le Palais de Yıldız garde par les Soldats de l'armee Liberatrice," Taksim Atatürk Kitaplığı, Postcards Collection, Krt_000706.

Images 5.3 "L'Armee Liberatrice gardant le lac de Yıldız," Taksim Atatürk Kitaplığı, Postcards Collection, Krt_000865

As the past two chapters elaborated, the imperial harems consisted, with the exception of the Ottoman dynasty members, almost entirely of enslaved women, many of whom were coerced into and sequestered in the harems as enslaved children many years prior. Those who occupied the low-ranking positions were ordinarily kidnapped (by abduction, persuasion, or an imperial decree) and sold to the palace, examples of which can be seen in chapter three above.[48] The high-ranking positions (that is, the path to become a legal wife or a concubine to the sultan or one of his sons) on the other hand have become no more than an on-paper legal status and could even be deemed symbolic. By the late-nineteenth and early-twentieth centuries, the high-ranking posts were reserved mostly for Abkhazian girls of noble birth, who were sent to the palace as gifts, with the purpose of cementing bonds between the Ottoman dynasty and the Abkhaz nobility that settled in the Ottoman domains earlier in the nineteenth century. However, once admitted to the palace, they still had limited interaction with the outside world. Instead, they built their world around the things they earned or were given for their labor, sexual services, or simply put, "good deeds" they had done for the benefit of the Ottoman state. In some instances, these items were given to the women on important occasions such as the birth

---

[48] As late as March 1908 (only a few months before the constitutional revolution), the Ottoman officials were still visiting Circassian settlements across the country to recruit/levy young girls. For an example, see BOA, Y.PRK.ASK 255/2, 1326.S.11 (15 March 1908). For a case of abduction that took place after the revolution, see DH.EUM.THR 32/34, 1328.R.26 (7 May 1910), although in this case the abducted young woman was not sold to the imperial harem, but to a provincial government officer. See the article titled "Esir Ticareti" in *Sada-i Millet*, 8 Mart 1326 (21 March 1910), for a discussion on the connections between poverty and the perpetuation of slave trade in Ottoman Anatolia, in relation to kidnapping by persuasion.

Image 5.4 Leyla Açba Hanım, 1919. Image courtesy of *Bir Çerkes Prensesinin Harem Hatıraları* (Istanbul: Timaş Yayınları, 2010).

of a new dynasty member, death (mostly in the form of an inheritance from the slave-owning dynasty members to the enslaved), as well as weddings and circumcision ceremonies, religious festivals, and other similar occasions. Imperial birth (*veladet-i hümayun*) registers list items provided not solely to the woman who gave birth and her personal attendants but to a larger group of enslaved women in the harem.[49] The death registers (*muhallefat*) also contain itemized lists of "things" that dynasty members (as well as some of the enslaved women themselves) owned and used in their everyday lives. Following the death of a harem inmate (in fact, anyone who was a member of the *askeri* class of imperial administrators), her personal belongings and estate were customarily distributed among her inheritors, with a decent portion held by the Ottoman state. In this, it was common practice among female members of the dynasty to allocate parts of their assets to the slaves they owned. In one such example, the *muhallefat* register of Behice Sultan, one of Abdülmecid's daughters, provides a long list of items to be given to her enslaved servants following her death. Among common items such as garments, dishware, bathroom utensils etc., the list also includes less-expected items such as a sewing machine and two *kemançe*s (a type of bowed string instrument).[50] Apart from those that belonged to dynasty members, *muhallefat* registers of high and low-ranking enslaved servants also exist and help decipher their ownership patterns. For instance, the

---

[49] See BOA, TSMA.d (Topkapı Palace Museum Archives) no. 971 and 974 for two examples of birth registers. Most of the items listed on the registers are birth related, such as cradles, washbasins, linens, etc., but there is a mention of jewelry, garments and gold coins also.

[50] BOA, TSMA.d no. 997. The register does not specifically note which item was given to whom, thus making it not that useful to understand the hierarchies attached to this process, but it nevertheless gives an idea about types of items that changed hands after the deceased slave holders. This particular list does not contain any jewelry or other valuables, hinting at the fact that those were distributed through other means, or at times were not distributed at all.

219

register for one of Esma Sultan's chief attendants, Nesim Saba Kalfa, demonstrates that these women owned not only precious items but also things for plain everyday use, such as copperware or mattresses, perhaps like those that were to be sent to Cerrahpaşa Hospital a couple of decades later.[51] In that sense, their ownership of things were not limited to things that had monetary value, that they were given on special occasions, or received as salary, although precious items such as jewelry and money (together with distinctly expensive fabrics and ornamented garments) functioned as markers of the harem inmates' rank within the highly hierarchical harem organization. When describing the *hazinedar*s in the harems,[52] Şadiye Sultan, one of Abdülhamid's daughters noted how distinct types of staffs, made of ivory and ornamented by different sorts of precious stones set the chief *hazinedar* apart from both other members of the harem and lower ranking *hazinedar*s.[53] In other instances, these items also pointed at unspoken or informal hierarchies. Such was the case with Pervin Kalfa, both an attendant and a concubine to Abdülhamid II's son Abdülkadir. Even though she was not one of his official wives, Pervin had been Abdülkadir's servant and concubine since adolescence, and according to one of the prince's wives, Mislimelek Hanım, also the most favored. Reportedly, she

---

[51] BOA, TSMA.d no. 7829. Also see TSMA.d no.7768, for a list of all expenses made for an enslaved woman named Tavrıfelek. Similarly, the list includes various items of every day use, such as coffee cups, dishware, etc.

[52] Literally meaning treasurer, the word denotes the highest rank of service (except sexual services) for enslaved inmates within the harem organization.

[53] Şadiye Sultan binti Abdülhamid Had, *Hayatımın Acı ve Tatlı Günleri* (Istanbul: Bedir Yayınevi, 2000), 16. Şadiye Sultan states lower rank *hazinedar*s also carried staffs, though less ornamented ones compared to that of the chief *hazinedar*. All *cariye*s in elite households were elegantly dressed, and decorated with jewelry. In his elaborate biographical study of Refia Sultan, Ali Akyıldız mentions weddings and other similar festive events during which the palace servants were given gifts, most notably precious fabrics. Ali Akyıldız, *Mümin ve Müsrif bir Padişah Kızı* (Istanbul: Tarih Vakfı Yurt Yayınları, 1998), 29.

received more gifts and owned significantly more jewelry than the official wives and was granted freer access to tailoring and embroidery services provided by the palace tailors.[54] Thus, the questions related to the dissolution process and whether these women should be allowed to keep their personal belongings or not also referred to their rank and political power within the harem in particular and the Ottoman court in general. In other words, what they were forced to leave behind not only comprised their jewelry, garments, or musical instruments (with practical, measurable value) but also any rank, position, and influence attached to those items. The wives, concubines, and servants of the sultan and his sons saw themselves not merely as wives and servants, even less as "pleasure fairies" that served a lecherous sovereign, as the *Resimli Ay* journal suggested, but as agents who took an active role in the perpetuation of the Ottoman dynasty and the well-being of the sovereign, which meant, for them, the Ottoman state.

It was not that the ownership of "things" was ever given to the *cariye*s indefinitely. In his account of Abdülaziz's dethronement in 1876, Ziya Şakir provided a detailed description of what dethronement meant in physical space, particularly for the female members of the palace. As soon as Murad V's accession to the throne was announced, Ziya Şakir wrote, the imperial harem was claimed by Murad V's mother Şevkefza Sultan, who effected the removal of Abdülaziz's mother, wives, concubines, and servants within the same day.[55] The latter were expelled from the palace forcefully and all of their property was confiscated by the new *valide sultan* Şevkefza, on behalf of

---

[54] Mislimelek Abdülkadir, *Haremden Sürgüne Bir Osmanlı Prensesi*, 94–96.

[55] Ziya Şakir, *Çırağan Sarayı'nda 28 Yıl: Beşinci Murad* [28 Years at the Çırağan Palace] (Istanbul: Kaknüs Yayınları, 2007), 108–109.

her son Murad V. According to Ziya Şakir's account, the expelled women were not allowed to take anything with them, except for the dresses they were wearing and had to worry about where they would sleep and what they would eat from then on.[56]

What started with the constitutional revolution in 1908 and Abdülhamid II's dethronement in 1909 was not new to the harem inmates in essence. What is important here is that the dissolution process carried out by the constitutional and republican regimes went against the harem inmates' understanding of what the Ottoman state was and the hierarchical order it was based on, both within the harem organization and in the ways it related to the world outside, in the form of a rigid divide between *sarayis* and *şehirlis*.[57] Safiye Ünüvar, a tutor hired for the education of the young princes and princesses (along with their enslaved playmates and servants) noted how these two groups were even referred to as two "distinct races" from time to time.[58] When praised by a *sarayi* for being "just like them," Ünüvar rebuked her as follows:

> My dear *kalfa*, who are the *şehirlis* and who are you, the *sarayis*? Are you not one among the people also? You should know that had the people [of the city] not exist, the palace would not exist either. We should do away with this sense of discrimination [...] A people without a state [understood here as the Ottoman dynasty and the court] would endure, while a state without a people would cease to exist.[59]

---

[56] Ziya Şakir, *Çırağan Sarayı'nda 28 Yıl*, 109.

[57] Literally, city dwellers, *şehirlis* constituted everyone who lived outside the palace and who has never been part of the court.

[58] Safiye Ünüvar, *Saray Hatırlarım* (Istanbul: L&M Yayınları, 2007), 62–63.

[59] Ibid., 62–63.

Image 5.5 Mislimelek Hanım (left) , 1897-98. Image courtesy of *Bir Çerkes Prensesinin Harem Hatıraları* (Istanbul: Timaş Yayınları, 2010).

Writing in the early republican era, Ünüvar's account [and this particular statement] here is not untouched by the republican portrayal of the Ottoman dynasty. Nevertheless, not only the dynasty members but all *sarayi*s considered themselves to be essential part of the Ottoman state, by virtue of being part of the extended Ottoman court and for having been given the authority in safeguarding its well-being. The material world they built for themselves was considered proof of this authority. It was in this context that for Nazikeda Kadınefendi and Leyla Açba, who told the story, being forced to leave the country by the republican regime, "as if [they] were traitors" as the former put it, was utterly inconceivable.[60]

The emergent perception of the palace and the harem as public space and their contents as public goods became sharper in the decades that followed the constitutional revolution and reached its peak in two steps; in 1922 and 1924, when the nascent republican government abolished the sultanate and caliphate respectively, consequently exiling all members of the Ottoman dynasty, removing all enslaved servants from the palace and confiscating imperial property in its entirety. What the constitutionalists hesitantly started in 1908–1909, was brought to a culmination by the republican regime that consisted of a new group of administrators who drew their legitimacy from a sequence of wars, most notably as mentioned above, the National Resistance. As the charter and the bylaws of the ruling Republican People's Party (*Cumhuriyet Halk Fırkası*) put it, this new group would do away (at least in theory) with the privileges granted to "any family, class, congregation, or individual," a point that was brought up

---

[60] Açba, *Bir Çerkes Prensesinin Harem Hatıraları*, 172.

during the debates about the incompatibility of the allowances paid to the royal family by the republican order.[61] The discussions on the palaces and the remainder of the Ottoman dynasty intensified in the early months of 1924 and continued to center on the allowances granted to the dynasty members. In an effort to make sense of or justify the payment, Istanbul deputy Yusuf Akçura suggested to provide an itemized version of the budget allotted to the royal family. This suggestion, however, yielded an even more unjustifiable result, as the itemized budget contained a sizable list of *cariye*s also, with their "incomprehensible, difficult to read names constructed from Persian, such as Mihridil, Dilşadan, Bedrifelek," Akçura noted with an annoyed tone.[62] The discussions that followed the budget-related debates increasingly emphasized the incongruity of paying large sums of money to those who could not even be called citizens, let alone civil servants.[63] In a tone similar to the *Resimli Ay* article that opens this chapter, which condemned imperial harems as "sources of prostitution and disgrace," the deputies stated that the caliphate[64] had no place in a national budget, drawn up and approved by the National Assembly, and sustained by the people.[65] "You say dynasty," the Denizli deputy Mazhar Müfid exclaimed, "but dynasty is no citizen, it is dynasty," and the burden was

---

[61] Cumhuriyet Halk Fırkası Nizamnamesi (Ankara: 1923), accessed through TBMM Library Open Access Collection. TBMMZC, 27.9.1339 (1923), 292, 310; TBMMZC, 27.9.1339 (1923), 327–328. After the abolition of the sultanate, the Ottoman sultans were considered to be caliphs only. In the budget-related debates, the allowance paid to the royal family is said to be paid only as a token for their respect to the religion of Islam and nothing else.

[62] TBMMZC, 25.2.1340 (1924), 345. Akçura here refers to the palace/harem practice of renaming all enslaved servants with exceedingly ornamented Persian phrases.

[63] TBMMZC, 25.2.1340 (1924), 346.

[64] Understood not so much as religious title here but a disguise for sultanate and the luxurious/extravagant life still maintained at the palaces and imperial harems.

[65] TBMMZC, 27.2.1340 (1924), 415.

related not only to the amount paid in allowances, but this very definition of who had the right to be a citizen and what constituted the Turkish republican state.[66] Consequently, when the law regarding the abolition of the caliphate and exile came on March 3, 1924, its basis (or, at least its primary concern) was precisely this inconsistency.[67] Yet, this was not the whole of it. Besides determining the lines of exclusion for the Ottoman dynasty, the Ottoman government simultaneously rearranged its legal institutions, reducing, as Judith Tucker described it, "what had previously been a vast body of somewhat disparate interpretation and opinion on family matters to a standardized code that aimed to establish clear and universally applicable rules for family life and gender relations."[68] The following section will explore how the republican government dealt with what came to be know as the legal "remnants of the caliphate and sultanate."[69]

The Legal Remnants of the Ottoman Past

As the republican state emerged as "a particular type of rationality in governmental practice," in which it is "at once that which exists, but which does not yet exist enough,"[70] it strived to set the boundaries of citizenship and determine who was entitled to be a republican citizen and who was not. Throughout the process, the palace

---

[66] TBMMZC, 27.2.1340 (1924), 429.

[67] For a lengthy debate on the dangers of keeping and the necessity of abolishing caliphate, see TBMMZC, 3.3.1340 (1924), 27–69.

[68] Judith E. Tucker, "Revisiting Reform: Women and the Ottoman Law of Family Rights, 1917," *The Arab Studies Journal*, Vol. 4, No. 2 (Fall 1996), 5.

[69] TBMMZC, 17.2.1926, 232.

[70] Michel Foucault, *The Birth of Biopolitics: Lectures at the Collège de France, 1978–79* (New York: Palgrave Macmillan, 2008), 3–4.

and the Ottoman dynasty, as well as their "human extensions" such as the enslaved servants of the imperial harem, again became a matter of contestation in which many of the republican views about the newly emerging mode of governance crystalized. The *de facto* dual nature of the republican political order and the present danger of people's increasing support of the caliphate over the republican government made the abolition of the caliphate a necessity, even though it was deemed to be a "1300-year-old institution [...] inherited through a long line of "glorious predecessors" of the Rashidun Caliphate, the Umayyids, the Abbasids, and the Fatimids..."[71] After all, the Minister of Justice Seyid Bey argued, there were no *Şer'i* or religious obstacles but only political ones that impeded its abolition, as Islam neither attached spirituality (*ruhaniyet*) to its administrative institutions nor attributed holiness to its religious dignitaries. In essence, Islam did not necessarily have religious governance (*teşkilat-ı diniye*) either and left its administration to the Islamic community itself.[72] In a highly intricate and technical discussion, Seyid Bey informed his audience in the parliament that the Islamic jurists in the past defined caliphate (*hilafet* and *imamet* used interchangeably) as the authority of a "deserving" (*istihkak*) person over public matters.[73] In language reminiscent of religious debates on the Islamic institution of slavery (partially explored in the previous chapter), yet completely oblivious of it, the minister defined caliphate as a type of guardianship [*velayet*, Ar. *walayat*], which is voluntarily granted by the people to an individual:

---

[71] TBMMZC, 3.3.1340 (1924), 35, 65.

[72] Ibid., 50.

[73] Ibid., 51.

The *ulema* defined guardianship as "*tenfiz-ül kavle alel gayri şae ev eba*,"[74] which meant to have others obey one's words, whether they agreed or not. [...] This means to have others obey by force and this means nothing but domination. Is domination lawful, from the viewpoint of the *Şer'i* law? If one attempts to subdue others by force through illegitimate means, then it should be called domination [*tahakküm*], or tyranny [*tagallüb*] and by definition [absolutist] reign. If that attempt is legitimate, on the other hand, it is called guardianship...[75]

For Seyid Bey, no one individual has been automatically granted such an authority in Islam, and no one had the right to subdue others by force either.

No person has the right to tell the others what and what not to say or where and where not to go. Everyone is free to live anywhere he likes, move in any ways he pleases. Each individual himself is honorable and immune from assault and aggression. So is the case with the right to property ownership. Every man is free to put his property to use in any ways he desires and that property is also immune from assault. Every one is equal before the law, that there are no such things as class privilege or aristocracy. Islam, in the true sense of the word, is a democratic religion that refuses to endorse any one person's prerogatives.[76]

The institution of slavery, sanctioned by the Islamic jurisprudence up until that time (possibly still so, at the time of the minister's address), was completely erased from the discussions and was not brought up by any other deputy either. The Justice Minister further argued that the only person that held a right to forceful guardianship as an

---

[74] This Arabic statement was the classic definition of *velayet*, literally meaning the enforcement of a statement in relation to others, whether they agreed or refused.

[75] TBMMZC, 3.3.1340 (1924), 52.

[76] Ibid., 52.

acceptable/legitimate practice was the father over his children. The justice minister's argument did not go far from the father-child analogy and was instead hastily tied to a general discussion that aimed to fit Islam into the republican view of governance. That "fitting," however, could be achieved only by erasing contradictory or problematic aspects of Islamic law, the most important of which was about slavery.[77] In many respects, the minister's speech was reminiscent of the Ottoman slaves' claims to freedom in the preceding decades, who indefatigably emphasized the incongruity (as well as the undermining effect of) of such forceful "subduing" with the constitutional order.

At the end of a long debate, the abolition of the caliphate was accepted by the parliament, and the law pertaining to the exile of the Ottoman dynasty members was resolved.[78] According to this law, the dynasty members were to leave the country within ten days and the ownership of all imperial property including palaces, mansions, and various other types of real estate, furnishings, art works, and other items found within those premises were to be confiscated for the use of the "people."[79] What started as an elaborate and highly technical discussion led by the Justice Minister was followed by a series of congratulation notices sent to the parliament (by local administrators, businessmen, educators), which condemned the caliphate as an institution. Even the *sufi* leaders and religious officers (the *kadı* and *müftü*) condemned the institution, some

---

[77] Ibid., 53.

[78] See ibid., 67 for a debate against the exile of female members of the dynasty.

[79] Note Tunalı Hilmi Bey's correction of terminology: it was no longer imperial (*mal-ı miri*) but republican property (*Cumhur malı*). TBMMZC, 29.11.1339 (1923), 647.

blaming it for sucking the blood of the people for so many centuries, and others arguing that it was never a legitimate institution in its long history to begin with.[80]

What the republican state set out to do was to redefine its political and legal institutions, eliminating both the political dualism mentioned above and the institutional bifurcation in the legal realm. As has been partially discussed in previous chapters, family law, which also regulated slavery, was exempted from earlier attempts of legal reform, due to a fear on the Ottoman government's side that it would cause unrest among the Muslim populations of the empire.[81] The *Mecelle* Commission, which oversaw the codification process of other areas of law had been the target of *Meşihat*'s attacks earlier in the mid-nineteenth century. Being a "thornier" area than criminal law, insisting on a reform of family law would produce only more strife and bring on more attacks by the office of the *Şeyhülislam*.[82] Only a year before the empire's collapse, the Ottoman government made any attempts towards the codification of Ottoman family law, which yielded the Ottoman Law of Family Rights of 1917. Having been promulgated at the very end of the empire's existence and in the midst of World War I, the new arrangement was inevitably short-lived and according to the republican deputy from Sinop, Yusuf Kemal Bey, it was unconstitutional as well, as it was not drawn up by the legislature (understood as "the people"), but as a governmental order:[83]

---

[80] TBMMZC, 6.3.1340 (1924), 136–137.

[81] M. Akif Aydın, *İslam-Osmanlı Aile Hukuku* (Istanbul: Marmara Üniversitesi İlahiyat Fakültesi Vakfı Yayınları, 1985), 133.

[82] Aydın, *İslam-Osmanlı Aile Hukuku*, 134. Aydın further argues that the urgency of such a legal arrangement was not high. This was not the case, at least for slaves, of course.

[83] TBMMZC, 17.2.1926, 233; The order was signed by the Ottoman sultan Mehmed Reşad, the Grand Vezir Talat and Justice Minister Halil (Menteşe) as a temporary law (*muvakkat kanun*) on

230

Even in the Constitutional era, the Family Law did not pass through the Parliament but rather enacted as a governmental order. [...] *Mecelle* is before us. All of its items were accepted/enacted through imperial decrees. The Family Law is before us, it too is an order. Regulations on the Criminal Proceedings (*Usul-ı Muhakemat-ı Cezaiye*) is a governmental order. Regulations on the Legal Proceedings (*Usul-ı Muhakemat-ı Hukukiye*) is also an order. The Commercial Law is via imperial edict. In short, none of these were discussed and voted at the parliament. Now we should accept this [the Civil law of 1926] with full courage and responsibility, and again with complete courage we advocate it to the people. [...] It is important to note however that for the well implementation of this law, there are several institutions that needs to be established. These should be established at once, and we as the parliament should support it as much as we can."[84]

The bifurcation within the legal practice, which characterized the Ottoman legal realm for most of the nineteenth century, did not solely emerge because there were simply different legal systems that conflicted with each other. In the aftermath of the 1908 revolution, for instance, the fight between the Ministry of Justice and the office of the *Şeyhülislam*, particularly visible in regards to the cases related to slavery and freedom, was not only due to a set of conflicting views on slavery and abolition but also these two institutions' efforts to maintain their respective areas of influence and control in administering law and justice. While the Ministry of Justice tried to extend its jurisdiction to the maximum (including the matters related to family and slavery), the

---

25 October 1917, and was printed in the *Takvim-i Vekayi*, the official journal of the Ottoman government on 31 October 1917. The order/law was also printed as a booklet the same year with the title *Hukuk-i Aile Kararnamesi* (Istanbul: Kader Matbaası, 1333 R/ 1917) accessed through İ.B.B Atatürk Kitaplığı, Ali Ulvi Ermiş Collection, AUE_00463, 297.522 HUK 297.522 HUK 1333 R/1917 1; Also see the minutes of the Ottoman Senate (Meclis-i Ayan Zabıt Cerideleri, MAZC).

[84] TBMMZC, 17.2.1926, 234.

office of the *Şeyhülislam* clung to its only remaining area of authority, producing an institutional duality which was carried over "into the Republican period, as part of the Ottoman legal heritage," and remained part of it until the Republican civil code promulgated in 1926.[85] This was particularly apparent in the parliamentary debates that related to the proposed takeover of the *Şer'i* courts by the Ministry of Justice, which also took place in 1917. When the items of the proposed law were debated and voted in the parliament, it was clear that despite the prospective takeover, *Şer'i* courts were expected to maintain their specific procedures and regulations. The goal was not to attain a procedural uniformity in adjudicating legal cases, but rather an institutional blending for administrative purposes. Even after these two institutions merged, however, the Ottoman legal system could not rid itself of its bifurcated character. For instance, the article 7 of the proposed law came in two versions; one was proposed jointly by the government and the Islamic clerics and the other by the Ministry of Justice. The Ministry of Justice suggested that following the merge/takeover, all legal procedures should be under the authority of the ministry alone. The government and the *Ulema* on the other hand suggested that, the Justice Minister and the *Şeyhülislam* should both have authority over this seemingly unified legal realm and the law was enacted in accordance with the latter suggestion.[86] In other words, the Ottoman government (as it had done previously in all slavery-related debates and arrangements) once again sided with the Islamic legal body, over the Ministry of Justice. In that sense, the foundation of the new legal institutions, which Yusuf Kemal Bey deemed crucial for the implementation of the newly enacted

---

[85] İlber Ortaylı, "Ottoman Family Law And The State In The Nineteenth Century," *OTAM* (Ankara Üniversitesi Osmanlı Tarihi Araştırma ve Uygulama Merkezi Dergisi), no.1, 1990, 332.

[86] TBMMZC, 11.2.1332 (1916), 299.

Civil Law in 1926, did not only point towards the necessity of establishing new legal institutions. It also meant doing away with these tensions, which had resulted more often than not in institutional crises in the past.

The legal arrangements of 1917 were partial efforts to reorganize the legal system and codify the family-related legal rules and regulations within the Şer'i law. The enacted Family Law covered only marriage and divorce-related matters and did not make a specific mention of slaves and slavery. Only in article 90, it stated that it was prohibited for the families and relatives of the bride to demand payment (in cash or kind) from the groom, when they married or "surrendered" (teslim) their daughter to him.[87] Nevertheless, the order was significant not because it made specific stipulations in relation to slavery. Rather, its importance came from the fact that it gave the authority to adjudicate family-related cases to the Ministry of Justice.[88] Although the Şer'i courts were still partially governed by the office of the Şeyhülislam, this was rather an unprecedented move on the Ottoman government's side, who traditionally had, as has been argued in the previous chapter, ample reluctance in the matters related to Şer'i law. This reluctance was still not entirely overcome by the time that 1917 legal adjustments were made. When these changes were debated in parliament, for instance, one of the core questions was related whether the Şer'i courts, now operating partially under the authority of the Ministry of Justice, would follow Islamic jurisprudence or not. The

---

[87] *Hukuk-ı Aile Kararnamesi*, article 90. This may lso relate to such marriage practices as bridewealth (*başlık*). Akif Aydın argues that the commission which prepared the 1917 Family Law was aware of its incompleteness and reported on their continuing work to codify the remainder of the family related rules and regulation. M. Akif Aydın, *İslam-Osmanlı Aile Hukuku* (Istanbul: Marmara Üniversitesi İlahiyat Fakültesi Vakfı Yayınları, 1985), 219.

[88] *Hukuk-ı Aile Kararnamesi*, article 107.

Justice Minister Halil Bey had to assure those who had "doubts" about the takeover, by saying that there was not even need to pose such a question, and added that "of course" the Islamic rules and regulations would apply to all Şer'i procedures and thinking otherwise was simply preposterous.[89] Moreover, not only the government's, but also the majority of the deputies' choices/approvals/rejections were characterized by a similar kind of reluctance and hesitation similar to those in the immediate aftermath of the 1908 revolution. Concerned about the takeover of the Şer'i courts by the Ministry of Justice, the Denizli deputy Mehmet Sadık Efendi expressed his fears that this merge might yield a "terrifying [legal] void."[90] For the Mamüratülaziz deputy Mehmet Said Efendi on the other hand, the real concern was to make sure that the "divine" aspects of the law would endure.[91] In sum, that the family or civil law was largely exempted from all the legal developments of the nineteenth century mainly had to do with this general "conservative" character of the late Ottoman government. As Akif Aydın argues, in addition to the political circumstances, the eventual annulment of the Family Law in 1919 was brought upon by a conservative group led by the Şeyhülislam himself, as they tried to reconcile new legal adjustments with the political reality of their time.[92]

When the 1926 Turkish Civil Code was eventually unanimously accepted at the parliament, it was not only that the law itself (a comprehensive one, adapted for the most

---

[89] TBMMZC, 11.2.1332 (1916), 289.

[90] Ibid., 288.

[91] Ibid., 287.

[92] Aydın, İslam-Osmanlı Aile Hukuku, 134, 224. The abolition of Family Law was followed by two other attempts to enact a comprehensive Family Law in 1923 and 1924, although both were of limited scope in ways similar to the 1917 law.

part from the Swiss Civil Code) was different but also the political reality of the republic was different. While the issue of slavery did not appear in its own terms, neither in the code itself nor in the parliamentary debates about it, the Justice Minister Mahmut Esat (Bozkurt) Bey inadvertently drew the connections. "In my view, the saddest figures of the Turkish history are the Turkish women," he maintained, and "the family and inheritance related provisions of the new bill will honor those [...] who had ordinarily been dragged here there like a slave."[93] The new law banned many of what the Aksaray deputy Besim Atalay Bey called "the rotten legal remnants of caliphate," among which was polygamy. With a touch of regret in his voice, Şükrü Kaya Bey reminded his colleagues that this was not a consequence of the civil code, but rather a necessity of the civilization.[94] The practice of slavery as another "rotten" remnant of the empire was never dealt with in actuality, until its abolition was finally resolved in parliament and the respective law was promulgated in 1933. By then, slavery had already become no more than a remote international problem (and presented at the parliament and in the bill strictly as such), the solution of which was again a matter of civilization.[95] "A number of countries including ours, where the practice of slavery virtually does not occur," the bill stated, "we have come to an agreement to prohibit the practice and trade of slavery in support of this humanitarian cause."

---

[93] TBMMZC, 17.2.1926, 230.

[94] Ibid., 232.

[95] "Esaretin meni hakkındaki mukavelenin tasdikına dair I/467 numaralı kanun layihası ve Hariciye ve Dahiliye encümenleri mazbatalari," (26.12.1932) in 5.6.1933.

Conclusion

The abolition of the caliphate, the dissolution or disposal of the physical, political, or legal remnants of the Ottoman Empire, and the corresponding laws had somewhat clear-cut descriptions. In practice, however, they were laden with ambiguities, for the Ottoman heritage was not wholly undesirable but only partially so. Thus, the debates about erasing the markers of the Ottoman past carried a great degree of ambivalence also. For instance, the proposal to remove all Ottoman coat of arms and imperial seals/signatures from government buildings, schools, hospitals, etc., met as much objection as support in parliament.[96] Another instance of this ambivalence was related to the manner the items/furnishings found at the palaces/harems put into reuse. Shortly after the abolition of the sultanate in 1922, many of the palaces/harems were already partially emptied. Such was the case with Fer'iye Palace for instance, when the harem inmates of then runaway sultan Vahideddin was relocated there.[97] Shortly after the abolition of the caliphate, parliament began debating about turning the Dolmabahçe Palace (the abode of many, but particularly the last Ottoman sultan) into a museum,[98] while their contents began flowing to and decorating the ministries in the new capital city of Ankara, public schools, or hospitals across the country, as well as embassy buildings across the globe.[99]

---

[96] TBMMZC, 5.1.1340 (1924), 665–666. Also see TBMMZC 9.3.1340 (1924), 203 for Rıza Nur's proposal to turn the Dolmabahçe palace into the museum of "Turkishness," that will contain and display the evidence the progress and "contribution of the 'Turks' to world civilization."

[97] Açba, *Bir Çerkes Prensesinin Harem Hatıraları*, 152.

[98] TBMMZC, 9.3.1340 (1924), 203.

[99] There is abundance of documents at Başbakanlık Republican Archives (BCA), in relation to the flow of items. Refer to, for instance, 30 18 1 2.31.66.17 / 132–117, 30 18 1 2.2.15.22 and 30 18 1 2.14.68.15 /132–95 to see how the residence of the president was furnished by the items brought over from Dolmabahçe Palace. The National Assembly building was also partially furnished by

236

The portraits of the sultans were to be removed from display in Dolmabahçe Palace,[100] but apart from those, most other items of artistic value were made public at the newly established museums or were put into use in state/public institutions/buildings etc. The items that matched up with the imagined majesty of the Ottoman past continued to ornament the republican banquets or the museum displays, while the unwanted part of that history was condemned and erased. That an emerald pin, a set of diamond earrings, a gold layered bowl, or a mahogany-colored piano (given to the court women for, among other things, their sexual services) were once embodiments of the Ottoman state had no place in the republican imagination. When comparing two different modes of rule, Naciye Meyyal, the wife of an elite imperial administrator, measured the Turkish state's might with the number of furnished buildings, offices, etc. it had in its possession, ready to be utilized at any time by those who served the state.[101] If the old regime lost credibility in the eyes of its people, it was, for Naciye Meyyal, due to its failure in functioning as a state organization and lack of authority in putting its assets in use, particularly of its ruling elite. The "might" of the republican state came from the material world of the old regime as well as the ways in which that material world was dissociated from its political significance.

The initial perplexity of Nazikeda Kadınefendi (one of Sultan Vahideddin's wives) and her *cariye* Leyla Açba soon turned into a peculiar and arduous episode of

---

items brought from Dolmabahçe Palace. See 30 18 1 1.30.63.20 / 132–34 and 30 18 1 1.26.63.15 / 132–34. For an example of paintings/artwork sent to the embassy building in Moscow, see 30 18 1 1.20.47.18 / 132–34.

[100] BCA, 30 18 1 1.15.53.2 / 50–4

[101] Naciye Neyyal, *Mutlakiyet, Meşrutiyet ve Cumhuriyet Anıları*, 105–106.

dislocation.[102] In the days that followed the law of exile, Fer'iye palace, where they were virtually held captive, were raided by a group of men, who took away all the remaining items, including the women's clothes and shoes, although many of them reportedly managed to hide away their jewelry.[103] Leyla Açba too, had a few valuable items, some of which she quickly chose and hid under her dress, particularly those she thought to be the most precious, such as a badge given to her by Sultan Vahideddin himself.[104] On March 10, 1924 Leyla Açba's mistress Nazikeda Kadınefendi left for San Remo, leaving Açba and many of her *cariye*s behind. Those who had families or relatives reportedly went to live with them, whereas another group of older *cariye*s managed to obtain a house for themselves and left to live there.[105] Leyla Açba was among those who had no family, although she owned a house that she inherited from her father. When she and two of her colleagues went there, however, she found out that the house was confiscated by the new government.[106] By March 15, 1924, she reported, they were left both "without a master or a home." Like many of their colleagues, the young women had to leave Istanbul and eventually took up residence in the provincial town of Sivas, where Açba's aunt lived, and where her perplexity lasted until her death (roughly about six months before of the official abolition of slavery in the Ottoman Empire), evident in the way she

---

[102] A similar sort of perplexity is also mentioned by Mislimelek Hanım in Mislimelek Abdülkadir, *Haremden Sürgüne Bir Osmanlı Prensesi*, 207.

[103] Açba, *Bir Çerkes Prensesinin Harem Hatıraları*, 175. Açba states that these items were given to them for their service at the harem.

[104] Ibid.

[105] Ibid., 183–184.

[106] Ibid., 187–188. This was possibly due to the political associations of Açba's father.

concluded her memoires. "If a government fails to provide a *sarayi* with a home" she wrote, "does it not mean the whole new order is wrong?"[107]

---

[107] Ibid., 188.

Conclusion

I began writing this dissertation when the conflict in Syria was gradually turning into a full-fledged, vicious war that eventually killed and uprooted (and to this day continues to do so) millions of Syrian men, women, and children, the biggest toll of which has fallen on those who were least able to bear it.[1] As the fights were turning more brutal, bloodier, and more systematic than the prior sporadic clashes, an article appeared on BBC News, which in the ensuing months would be followed by numerous others. The article told about young Syrian refugee women and children, who were being sold for marriage in Jordan. One refugee among 500,000 in the country (the vast majority of whom were reported to be women and children), an 18-year old girl named Kazal faced harsh conditions of refugee life since she and her family fled Homs and came to Amman; conditions eventually forced Kazal to consent to what the article called "survival sex" and marry a 50-year-old man from Saudi Arabia in exchange of $3,100. It was not that these marriages between young Syrian girls and older men from the Gulf did not happen before the war, but as Kazal's mother asserted, many of the families would not turn to such measures, had they not been forced by the difficult conditions of the war. Kazal's mother reported how hard their life as refugees have been and that they received very

_____

[1] As of July 2015, the registered number of Syrian refugees is given as 4,015,065 individuals, 1,805,255 of which are in Turkey. See http://data.unhcr.org/syrianrefugees/regional.php for a more detailed breakdown. For two examples of refugee children's vulnerabilities, see "To be young, Syrian and a refugee in the streets of Beirut,"
http://america.aljazeera.com/articles/2014/7/18/to-be-young
syrianandarefugeeinthestreetsofbeirut.html and
http://www.ozgur-gundem.com/haber/138965/iste-buyuk-ekonomi-budur.

little aid. They could not afford to pay the rent or buy food. "So I had to sacrifice Kazal" she said, "to help the other members of the family."[2]

Kazal's marriage was arranged by an NGO that normally provided aid to the refugees, in the form of cash, food, and medicine, but there were other types of agents arranging these marriages as well. For one, a certain Um Mazed, a 28-year-old Syrian woman who called herself a matchmaker, also a refugee from Homs, presented more than a hundred Syrian girls to older Arab men, most of whom were between 50 and 80 years of age. Most of these men asked for girls who had white skin and blue or green eyes and demanded that they be no older than 16 years old. They paid Um Mazed an amount $70 for an introduction, and $310, when it resulted in a marriage. If the marriage ended with a divorce in a short while, it was not Um Mazed's fault, as she was only a matchmaker. What the girls consented to did not count as prostitution, she contented, as there was a "contract between the groom and the bride." Still, Um Mazed was not proud of what she was doing, the article reported, but she claimed she had no other choice.

The story of Kazal and her family, and that of Um Mazed for that matter, looks only too familiar to that of Müzeyyen, Sıdıka, Şirin, Fatma Leman and many others that this dissertation talked about. Like that of Kazal and Um Mazed, their stories too were shaped or given new meanings during such instances of crisis as the Circassian expulsion in the 1860s, the Russo-Turkish war in 1877–78 and the Armenian genocide in 1915, during which ethical boundaries in relation to power, coercion, violence, slavery, or

---

[2] Beth McLeod, "Syrian Refugees 'sold for marriage' in Jordan," *BBC News*, 10 May 2013, accessed online 18 May 2013. Similar stories, pertaining to the Syrian refugees in Turkey appeared in Turkish press also. See "Suriyelilerle evlilik ticarete dönüştü," in *Milliyet*, 27.1.2014, or "Suriyeli kızlar yaşamak için evlendiriliyor," in *Al Jazeera Turk*, 27.1.2014.

freedom among other things were severely altered. During the Circassian expulsion, for instance, many families and their "white skinned, blue-eyed" daughters fell prey as much to men and women like Um Mazed, who took advantage of their peculiar "insider" positions, as to professional slave dealers. Similarly, in the aftermath of the Russo-Turkish war, abductions or kidnappings abounded in number. In one of these cases, which opens chapter 3, a band of three "amiable" abductor women used their own freed-slave experiences (not without ample amount of despair on their side) and connections to persuade a number of poor immigrant families to surrender their "flaxen haired" and "blue-eyed" (or, *ma'iye meyyal,* "blue inclined," as an interrogation report poetically put it) daughters to them, whom they sold not only to various prominent households in Istanbul, Cairo, and Baghdad, but even to the imperial harem. In the aftermath of the Armenian genocide, abducting of young Armenian women and children and placing them in Muslim households took on new meanings and became a government policy that delineated the female body as a "site of vengeance" as Lerna Ekmekçioğlu called it.[3] Nevertheless, these new meanings also built on familiar structures exploited by the longstanding practice of slavery in the Ottoman Empire.

This dissertation told the story of the legal making and perpetuation of "Circassianness" as an "enslavable" ethnic category, although African slaves are not

---

[3] Lerna Ekmekçioğlu, "The Female Body as Site of Vengeance: Armenians and Turks at (Great) War, " paper presented at the 47th MESA Annual Meeting, October 10–13, 2013. New Orleans, LA. For excellent accounts of the abduction and sale of Armenian women and children and international humanitarian discourses and campaigns organized around those incidents during and after the genocide, see Keith David Watenpaugh, "The League of Nations' Rescue of Armenian Genocide Survivors and the Making of Modern Humanitarianism, 1920–1927," *The American Historical Review*, vol.115, no. 5 (2010); Lerna Ekmekçioğlu, "A Climate for Abduction, a Climate for Redemption: The Politics of Inclusion during and after the Armenian Genocide," *Comparative Studies in Society and History*, vol. 55, no. 3 (2013).

entirely absent from it. In the first chapter, for instance, they come in to help emphasize the contrasts between different modes of enslavement and their relation to Islamic state-building and expansion processes, particularly the deployment of *jihad* ideology, to demonstrate that Circassian slavery was not necessarily Islamic, and if it was, it became so during the course of the five decades long Russo-Circassian war. In the second chapter, they have an indirect presence as references to Circassian claims to freedom in the aftermath of the Circassian expulsion. In the remainder of the chapters they come and go, at times appearing as a pivotal actors within the practice. Such is the case with Şirin Kadın in chapter 3, a manumitted African slave turned slave dealer, who ran a clandestine slaving business together with a manumitted Circassian slave, for instance. She is central to the story, especially in regards to her remarkable network that included her husband in Cairo who oversaw her "exports" to that city, a number of manumitted slaves living in different neighborhoods in Istanbul who alerted her about the "eligible" young girls in their vicinity, captains of merchant ships that docked in Tophane port, as well as a eunuch from the imperial harem, who bought slaves on behalf of one of the *kadınefendi*s (official wives) there. Even then, however, the focus remains on the Circassian slaves (and occasionally prostitutes) she traded and handled, with a particular effort to come to an understanding how the ethnic boundaries were drawn within the trade.

This decision of giving Circassian slaves a primary presence throughout the dissertation requires a brief contextualization and explanation. First and foremost, to reiterate the obvious, this is not to imply that their presence or experiences bore any more significance than that of African slaves in the Ottoman Empire. As has already been well established, particularly by Ehud Toledano but others as well, African slaves exceeded the Circassian slaves in number particularly in the nineteenth century and their predicament was by no means milder, either.[4] In fact, recurrent depictions in both archival and literary sources illustrate their vulnerability and exploitation to be exceeding that of the Circassian slaves. All in all, the reason why Circassian slaves have a larger presence is not due to the numbers involved, the severity of the work they performed or the physical and psychological coercion they were subjected to (the major traits that characterized slavery in the boom-time antebellum South, for instance), but to the Ottoman non-adherence to strict racial boundaries as well as its rigor in making and "consuming" black and white slaves with similar ease. This ease, however, is not taken here as a general laxness or lack of race consciousness or classification in the Ottoman Empire. On the contrary, the Ottoman government's ways of marking blackness and whiteness, the slave traders' ways of determining their price in the market, and slave-holding intellectuals' ways of portraying them in literary sources all constitute proof that this was not at all the case. Rather than laxness or indifference, their seemingly indiscriminate attitude is read in this dissertation as a decision on the Ottoman policy makers', slave traders' and slaveholders' side to deliberately extend the practice to everyone who was vulnerable enough (or made so, through political processes, as in the case of Circassian expulsion or Armenian genocide). Probing this deliberate decision and the ways it interacted with liberalism as a new and specific form of governmentality taking root (or failing to do so) in the Ottoman Empire during the second half of the nineteenth and early decades of the twentieth centuries, is the primary objective of this

---

[4] As one British consular report stated in 1869, "the respective totals of the two categories are nearly balanced." FO 195/946 from Palgrave to Clarendon, 21 September 1869.

244

dissertation. It is my conviction that this objective helps to place slavery more firmly within a context of "power and exploitation," the importance of which has been insightfully argued in a discussion a decade and a half ago, where David Brion Davis's call for a transnational approach to study slavery was complemented by a claim "to reconsider not just how [to] teach and write about slavery, but how [to] think about past boundaries of all kinds," made by Peter Kolchin, Rebecca J. Scott, and Stanley L. Engerman.[5] The present study is an effort to think along similar lines, in that it proposes an account of slavery that is delineated not only along racial but also ethnic boundaries, which were simultaneously mediated and manipulated by social, political, and legal practices. To add to Davis et al.'s statement is the question highlighted by Dylan Penningroth about the viability of the pursuit of "a solid and unified 'subaltern presence'," which has increasingly been posed by historians with different temporal and geographic focus. As Penningroth writes:

> [B]lack churches have grappled with conflicts over gendered
> "respectability," "[a] leader of a movement can. . . go home and beat up a
> wife or children," colonized people could be colonizers themselves, and
> some of the strongest resistance to European colonialism came from
> slaveholding Africans. It would be a mistake to assume that such power
> relations merely echo, or are ultimately less meaningful than, the story of
> white-on-black oppression—or that studying the former necessarily means
> downplaying the latter. Probing the internal dynamics of subaltern families
> and communities—issues of conflict, authority, and change over time—
> demands new interpretive frameworks that can complement the familiar

---

[5]See the forum entitled "Crossing Slavery's Boundaries," in the *American Historical Review*, Vol. 105, No. 2 (Apr., 2000).

dyads of race and resistance: master and slave, colonizer and colonized, white and Other.[6]

In this context, limiting the scope of this dissertation to the Circassian slaves allowed me to better investigate these dynamics in general and trace the legal making and containment of the ethnic category of "Circassianness," in particular. Secondly, in a more practical sense, my aim is to demonstrate how two distinct systems of slavery, that is Islamic and Caucasian, underwent change when they merged following the Circassian expulsion. The existence of more than one systems of slavery, combining with the policy change with the ban of trade in African slaves, shaped not only the practice of slavery but also the Ottoman polity as a whole in the subsequent years. Last but not least, focusing on the Circassian slaves is also conducive, as the fourth chapter below explores, to probe "the internal dynamics of subaltern families and communities" who struggled to come to terms with their enslaved status, freedom promised by the constitutional regime, and their "Ottomanness" and "Circassianness" at once.

Despite the fact that the Ottoman slaves' attempts were largely unsuccessful, their strategies and the sophisticated debates they made offer highly transparent cases to study multiple political and social dynamics in the late Ottoman Empire and early Turkish Republic. Once placed properly in its political context, slavery emerges as a practice jointly produced and perpetuated by a pluralistic legal system with inner conflicts, a government that was "conservative" particularly in protecting male and Muslim (to be more specific, powerful and Sunni) prerogatives, as well as its strict adherence to a

---

[6] Dylan C. Penningroth, "The Claims of Slaves and Ex-Slaves to Family and Property: A Transatlantic Comparison," *The American Historical Review*, Vol. 112, No. 4 (Oct., 2007), 1045.

corporate notion of citizenship. That the Ottoman government was caught between its old habits of rule by coopting the local elites (that it preferred to side with Circassian chieftains over slaves' claims, for instance) at the expense of undermining the new political and legal order it aspired to attain in the post-Reform Edict Ottoman Empire, is a good example of the conditions of this "joint production," as chapter 2 illustrated.

Placing the Ottoman practice of slavery within a larger political context, as the above chapters sought to do (rather than portraying it as an anomalous practice that existed in and of itself that happened and ended in the past), is important for a variety of other reasons as well. For one, doing so provides hints as to how Circassian slaves perceived themselves as Ottomans, Circassians, and Muslims at once. Unlike the non-Muslim or heterodox communities of the empire, Circassians (being Sunni Muslims, however nominally) considered themselves entitled to be full members of the Ottoman society, as evinced by the many slave petitions that support this study. In that respect, tracing their aspirations and setbacks offers insight to understanding what the Ottoman and Turkish state on the one hand and the slaves on the other, understood of slavery, freedom, or citizenship. Moreover, "de-exoticizing" slavery, as this dissertation aims to do, also helps in connecting different instances of coercion and violence in the late Ottoman Empire and early Turkish Republic. For instance, such is the case, as chapter 4 suggests, with the stories of the enslavement of Armenian girls during and after the Armenian genocide in 1915. The "climate for abduction," as Lerna Ekmekcioglu calls it, emerged not independently from earlier "climates."[7]

---

[7] Lerna Ekmekçioğlu, "A Climate for Abduction, a Climate for Redemption: The Politics of Inclusion during and after the Armenian Genocide," *Comparative Studies in Society and History*, vol. 55, no. 3 (2013).

This dissertation ends in 1933, when the republican government promulgated a law that prohibited slavery and slave trade in the Turkish Republic. This was done, in the republican government's own words, to give support to a "humanitarian cause" that remotely happened elsewhere. Written off as a "rotten remnant" from the Ottoman past, slavery was erased and forgotten in congruence with the republican "project of regulated amnesia."[8] In the following decades, slavery as a practice was at best forgotten or exoticized and at worst denied, but never confronted in the Turkish Republic. Like other cases of state-produced (or, at least state approved) coercion and violence, it continued to reproduce itself whenever the conditions allowed it. For one, the forced schooling of young girls in Dersim in the aftermath of the Dersim massacre of 1937–38 bears striking resemblances to the enslavement of young girls in the previous century.[9] More recently, the stories of coerced migration of the Kurds continue to be interwoven with that of the descendants of African slaves, in such poor neighborhoods as Kadifekale in Izmir.[10]

Roughly around half a century earlier than this present story began, another (and no doubt a more potent) one culminated on the far side of the Atlantic. "If we live in a world in which democracy is meant to exclude no one," Laurent Dubois has stated, "it is in no small part because of the actions of those slaves in Saint-Domingue who insisted

---

[8] Murat Ergin, "'Is the Turk a White Man?' Towards a Theoretical Framework for Race in the Making of Turkishness," Middle Eastern Studies, 44:6 (2008), 837.

[9] Zeynep Türkyılmaz, "Nationalizing through Education: The Case of 'Mountain Flowers' at Elazığ Girls' Institute," (MA Thesis, Boğaziçi University, 2001).

[10] For an overview of these interactions, see Michael Ferguson, "'It's Not Destruction, It's Urban Renewal': The Transformation of Urban Space Atop Kadifekale, Izmir." Paper presented at the Quatrième Journée d'étude du groupe d'études turques et ottomanes (GÉTO): « La République Turque : histoire, culture, société », Université du Québec à Montréal, Montreal, Quebec, Canada, 8 March 2013.

that human rights were theirs too."[11] We do not know whether the enslaved men and women of the Ottoman Empire, who seem to be concerned more with their own immediate lives, ever heard of a group of enslaved men, who succeeded in "creating a society in which all people, of all colors, were granted freedom and citizenship."[12] Drawing direct connections between the motives and actions of the Haitian revolutionaries and the Ottoman slave representatives or insurgents may be far-fetched, but whenever the latter claimed what they believed to be their rights, their voices resonated with their Haitian counterparts.

---

[11] Laurent Dubois, *The Avengers of the New World: The Story of the Haitian Revolution* (Cambridge, MA: The Belknap Press of Harvard University Press, 2004), 3.

[12] Ibid., 6–7.

www.ingramcontent.com/pod-product-compliance
Lightning Source LLC
Chambersburg PA
CBHW072145060526
44654CB00046B/1177